BROKEN BUILDINGS, BUSTED BUDGETS

BROKEN BUILDINGS, BUSTED BUDGETS

How to Fix America's Trillion-Dollar Construction Industry

BARRY B. LEPATNER

WITH TIMOTHY JACOBSON AND ROBERT E. WRIGHT

THE UNIVERSITY OF CHICAGO PRESS · CHICAGO AND LONDON

BARRY B. LEPATNER is founder and partner of LePatner and
Associates LLP.
TIMOTHY JACOBSON is partner of Withrop Group.
ROBERT E. WRIGHT is clinical associate professor of economics at
New York University.

The University of Chicago Press, Chicago 60637
The University of Chicago Press, Ltd., London
© 2007 by The University of Chicago
All rights reserved. Published 2007
Printed in the United States of America

16 15 14 13 12 11 10 09 08 07   1 2 3 4 5

ISBN-13: 978-0-226-47267-6   (cloth)
ISBN-10: 0-226-47267-1   (cloth)

Library of Congress Cataloging-in-Publication Data

LePatner, Barry B.
  Broken buildings, busted budgets : how to fix America's
trillion-dollar construction industry / Barry B. LePatner, with
Timothy Jacobson and Robert E. Wright.
       p. cm.
  Includes bibliographical references and index.
  ISBN-13: 978-0-226-47267-6   (cloth : alk. paper)
  ISBN-10: 0-226-47267-1   (cloth : alk. paper)
  1. Construction industry—United States—History.
2. Construction industry—United States—Management.
I. Jacobson, Timothy, C., 1948– II. Wright, Robert E. (Robert
Eric), 1969– III. Title.
  HD9715.U52L46 2007
  338.4'76900973—dc22
                                        2007019034

Imagine an automobile assembly line where each step along the line is undertaken by a different company with its own financial interest and separate labor union! . . . Present [construction] practice is impossible. The client asks an architect to design something specifically for him. In making drawings the architect will specify various components out of catalogues. He is nearly always restricted to elements that are already manufactured. Then the contractor, who has usually had nothing to do with the design process, examines the drawings and makes his bid. Industry supplies raw materials and components and has little contact with the contractor. The various building material manufacturers make their components totally independent of each other. . . . It is an absurd industry.

MOSHE SAFDIE, internationally renowned architect

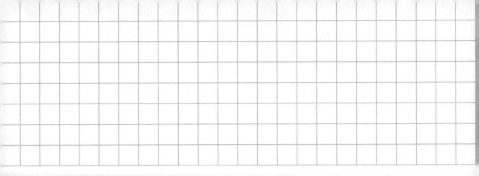

Contents

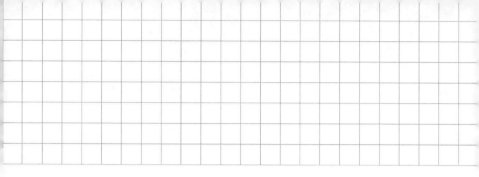

Figures

Acknowledgments

This book is the product of several years of development and countless discussions with many in the industry who graciously shared their insights and experiences. As I began writing what would become *Broken Buildings, Busted Budgets*, I was fortunate to have associated with Timothy C. Jacobson and Robert E. Wright, historians and economists of note in their own right and my coauthors, who rigorously challenged my early assumptions and asked probing questions to lead us forward to more definitive answers. Working with them has been an intellectual challenge and broadened my own perspective on how the construction industry got into the shape it is in today.

I am blessed with partners and associates at LePatner & Associates LLP who are creative, analytic problem solvers. Through the many drafts of this book they contributed comments that framed my thinking and opened up new avenues to pursue. Their insights are embedded throughout. It would be remiss of me not to single out Brad Cronk who serves so admirably as our firm's head of project management services. His comments and suggestions added immeasurably to the final editing process. Tadhg O'Connor, my assistant and head of information technology, valiantly waded through numerous drafts of the book, always keeping everything where it was supposed to be.

When all was seemingly in place, the book benefited greatly from the insightful comments and restructuring put forth by David Pervin of the University of Chicago Press.

Finally, I cannot minimize the importance played by my three children. Instead of groaning that their father, who already had a full plate of commitments, was off on a new venture, each supported my efforts at every stage. Being with them has always been my greatest pleasure. Their backing for this work has been an enormous satisfaction.

Barry B. LePatner

May 2007, New York City

Introduction

How could a nation as technologically advanced and business oriented as this one care so little about how it spends upwards of $1 trillion on construction each year? All too frequently, construction projects of all sizes and types are plagued by massive cost increases that were totally unanticipated at the outset of the work. We have become almost immune to the fact that most construction in this nation will result in serious cost overruns and schedule delays. Executives of major U.S. corporations, the leaders of public institutions, and millions of American homeowners are routinely held hostage by the construction industry to pay up or face even greater costs and delays. All too often, corporate executives, who retain business advisors and consultants to oversee and coordinate every phase of their daily business activities, readily cede control to a construction manager with an overt conflict of interest in structuring the cost of a project. These realities have stymied me for many of the thirty plus years that I have served as construction counsel to real estate developers, national and international corporations, educational and healthcare institutions, and countless architects, engineers, and homeowners.

When questioned as to why they feel they have no control over what they spend for their hospital, school, or hotel project, business leaders express anger, frustration, or denial. Often few have any good answers to why it costs so much and takes so long. Yet runaway projects and pricing continue unabated. Whether a stadium for a football or base-ball team, a new bridge or tunnel, or a hospital or school, all too often owners concede that neither the budget established by the contract nor the original scheduled completion date is under control. Knowl-edgeable construction executives, in defense, are quick to point out that each project is custom made, a veritable "one off." When events miraculously transpire so that a project actually is completed on time and on budget, few clients can explain how this happy event occurs. In short, I came to realize that no one involved in the process has a clear understanding of why our nation's construction world works the way it does.

It does not work like anything we are familiar with. When any of us go shopping for a car we make our decisions based on masses of in-formation that enable us to compare models, options, pricing, and the like. The automobile industry spends hundreds of millions of dollars annually to convince us that their product is right for us. If they give us a fair representation of our expectations after we buy that Ford or Toyota, then the industry has a fair chance of securing the second part of their carefully orchestrated game plan: when it comes time for us to buy anew, we buy that next car from the same company. In a sense, the automobile industry, which is a very competitive industry, hopes to ensure our loyalty so that they do not need to compete for that sec-ond chance with each customer.

Not so the construction industry. While repeat business and repu-tation are important to most contractors, as to most businesses, the probability of a contractor getting a second and third project from a typical corporate, institutional, or individual owner is small. This is so for several reasons. To secure the initial project, a contractor is required to compete with many other contractors, some of whom may need the project more desperately than the others. Hence, the desperate con-tractor's bid may be intentionally designed *not* to secure a known profit at the outset. Instead, it may be made with the strategy of getting the commission and then employing a number of tactics to create a profit during the course of the project. This is a major cause of the cost over-runs, delays, and change orders that plague many owners.

Another reason repeat business is not as big a factor in construction as it is in other consumer or service industries is the passage of time. Most corporate and certainly most individual owners simply do not build often. Their projects may be spaced years apart. In the interval, markets change, tastes change, finances change. There are abundant reasons why an owner would not return to a prior contractor even if the initial experience was satisfactory.

But the foremost distinction between the auto and construction industries is that for the contractor, the current project is critical to ensure his ongoing cash flow. In managing their day-to-day workload, most contractors do not have the time or funds for ongoing advertising expenditures to ensure brand loyalty. Besides, on the next project for that same client, there will be new competitors, some of whom may be more desperate for the project, and his low bid may not be low enough to secure the job.

Once awarded the contract, the contractor then changes hats. From occupying the highly competitive world needed to secure the project, the contractor now becomes a monopolist insofar as the owner is concerned. As a monopolist, the contractor is in total control over the project: its costs, its schedule and the manner in which it is run. Typical owners often have no good option for recourse when faced with spiraling costs and delays. In no other industry does this happen.

My own journey in this world started as a young lawyer assigned to represent architects and engineers whose projects, for one reason or another, faced problems associated with their design drawings. Traveling the nation and learning the intricacies of the design process that had been taught the same way in schools for many decades, I came to respect and admire the talented men and women who envisioned then brought to physical form their concepts for how we live and work in the built environment around us.

By the late 1980s I had started what became the first law firm in the United States solely serving as business and legal advisor to the design professions. In 1983 I coauthored a book that traced the case histories of thirty-two actual projects that had experienced design and construction problems.[1] As a result of the book's publication I was asked to testify before a congressional sub-committee headed by a then-young congressman from Tennessee, Albert C. Gore, Jr. The Committee on Science and Technology was considering legislation to require architects and engineers to certify that the buildings they designed were, in fact, built in accordance with the design documents they had prepared for the owner. I was the only nondesign professional called to testify and spoke out strongly against the legislation, outlining to the subcommittee that owners did not customarily retain design professionals to be on site often enough to provide such assurances. The proposed law was not enacted.[2]

I began to represent corporations and developers, highlighting to them the importance of preparing a business plan for their projects that would be the blueprint for selecting the various team members (to name a few: the architect, structural engineer, mechanical engineer, specialty consultants, construction manager, contractors and suppliers). I also began negotiating what I came to call "Equitable Risk Allocation Agreements" that precluded the unwarranted claims for delay and extra costs that plagued the construction industry. It was the start of a journey that led to this book.

The overwhelming majority of contractors and subcontractors in our nation accomplish enormous unheralded tasks that deserve admiration from us all. All too often, when a project is beset by serious challenges to timely completion, these talented individuals bring their expertise to bear with fresh ideas and energy that make working with them a special experience. Whether working with the largest construction management firms or the many small firms that make up the majority of our nation's construction industry, one cannot but be impressed by the dedication they bring to producing a quality product. Yet the deck is stacked against them. They are ensconced in an industry that is an anachronism, encrusted with an attitude that advertises that "this is the way it's always been done" since time immemorial, and there is no better way. But, in the course of my career, through discussions with countless professionals in the field, I came to realize that there is a better way for all.

Many will challenge the findings in this book. Some will assert that everything is fine just the way it is. Any uncertainty and fear on the part of the construction community as to what is reported in this book is and will be entirely justifiable. The change that lies just ahead will threaten long-established firms, careers and institutions. No one can hide from it. Some will read these chapters and see the opportunities they portend. Much like the flattening of the world described by Thomas L. Friedman, the impending use of the latest technology, global implementation of new materials and building systems, and long overdue research and capital investment will radically alter the construction landscape in the next ten to twenty years.[3] The construction industry today is the last major industry in our world to remain "mom and pop." It is an industry that shuns risk at all levels and hordes information on its day-to-day operations. Outsiders are not welcomed and the throwback to the days of the guild is omnipresent.

5

This situation will not last, for the costs have finally become too high. Change will come, mandated by law or the marketplace. It will threaten some. To others it will offer only opportunity. None of the recommendations set out in this book are radical departures. Together, they serve to liberate anyone who builds anything from fear of paying too much, waiting too long, and not getting what was paid for.

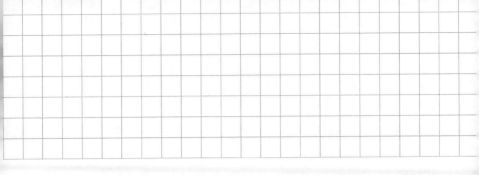

Overbudget and Overdue

Every American lives in the long shadow cast by our nation's construc- 7
tion industry. While few of us recognize just how many dollars are
spent annually on construction, each of us lives from infancy through
old age in buildings designed and constructed by a coterie of architects, engineers, and contractors. All of their efforts are funded by
monies generated by private or governmental financing.

Construction is an enormously important part of any economy,
often accounting for approximately 5 percent of aggregate output
(Gross Domestic Product) and employment. In the United States today,
construction is a *trillion* dollar business that employs over 7 million
Americans. According to a series of studies by McKinsey and Company,
the U.S. construction industry is one of, if not the, most productive
in the world. But before we congratulate ourselves we need to realize
that the construction industries of most other countries are extremely
inefficient. Most of the world's construction is done by small-scale
builders using traditional materials and methods sometimes unchanged for centuries. Only about 5 percent of total construction is
undertaken in a fully international, competitive market.[1]

According to the latest census information, the United States population of 300 million will increase by over 70 million by the year 2030.
Between 2000 and 2030, the number of Americans over the age of 65
will more than double. According to a recent study from the Brook-

ings Institution by Arthur C. Nelson, population growth coupled with the continued movement of people to the south and west will result in 100 billion square feet of new homes.[2] Commercial and industrial square footage will increase even more rapidly in the next twenty-five years. Other studies predict that America is poised to embark on a $25 trillion construction binge that will sweep every sector of the nation. Local school districts will expand; health and hospital will grow with our aging baby boomer population; and new offices, retail, and entertainment complexes will abound as never before. Nelson predicts that by 2030, almost 58 percent of our nation's total building stock, some 427 billion square feet, will have been built after 2000. The time for change in the construction industry could not be more urgent.

For home builders, the years since the early 1990s have been some of the most frenzied in U.S. history. Large-scale home builders, such as Toll Brothers and Pulte Homes, have "transformed the American home into a corporate product—probably the last item in our $11 trillion economy that has yet to be marketed and branded on a national scale to consumers."[3] While the large home builders currently account for one out of four new homes in the United States, Wall Street analysts currently estimate that within ten years this ratio will change so that large home builders will be building half of all homes in the nation. This growth would be welcome were it not for the dismal performance that all too often marks how the nation's buildings are designed and constructed.

Yes, we build big in America, but *caveat emptor.* Very few of the corporations, institutions, governmental entities, or individual homeowners undertaking a construction project have a clue about the process they are about to embark upon.

To most educated, office-bound Americans, this world of construction is foreign territory. These men with the hardhats and big boots look a rough crowd: sweaty, swearing, with unfashionable views on matters like sexual harassment. Many construction workers, especially in the northeast, are unionized. Therefore, as the image has it, they spend most of the day standing around hardly working and then knocking off by 2:00 PM. About their bosses, called general contractors, hovers similar lore. At the turn of the twentieth century, muckrakers portrayed the contractor as "a burly, uncouth figure with an enormous cigar stuck in his pig-like mouth and his big paws handing out boodle to public officials."[4] The cigar and swinish countenances are largely gone, but not the payments and roguish air.

That's the cynic's view, but we are also romantics. Remember when you were a child and the excitement when a new building started to go up in town, whether you lived in Metropolis or in Popperville? In Metropolis let's say it was a tall office building; in Popperville let's say it was the town hall as imagined in Virginia Lee Burton's 1939 classic children's tale of construction and civic virtue, *Mike Mulligan and His Steam Shovel.*[5] The gee-whiz thrills of childhood go down through generations: the trip to the boarded-off construction site with viewing holes cut at various heights to accommodate children of all ages. There we glimpsed a world of burly men, big, steam-chugging machines, the beginnings of massive concrete footings and soaring steel frames. Strength, power, awe. What, we wondered, would it finally look like? How tall would it be? How soon would it be finished?

How to reconcile these two drastically different views of the construction industry? Both are true. We absolutely, positively *need* houses, malls, airports, park-like boulevards, and skyscrapers. We deeply *desire* beautiful, functional spaces for work and play. As it turns out, we desire them so much, so pressing is our need, we seem willing to pay far too much for them.

We live in an era when economic power has broadly and decisively shifted from suppliers to consumers. The availability of information on products and cost has exploded geometrically in recent years. Choices as to where a consumer can obtain products have multiplied. It is not nearly as easy as it once routinely was to get away with peddling expensive junk. Just ask GM and Chrysler, or if you could find them, RCA and Philco. Companies propose. Consumers dispose. Don't like something—no, make that *anything*—you took home from Wal-Mart or Target yesterday? Take it back tomorrow and an "associate" will return your money with a smile. We speak here not just of toothpaste and iPods. Even in hoary citadels of professional privilege like medicine, consumers (patients)—at least in countries like the United States—exercise choice at levels unthinkable a decade or two back, and providers (doctors on down) have no choice at all but to try hard to satisfy them.

If there's anything that Americans are more cynical about than politics, it is construction. And with good reason. In politics at least we get an opportunity to vote and turn out one set of rascals for another—the appearance of change anyway. In construction we do not seem to have even that much choice. It always costs more and always takes longer than the owners thought. And always, if they want their building finished, owners put-up and pay-up.

"Always" exaggerates, but not much. How did it go when you added a room or two to your house for the new baby, or your company built its new headquarters, or your town erected a new elementary school? The same way, probably, it will go when New York City starts to build a proposed new tunnel under the East River connecting Brooklyn with downtown Manhattan. We hear this will take $6 billion and eight years to complete.[6] Almost certainly the final numbers will be significantly higher. Between the mother-in-law apartment and the most massive infrastructure work, only the scale differs, not the problem that curses them both. Large project or small, chances are high that you, the owner, will have paid more than the contract said you would pay and will have waited longer than the contract said you would wait before you get what is often only an approximation of what you thought you were buying.

Like as not, construction is likely to be the only experience where otherwise sophisticated, business savvy owners feel distinctly uncomfortable with the process because of their inability to understand and control it. Perhaps a classic explanation of this phenomenon was recently presented by Malcom Gladwell, author of *The Tipping Point* and *Blink: The Power of Thinking without Thinking*. In his article, "Open Secrets," Gladwell discussed the prosecution's case against Enron's now incarcerated CEO, Jeffrey Skilling.[7] In a novel, almost contrarian manner, Gladwell challenged the conventional wisdom that Skilling and other Enron officials withheld information and misled investors and regulators about the company's inventive financial chicanery. Gladwell demonstrates not that "we weren't told enough," but that we were told too much. According to Gladwell and others he cites, trying to solve a problem without having enough information is a puzzle, while trying to solve a problem with information at hand is a mystery. In the Enron example, the prosecutor framed its case as a puzzle, that is, arguing Enron withheld key information, without which their true financial condition could not be understood. Gladwell argues, in fact, that Enron was a mystery; all its information was there to see publicly, it was simply a matter of analyzing and understanding it. Gladwell cites Yale law professor Jonathan Macey, whose landmark law review article around this distinction triggered a major rethinking of the Enron case.[8]

11

Similarly, a careful study of the construction industry reveals that this sector of the economy exhibits the characteristics of a mystery more than those of a puzzle. While there will always be instances when a contractor misrepresents or withholds from the owner certain cost information (a puzzle), in most projects, the owner needs to know how to interpret the cost information he is already looking at (a mystery). Is the contractor's $25,000 estimate for carpentry a bargain or a rip-off? What about the rest of the estimate line items? How does the owner make that judgment?

As we shall see in later chapters, owners, whether building hospitals, office towers, or public schools, become totally reliant on information provided by their contractors. From the contractor's perspective, the contractor provides the owner substantial financial information detailing what the owner believes will be the cost of the project. Often, the contractor is up front with the owner about the high potential, even certainty, that there will be additional costs of an unspecified amount before the project is completed. Rare, however, is the owner (or its consultant) who can analyze the contractor's information capably enough to predict or prevent those additional project costs and delays. Given the average owner's lack of construction experience and ability to accurately interpret information presented by its contractor, is it any mystery why the owner experiences such discomfort with the whole process?

The mystery deepens when we realize that, despite the appearance that each building is unique, the process by which most are built is not. Snazzy looking buildings abound, but for the way they are built they might as well be log cabins. True, they may be complex log cabins filled with all sorts of high-tech gizmos to make us comfortable and secure, but log cabins just the same, at least in process. Buildings do not happen, they do not come into existence the same way cars or computers do. This is because they are not built by big companies but by thousands of little firms. Ask a contractor and he will tell you that each building represents a "job" that is unique and handmade, which once finished will never be replicated exactly the same way again. Or so long habit has taught us to understand the construction process. It is a bad habit and a costly misunderstanding.

This book is about how owners can find a way to gain control of what they want to build and what it will cost. To prevent your organization—your business, your government agency, your family—from paying more than it has to for its physical infrastructure, it is absolutely essential that you understand the construction industry's history, its economic structure, and the incentives facing its major players. *Broken Buildings* does not present yet another banal list of business dos and don'ts. Such a list would have a short shelf life, because contractors could quickly adapt to it. Instead, *Broken Buildings* has been written to help you, the potential purchaser of an office building, a home, a highway, a dam, to understand how the construction industry functions and why it is so inefficient and so likely to try to bust your budget or expose you to unwarranted surprises. Armed with the most powerful weapon in anyone's business arsenal—understanding—you will have a fighting chance to get the building you want, when you want it, for the price you originally agreed upon.

After laying out just *what* is at stake here—hundreds of billions of dollars, *your* dollars, the very lifeblood of your organization—the book applies economic analysis to the industry's institutional failures to explain why it functions so poorly. As the reader will learn, the construction industry experienced some frustrated early starts at reform and developed enduring barriers to change. The concluding chapters set forth a prescription for fixing the industry's failures and guide the reader conceptually through a new model contract that can restore transparency to a complex, but no longer mysterious, business. In the final chapter, the reader will be provided with concrete suggestions to save you or your company or institution time, hassle, and expense on your next project.

13

Most of all, this book has been written to call attention not only to the importance of the construction industry to our nation's economy, but to the critical need for reforming this industry that time has forgotten.

Tales of Woe

Many Americans have construction horror stories: adding the screened porch, remodeling the kitchen, maybe even building a whole house. Many projects are over budget, late, or of poor quality. Contractors have a severe customer-relations problem. Of course there are good ones, but a load of bad ones too. And by bad we do not just mean fast-traveling shysters stealing money from elderly victims of Florida's horrific 2004 hurricane season either. Unfortunately, there are those that regularly take advantage of the fact that owners do not have the knowledge of costs or the experience to enter into good faith bargaining.[9]

Anyone who pays attention to the news will know that this indictment is not limited to the panel-truck contractor who lives the next street over. Even the big operators, the heavy construction firms, the commercial builders, the public works companies, often come in over budget and past deadline.

One of the most notorious recent examples is the Big Dig, an ambitious underground highway system in downtown Boston. It was a boondoggle of epic dimension, $12 billion over budget and years late, even before the highly publicized failure of the concrete ceiling panel that killed a motorist in 2006. After a yearlong investigation, the *Bos-*

14

ton Globe found that over $1 billion of waste was caused by errors committed by the project's managers, Bechtel Corporation of San Francisco and Parsons Brinckerhoff of New York. Some of the errors, like the omission of the 19,600 seat Fleet Center from its own design drawings, a "minor" oversight that cost taxpayers an additional $991,000 in design fees and Boston commuters untold months of delay, led some to conclude they had been intentionally omitted to increase fees and the project's cost. And—who is surprised?—the thing leaks. Such behavior is not unusual in the construction business, again not because contractors are bad people, but because owners and governments allow them to get away with it.[10]

Two Broadway in Manhattan, where the Metropolitan Transit Authority, an organization with 175,000 employees and a budget in excess of $5 billion a year, built its new headquarters, is another high-profile fiasco. The project, which has spurred court battles and accusations of graft, was $300 million over budget and years late. The drama has it all: money laundering, false invoices, mob ties, guys with broken noses, Russian immigrant taxicab drivers turned real estate moguls, emergency flights to Europe on the Concorde, and pricey legal fees in excess of $8 million. This is not a joke. You don't need fancy economic analysis to figure out where the burden of this waste will fall: higher fares for New York commuters. And this job leaks too.[11]

In Las Vegas, where missed deadlines translate into millions of dollars a day in lost casino revenue, the $1.5 billion Venetian Resort Hotel Casino saw one of the most costly construction litigations in recent memory. After finally opening in 1999, the Venetian sued Bovis Lend Lease, the construction manager, for delays and construction defects. Bovis Lend Lease countered with a $140 million suit on its behalf and that of its many subcontractors. The length of the trial was a record for Nevada and raised numerous issues attesting to the claims for inefficiencies, defective construction, and the numerous increases to the original guaranteed maximum price contract.[12] After twelve months in court, the Venetian and Bovis Lend Lease reached an agreement to resolve the construction litigation.[13]

Those are the celebrity cases, but reports on the frequency of construction cost overruns for all size and scale of projects abound. Consider just this handful of headlines from across the country in the span of just a few weeks from early 2007:

"City That Loves Mass Transit Looks to the Sky for More," William Yardley, *New York Times* (January 29, 2007): The construction cost for the Portland Aerial Tram soared from $15M to over $57M by the time it was completed, resulting in a passenger fare of $4, twice initial estimates.

"Costs Jump for New Meadowlands Stadium," Janet Frankston Lorin, *Associated Press* (January 26, 2007): The price of the new football stadium for the New York Giants and New York Jets has risen $600 million [or 43%] to $1.4 billion. Initial costs were estimated at $800 million.

"D-49 still on track to build despite cost spike," Brian Newsome, *Colorado Springs Gazette* (February 4, 2007): "Falcon School District 49 will build two high schools as promised to voters despite a multimillion [$10–$14 million] cost overrun. The district will use creative financing to avoid asking residents for more money."

"MTA Exec Threatens to Stop 7 Line Extension," Chuck Bennett, *amNewYork* (February 14, 2007): The No. 7 subway extension project is already $1 billion over its initial $2 billion budget, and construction has yet to begin.

"Overruns Add Up to Tax Hike for Richland 1," Lisa Michals, http://www.thestate.com (February 14, 2007): "Richland [South Carolina] taxpayers will pay as much as $35M of the $51M in cost overruns on school construction projects, school board members decided." The initial 2002 $381M budget included a $40M contingency.

Evidence that the construction industry is badly broken is not anomalous. The consensus, statistical and anecdotal, is broad and deep that this huge industry does not perform as it should. The men and women working in this industry every day, year after year, at every level, work within an industry that time has forgotten. The way we build today differs little from how our ancestors built churches and sphinxes hundreds and thousands of years ago. No one denies it. Everyone would prefer to do better.

The Process and Its Players

In a puristic sense, it is a simple task to define what each of the participants seeks from a project. The construction process that remains as predominant today as a century ago is "design-bid-build." In this linear process, the owner develops the parameters of the project, the architect prepares the design, the owner invites contractors to bid on the design, and the selected contractor then builds the design. It sounds simple. But there are numerous opportunities for the contractor to use its superior informational advantage to escape the confines of its original contract price.

In the typical building project, the owner and its business consultants conceive and outline the program (use, area, occupancy, etc.) of the project that meet specific business objectives. The owner must match its present and future needs to the site, budget and financing, and timetable available to complete the project.

In the design phase, the architect analyzes the owner's program and develops one or more conceptual designs for the owner to select for final development. Once the owner and the architect choose the final concept design, the architect proceeds through schematic design, design development, and finally construction document phases, securing the owner's approval after each. The architect, or occasionally the owner, retains additional design consultants as needed, such as structural engineers, mechanical engineers, lighting designers, and acousticians, among others, to develop a complete, coordinated, technically responsive design solution.

When the design is completed, or nearly completed, the owner and architect invite prequalified general contractors (GC) or construction managers (CM) to bid on the construction documents. Depending on the experience of the GC, it may estimate the cost of the work itself or in consultation with its preferred subcontractors in order to present the best possible competitive bid to the owner. A good GC will itemize its bid proposal for the owner following the industry accepted CSI (Construction Specification Institute) outline format (site work, concrete, masonry, carpentry, etc.). The GC then adds its markups for general conditions, insurance, and fees (the combined percentage of these markups is commonly 15–20 percent—it could be more or less depending on the scale and complexity of the project and the reputation of the contractor). Notably, the GC almost never specifies particular subcontractors for the CSI line items on its final bid proposal to the owner. The GC simply provides a cost estimate for that trade's scope of work. The owner (and perhaps the GC) does not yet know which subcontractor(s) will perform the work. When the GC bids on the architect's drawings and specifications, the bid documents, it assumes they are 100 percent complete. The GC's base bid represents a fixed price only on the information shown on the bid documents. The owner's bid documents and the GC's base bid form the foundation of the base contract.

After the GC is awarded the project, the "build" phase begins. But before actual construction begins, the GC must "buy out" contracts with the subcontractor trades necessary to the project: for example, excavators, masons, carpenters, electricians, plumbers, and painters among potentially dozens of others. Here, the goal of the GC is to buy out the subcontractors at a discount of 10–20 percent or more to the trade work CSI line item in the bid proposal. This difference is the "buy," and it can be a much-needed cushion if the GC makes a mistake or its subcontractor needs to be replaced during construction. But more often, the buy is a hidden profit center, much more significant than the GC's overhead and fee markup shown on its base bid. Within a few weeks after being awarded the job, the GC has usually bought all the trade subcontractors—many may have prior working relationships with the GC. Some GCs may wait until further into the project if they believe that they won't need a particular subcontractor until much later, such as a painter. Or they may take a calculated risk that they can buy that trade even cheaper at a later date than they had budgeted in their base bid proposal. Of course, the GC understands that trade and material costs may increase in price during that interval, leaving the GC with a "negative buy," that is, paying more for the trade than it initially estimated and agreed to in the base bid proposal. This is the kind of situation that leads even good GC's to look for any excuse to submit change orders.

A few years ago when my firm represented an owner renovating their downtown Manhattan office building, we witnessed the magnitude of the GC's buy. Typically, an owner pays its GC (or CM) based on monthly requisitions submitted to the owner. The requisitions include line items costs due subcontractors that correspond to the project completion percentage they attained that month. The owner pays the GC and the GC disperses payment to the subs. In this case, when the owner discovered that the GC had not distributed two requisitions worth of owner-paid invoices to the subcontractors, the owner audited the GC's books (which the agreement allowed) and discovered that the GC's average buy on each subcontractor ranged from 25 percent to 50 percent of total cost of the trade! Armed with that information, the owner struck a deal with the GC whereby on subsequent requisitions, the owner made-up all payments to the GC's subcontractors first before releasing any further payments to the GC.

Theoretically, there is nothing wrong with allowing the GC its buy. After all, the owner agrees to the GC's base bid price, and the GC should therefore be fully entitled to use its market expertise to make as much profit as possible on the project (provided it properly completes the structure as shown on the bid documents.) The problem with this, especially from the owner's perspective, is that the buy is only possible because of the huge asymmetrical information gap favoring the GC. Even if the owner is capable of comparing multiple GC bid proposals, it can never really know how much the hidden buys are inflating the project's costs right from the start.

Once construction starts, the GC is responsible for coordinating and scheduling its subcontractors, along with its own laborers and project management to keep the project on budget and schedule. It is during the "build" phase that conflicts, errors, and omissions are discovered in the design team's bid documents, unforeseen and concealed site conditions are uncovered, and myriad other minor and major derailments encountered. These conditions inevitably lead to delay claims and change orders submitted by the GC. The change order indicates the cost of additional work not shown on the bid documents or included in the base bid contract price. With a change order comes an increase in project costs. In almost all instances, a change order must be approved by the owner (and often the architect) and signed by the GC to be deemed valid. There are valid reasons for change orders, but illegitimate ones are also common. Change order costs are made up of the actual cost of the additional work plus previously agreed upon fees and insurance costs. But they may also include hidden premiums charged by the GC and its subcontractors since, having already been awarded the job, they now operate in a competition-free environment. The uncertainty of the change order process is the single biggest contributor to fixed-price construction contracts not being as "fixed" as they initially appear.

While more and more midsize ($1 million plus) and larger projects use a construction manager instead of a general contractor, the design-bid-build model is still generally followed. The primary difference between the CM and the GC is one of transparency. The CM shares with the owner, on an open-book basis, the subcontractors' contracts whereas the GC does not disclose to the owner its negotiated price with each subcontractor, or its buy. The CM therefore acts in the guise of a consultant to the owner and charges a percentage-based fee, commonly 2–4 percent, based on the cost of the subcontractor work and any direct project expenses incurred by the CM (such as its own labor, site equipment, and overhead, collectively known as the general conditions).

The CM typically enters into the construction agreement "at risk." This means that although the CM works with the owner on an open book basis, the CM enters into direct contracts with the subcontractors and remains solely responsible to the owner for their per-

20

formance, like a GC. Another version is where the CM acts as agent of the owner. In this arrangement, the CM incurs little risk as the owner enters into agreements directly with the subcontractors recommended by the CM while the CM simply manages the day-to-day construction. When a CM can serve as the owner's agent, it effectively has no independent liability to the owner as long as it acts within the scope of its retention.

The GC works on a lump sum basis, which includes costs for its subcontractors as well as its general conditions costs and fee. Unlike the GC, the CM does not give the owner a fixed price. Instead, it develops a Guaranteed Maximum Price, or GMP (a misnomer if there ever was one), from its own project cost estimates on design drawings that may only be 80–95 percent complete. It works with the design team and subcontractors to estimate the other 5–15 percent design intent missing from the bid drawings. The CM is contractually obligated to buy the entire project, that is, "actual" plus "intent," for no more than the GMP. As a result the project is frequently many months into construction before the drawings are 100 percent complete and coordinated and the owner has any assurances as to what the final cost of the project will be. Only then can the CM go back to the owner and, now subject to price fluctuations and other factors, provide a final cost. In practice, the GC's fixed price provides an element of certainty for the owner because the cost is based on a virtually complete, specific scope of work. Only additions to this specific project scope will increase the owner's cost. But with a CM and a GMP, there is no fixed cost from the outset of construction. Incomplete design, material cost fluctuations, a more protracted buyout process are some of the resulting uncertainties that can come back to plague the owner in the form of change orders and delays.

Some now say it does not really matter whether an owner uses a GC or CM. They are just as likely to experience delays and cost overruns with one as they are the other, since the design-bid-build process itself has not changed appreciably. The "fast-track" process, a more recent variation on design-bid-build, adds significantly greater risk to the owner. Fast-track projects seek to compress the overall project schedule by beginning construction significantly before the design is fully complete. Because of the overlap of the design and construction phases, a CM is always retained early in the project. Instead of issuing a single bid package all at once upon completion (or near completion) of the design as in design-bid-build, the CM issues awards to subcontractors and commences construction on multiple bid packages over several months. For example, the superstructure drawings are issued first for bid and construction. A month later, the exterior enclosure and mechanical system packages may be issued. A month later, the finish carpentry package, and so on. Obviously, the CM and the design team need to adhere to a rigorous design and construction schedule. There can be no deviation in the overall design plan for the building once the construction commences without serious cost implications. For this reason, the fast-track process is best suited for simple projects with little potential for design error. Most owners who choose this construction process are sophisticated enough to weigh the trade-offs: is the potential cost savings of an early finish offset by the potential for huge cost increases? However, the novice owner should beware of fast-track, especially if it is heavily promoted by its CM. The CM stands to make significant additional fees by managing the multiple bid process and construction instead of the construction alone. Their fees are based on the cost of the work and their general conditions: the more work, the bigger their fee.

An increasingly popular construction option is "design-build." Design-build combines the design team and construction team into a joint entity, solely responsible to the owner, in some cases even providing a turnkey, or move-in-ready solution, for a fixed fee. Contractors typically lead design-build efforts, either hiring design professionals directly or entering into a joint venture agreement with a design firm for the project.

In the past, design-build was typically utilized for such standardized projects as industrial warehouses and large-scale residential developments. Today, design-build has become a more popular choice for a range of construction projects. The advantages are compelling. Potential cost savings and shortened schedules are common. Minimized is the potential for conflicts between the designers and contractors, the root problem of design-bid-build projects that result in change orders and delay. On the one hand, the design-build process may be as close to a fixed cost contract that an owner can expect in today's construction world, notwithstanding whether the owner decides to add another floor after the design is complete. On the other hand, the information balance favors the design-builder since it controls both the design and construction of the project. If the owner knows with a high degree of certainty the general design, program, systems, and finishes desired, and is comfortable giving up a certain degree of control and micro–decision making, then design-build could be more cost effective than design-bid-build. But as to the discrete detailed costs of each element comprising the construction, the owner will remain largely in the dark.

Themes and Argument

The construction industry's woes are only partly a function of its multiple participants and processes. The central problem is structural. As illustrated in figure 1, the symptoms of our broken buildings and busted budgets are low productivity relative to other U.S. industries; the predominance of small firms fragmented across the industry; risk-averse and short-sighted management; an uncompetitive market; and most problematic, mutable-cost contracts. These symptoms are caused by the twin root problems of asymmetric information and the lack of real intermediaries.

ASYMMETRY AND THE LACK OF REAL INTERMEDIARIES

The construction industry is extremely fragmented. It consists of hundreds of thousands of firms, most of them very small.[14] "Mom and pop" is the tempting description, but to this day with so few women involved, "pop shops" is more precise. There are very few big firms, and they do not account for much output or employment. Every year, thousands of new firms enter the industry, and thousands of existing firms exit through bankruptcy or a deliberate winding-up of (usu-

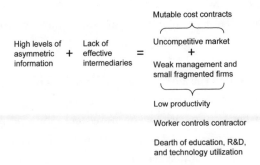

High levels of asymmetric information + Lack of effective intermediaries =

Mutable cost contracts

Uncompetitive market
+
Weak management and small fragmented firms

Low productivity

Worker controls contractor

Dearth of education, R&D, and technology utilization

FIGURE 1. The Equation of Existing Industry Failure. Source: Barry B. LePatner.

ally limited) business projects. At first glance, this looks like Adam Smith: a free market with many small companies where competition ensures that the good ones stay, and the bad ones get kicked out. Even if that were so, it wouldn't ensure that owners would get burned any less by contractors.

Alas, Adam Smith's model is just that, a model. It "works" when applied to markets that have a free flow of information, markets where buyers can easily discern price and quality differences, like markets for gold, wheat, and chewing gum. The flow of information in construction markets, by contrast, is sluggish at best. Dressing it up, economists would call the construction industry a classic example of market failure due to asymmetric information. Specifically, sellers (building contractors) have at their fingertips all of the critical information to establish the business terms with their buyers (owners), but the buyers do not. That is, the contractor possesses far superior technical and operational knowledge of the industry than all owners, except for those who develop or build as often as their contractors. We do not live in Smith's utopia because levels of precontract asymmetric information (adverse selection) and postcontract asymmetric information (moral hazard) remain high in favor of the contractor. Adverse selection in this context means that the owner's absence of complete information during the precontract (bidding) phase may result in him unknowingly selecting a contractor of dubious quality. And moral hazard in this context means that after the project is complete, the owner has no way of knowing whether the contractor honestly adhered to the agreement. The owner has no assurance because there is no effective, independent intermediary to assist him.

Markets characterized by asymmetric information can and do work, but only with the aid of intermediaries that create information available to buyers. A classic example is the stock market. When an individual wishes to purchase one or more stocks for a retirement account, no call is placed to IBM asking the company if this is a good time to buy IBM. Instead, an intermediary—a stockbroker or investment advisor—well versed in the needs of the purchaser and the stock market acts on behalf of the buyer. The market for used automobiles, a business about as low on the reputation ladder as construction or maybe insurance sales, is similar. Adverse selection is high because, in the famous model of economist George Akerlof, used cars come in one of two types, breakdown-prone "lemons" and highly reliable "peaches." The seller knows (or knows more) which category best describes his car, but most potential buyers cannot tell if the auto is a lemon or a peach. Kicking the tires or knowingly looking under the hood doesn't work. The buyers naturally offer the average price for used cars of the same make, model, and mileage. Here is the kicker: offended, the seller of the peach refuses the offer, but the seller of the lemon greedily accepts. As a result, only lemons trade and potential buyers soon "learn" that all used automobiles are untrustworthy. The market can be salvaged if an intermediary, like a used-car dealership, arises to reduce the asymmetric information. In exchange for a spread or markup between the seller's price and the buyer's price, the used-car dealership creates information about each car, charging less for the lemons and more for the peaches.[15] A truly independent intermediary is the universal antidote to asymmetric information.

Though still a far cry from perfect, the market for used automobiles functions better in the presence of knowledgeable intermediaries. And it has been improving in recent years with the entry of big corporate intermediaries like AutoNation, whose founder H. Wayne Huizenga—ironically enough the son of a Chicago builder—previously helped to consolidate the historically fragmented waste management

24

and video rental industries. It didn't take all that much either, in a grossly asymmetric business like used cars. Just let the buyer in on better information—well-inspected vehicles under reasonable warranties, fixed-sticker prices, no haggling—and you can look like a prince in a business where demand, as in construction, knows no limit. Many mom-and-pop shops go out of business (in truth many go to work for the new corporate entity), but the average consumer benefits because bigger more efficient companies reduce prices and/or raise quality.[16]

25

In construction, the real danger for an owner arises most frequently after the negotiated contract has been executed. To the unassuming owner—be it a sophisticated corporation, a university, or a homeowner—the contractor appears to submit a fixed cost for a defined scope of work as set out in the drawings prepared by the architect. Often, even the start and completion dates are clearly established. Postcontract asymmetric information, or moral hazard, is unusually high in construction. After the deal is signed and work has begun, the contractor has tremendous power over the owner, power that many contractors leverage to their advantage. As we shall see, this power is almost monopolist in nature, as it would be highly costly—in time and money—for the owner to fire the current contractor and seek new bids and even less reason to believe that the new experience would be any better. As most owners in this situation come to recognize, firing a contractor midproject only ensures that the project will certainly take longer and lead to highly increased costs for completion. With this kind of market asymmetry in place, a seemingly fixed-price contract at the outset of a project can quickly become a mutable one by the end of the project.

But all is not lost. Financial markets are also characterized by both adverse selection and moral hazard. Namely, the seller or borrower of securities knows whether his business is a peach or a lemon, but buyers or lenders of securities do not, and even borrowers may engage in risky behaviors after receiving a loan. So intermediaries like banks, brokerages, and insurance companies step in to create information about the borrower and its business, both screening applicants to reduce adverse selection and monitoring customers postloan to keep moral hazard at a minimum. Again, the result is not always foolproof (vide Enron), but financial markets work far better with the aid of intermediaries than they would without them. Nor will any Wayne Huizengas find much opportunity here, because the mom-and-pop financial shops long since have given way to big corporations.[17]

Those parts of the American economy that have enjoyed phenomenal success have all shared one trait—high levels of competition between producers. As *New Yorker* columnist James Surowiecki puts it:

> The story of the early days of the U.S. auto industry is not an unusual one. In fact, if you look at the histories of most new industries in America, from the railroads to television to personal computers to, most recently, the Internet, you'll see a similar pattern. In all these cases, the early days of the business are characterized by a profusion of alternatives, many of them dramatically different from each other in design and technology. As time passes, a market winnows out the winners and losers, effectively choosing which technologies will flourish and which will disappear. Most companies fail, going bankrupt or getting acquired by other firms. At the end of the day a few players are left standing and in control of most of the market.[18]

This is not what has happened in construction. The preponderance of asymmetric information favoring contractors has allowed small inefficiently operated firms to stay in business, even thrive, often despite a lack of traditional business acumen. The contractor's knowledge advantage over the owner creates perverse incentives whereby the contractor can be systematically rewarded for inefficient behavior since there are typically few real consequences to deter such actions. For example, the contractor can hold the owner hostage by slowing down or even ceasing work in order to pressure an owner to approve and pay for disputed change orders. Responsibility for a contractor error can similarly be shifted to an owner. The contractor can even control the rate at which he submits change orders to pressure the owner into coughing up more money, especially near the end of the project when the owner is desperate to move in and move on. Strikingly, this is allowed to happen, in part because the construction industry has no true independent intermediaries worth the name. These exist in other industries precisely to check the rise of an asymmetrical information advantage by one party over the other.

As a consequence, our market for buildings and other construction work is badly broken. No institution—the equivalent of a Zagat guide for construction—helps owners and developers to distinguish honest contractors from highwaymen. No *effective* intermediary on a nationwide basis exists to stop contractors from exaggerating, misrepresenting, or lying to owners to extract inflated and extra payments for both the base bid price and subsequent change orders. Most owners, even relatively big, sophisticated ones like the MTA, usually do not have the capability to properly determine whether the construction costs submitted by the contractor are fully legitimate. In this environment, even grossly inefficient construction companies can make a go of it. The companies that do the best financially are often not those that build the best, but those that are the best at bidding strategically to win the job for the right to subsequently induce owners to pay more than the amount specified in the base contract.

THE QUESTION OF COMPETITION AND INTERMEDIARIES

The construction business is deceptively uncompetitive. Construction companies profess to compete with each other to supply owners with the best buildings at the best price. Rather, they compete for the future right to increase the initial cost of their agreement with owners and to protect their anticipated profit against the reality that their projects are not always likely to meet the project's scheduled completion. In other words, they become monopolists after signing the contract. The competition at the bidding stage, therefore, is in a sense anti-competitive.[19] Getting the contract becomes the objective, not providing a superior product. We end up with many firms but little head-to-head competition on the big economic variables of time, quality, and price. And that, Nobel Prize winning economist Douglass North reminds us, is a recipe for stagnation if there ever was one.[20]

Ironically, so many small construction firms enter the industry each year because the market is *not* economically competitive, not because it is. Remember, people need and desire buildings and other physical infrastructure. There is a huge demand for houses, retail stores, office parks, dams, and roadways, even at high prices. Little firms can all get a piece of this inevitable action, if only by virtue of luck, proximity, or personal connection. In an economically competitive market, they would eventually lose out to bigger, better-managed companies. But in the current environment, where the purchaser of the end product has little experience or ability to challenge bidders, the little guys persist and everyone else pays for it.

There would seem to be some natural-enough intermediary candidates in construction. What about building inspectors, architects, the Better Business Bureau?[21] None though is capable of doing the job. The inspector's role is to ensure that the electrician or plumber complied with the applicable codes so as not to endanger life or property. But he will not tell the owner whether the contractor did a top-quality or a just-so job and if the price was fair.

Such judgments used to be the bailiwick of architects, but somewhere along the line, architects lost their grip on the grimy reality of construction. Architects were once big players in the construction process. They were just as involved in the construction phase as they were the design phase. They imagined a structure; they drew plans for it; they supervised construction and controlled costs. There was a time when they were referred to as the "master builder." They connected owners to buildings-in-the-making each and every step of the way.

Those days in architecture are long gone. Today, architects play a shadow of their former role. They shrank from their historic role as the owner's ombudsman charged, above all, with keeping an eye on the work of the contractors during the so-called construction administration phase. By the late 1980s, many architects had evolved into stylists; their designs often focused on achieving a "look," that sometimes forgot that most owners simply wanted a useable, functional building. By the mid-1990s the star architect, or "starchitect" attained celebrity status, branding his (yes, it is still a male-dominated profession at its upper echelons) characteristic style into a commodity that was marketable to corporations and developers alike. Rarely did the starchitects or the great majority of architects commit significant resources to the construction administration phase of their projects, often devoting less than 15 percent of their overall fee for such services. In their absence during the construction process, building owners have gotten well and truly lost.

If a contractor cheats an owner, the owner can complain to the Better Business Bureau or other information clearinghouses. The sad fact, though, is that most such organizations and services have little authority, especially in resolving disputes. Contractors that do manage to get bad reputations simply re-form under new names every couple of years.

Other pseudo-intermediaries have also come along, the most prominent of which is the construction manager. When dedicated to its work and incentivized to truly align its interests with the owner's, a good construction manager can keep a project on schedule and on budget. They can effectively rein in the overly enthusiastic architect who specifies materials that may inflate the budget or are unavailable for delivery in time to meet the project schedule. However, the idiosyncrasies of the individual rule, and not all construction managers are dedicated and good. When paid a salary by the owner, they are mere employees and like all employees may neglect their employer's interests. When their remuneration is put "at risk" or percentage-based, however, they may cavort with contractors to ensure the appearance of quality or provide excuses why a project was delayed.

The one process—competitive bidding—that is often held up by contractors as the means whereby owners get sufficient information to effectively discern price is of equally little aid. This is because contractors often fall victim to, and sometimes deliberately inflict upon themselves, the so-called "winner's curse." In layman's terms, they bid below their costs (including normal profits) in order to win the job. A few of them will eat the loss grudgingly. Many can't afford to absorb the loss, mainly due to their small size, so they will either perform substandard quality work, substitute inferior materials for those specified, or find other inventive ways to charge the owner extra through inflated change orders or delay costs. As will be discussed in chapter 7, this behavior is best controlled by contract language that precludes such chicanery.

This happens only because no one carefully minds the owner's store. Architects often contend that complete, fully coordinated sets of plans are not possible on large, complex projects. They assert that the fast-track process chosen by owners and construction managers precludes this from occurring. Almost always, contractors find that changes in the design during construction are necessary to actually get the thing built, and they subsequently charge large sums to make those changes just like Bechtel did for adding the Fleet Center to the Big Dig's drawings.

Even if an owner is astute enough to realize that changing from a medium grade laminated beam to a structural steel header is not worth $3,300, there is little or nothing he can do about it. Architects are rarely equipped to come to the aid of an owner in these situations. The only thing that is certain is that after work has gotten under way the contractor is a monopolist, or close to it. To shutter a half-completed project for even one month while alternate bids from other contractors are lined up costs much more than $3,300. So, inevitably work continues at or close to the price set by the contractor. If the contractor tries to pad the bill again, the owner might think about filing suit. But then again, lawyers do not come cheap and the project still isn't complete. A compromise is struck and the work proceeds as charges mount, often well beyond the project's true cost (and fair profits) for the contractor. The owner is out a tidy sum that he would have preferred to put to other uses and suffers from the uncertainty of not knowing what the project will cost until it is done. The contractor, in turn, learns that landing the contract is the most important thing because, after that, he can use his superior information and market power to make the project profitable. Essentially, contractors are incentivized to bid low to win the job, which will subsequently give them the exclusive right to bid high later. Unsurprisingly, many of them are very good at it.

Competitive bidding is therefore no panacea because it fails to determine the final cost or quality of the job. In order to jumpstart construction productivity, we need two interrelated devices: 1) an intermediary with some teeth, and 2) a true fixed cost (a.k.a. "hard money" or lump sum) contract, where a contractor commits to build in accordance with the design intent for a precise sum. Once those are in place, hundreds of thousands of tiny construction firms, most of which do only one very specific task on a subcontracting basis, will disappear. There need not be panic about jobs, which will not go away. In fact, construction employment will likely soar as the industry's productivity increases because at lower prices individuals, governments, and businesses will choose to invest in more, better quality buildings and public works. However, instead of working for themselves, those employed will work for big corporations, the ones that have proven that they can deliver what they say, when they say, for the price they say, just like automobile or airplane or chewing gum manufacturers do.

The argument set forth is straightforward. Asymmetric information and mutable-cost contracts put owners at a substantial disadvantage compared to builders, who have every incentive to bid low on a project to get the job. Because the business is highly competitive *at the bid stage,* most firms (which are small to begin with and enjoy little financial safety net to absorb cost overruns) know that their low bid will not return an adequate profit. But *after a contractor is awarded a contract, the situation changes radically.* The contractor then becomes a monopolist, who will attempt to recoup through change orders the profits denied it by the bid process. This explains the pervasiveness of mutable-cost contracts. Owners realize that, even with a seemingly straightforward fixed-price contract, once they are embroiled in construction, they have few good options but to pay up in order to keep the project moving ahead so as not to incur even greater delays and costs. The industry is caught in this unvirtuous cycle. We take up these issues in the next chapter.

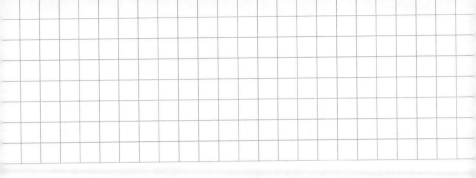

The Economic Context of Construction

As recently as March 23, 2005, the *Wall Street Journal* informed its readers of yet another round of "construction sticker shock," or yet higher prices for new buildings. The *Journal* portrayed the recent price increases as the effects of increased demand. Demand may be high, for sure, but the root cause of such double-digit increases runs much deeper and cannot be ascribed to the neat workings of supply and demand. On the contrary, the construction industry illustrates not a working market, but a failed one.[1]

   The subject is of global importance in every sense. In this chapter we will detail the construction industry's contribution to the economies of the United States and the rest of the world, and survey the strengths and weaknesses of the construction industries of other countries, some poor and some rich. We will conclude with a description of the construction industry's structure here at home.

The Construction Industry: Its Size and Importance

Historically, the construction industry has played a comparably hefty role in the U.S. economy, but it has not played it very efficiently. Its contribution to the GDP from 1959 to 1999 has remained steady just below 5 percent in comparison to most other private economic sectors, which have generally declined modestly during the same period.[2] In 2000, the construction industry's contribution to GDP was pegged at 4.7 percent.[3] Not much has changed in recent years. Today in the United States, construction accounts for 2 to 6 percent of employment and some 5 to 9 percent of GDP, depending on the figures used.[4]

The annual value of construction of all types (public and private, residential and commercial) is truly staggering. Since 1993, the value has doubled from $500 billion to more than $1 trillion.[5] The value created by the industry, both public and private, is about evenly split between residential and nonresidential construction.

Since 1998 the industry has employed between 5.8 and 7 million Americans annually.[6] Construction has long been a major employer of nonagricultural goods producers.[7] Construction has also traditionally been a major employer of labor of all sorts.[8] Construction is important in part because it is an extremely broad category, encompassing everything from the erection of skyscrapers and bridges to refinishing basements in single-family homes to maintaining existing structures of all types.[9] The fact that Americans spend more on building renovations and improvements than they do on building maintenance reveals both our desire to grow and our dependency on the industry.[10] In some form or another, be it erecting public buildings and infrastructure, building corporate edifices, or mere home remodeling, the construction industry is present in every U.S. community at every economic level.[11]

The Problem of Productivity

That presence adds up. By January 2007, construction was a $1.23 trillion a year industry in the United States. A one-time improvement in construction productivity of 10 percent would boost America's GDP by $123 billion. That sum, compounded annually at 3 percent for thirty years, would mean a real per capita income over $273 billion higher in 2037 than if the construction industry remains unreformed. Put another way, reform of the construction industry could generate enough economic growth to save Social Security as it is currently con-

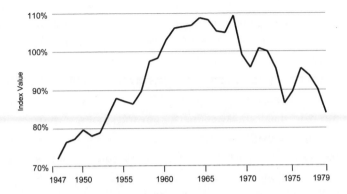

FIGURE 2. Productivity in the U.S. Construction Industry, 1947–1979. Source: J. E. Cremeans, *Construction Review* (May–June 1981).

stituted. (Not that we'd necessarily use the economic resources freed up in that way.)[12]

In theory, measuring productivity in construction is no different than measuring it in other industries. It is simply the ratio of output per unit of input over time. For example, in 1960, it took X hours or dollars (input), to complete construction job Y (output). Today it takes $X - j$ hours, where j is an extremely small positive number, or perhaps even negative, relative to X. In most other industries it now takes $X - k$ hours, where k is positive and a larger percentage of X. Less input + same output = increased productivity; the same input + same output = stagnation. In reality though, scholarly and industry arguments swirl over how best to measure construction productivity.[13]

Ominously, productivity in the U.S. construction industry has been stalled for a long time, and by several accounts the rate of productivity growth has never been very impressive especially when compared to most other economic sectors. Nevertheless, productivity increased at 2.4 percent per year after World War II, peaking in 1968. But, as shown in figure 2, it then declined by 2.8 percent annually between 1968 and 1978. (Other measures of productivity give broadly similar results, but the details are disputed.)

The Great Inflation of the 1970s might be the culprit here because it caused financing costs to soar and real wages to sag, both of which hurt demand for new homes. That led to a housing crisis.[14] Perhaps more importantly, inflation also hurt contractors on long-term projects because wages and materials prices soared between the bid and

36   the payment. In order to "come out whole at the end of the project," one recent study notes, contractors during the Great Inflation had to find ways to pressure owners for additional funds. In other words, "contractors had to make claims for any work not shown or implied on the documents."[15] But even after Federal Reserve chairman Paul Volcker dampened the fires of inflation, U.S. construction productivity continued to lag and American contractors continued to submit change orders under the mutable contracts signed with owners—or in other words to inflate the price of construction projects whenever they could. The more unscrupulous contractors made a business of bilking owners with extra charges rather than improving their core performance, so it is not surprising that productivity has continued to stagnate. In relative terms, the lack of robust productivity growth means the industry can only head in one direction: down.

While lack of worker productivity will be discussed later, suffice it to say that the stereotype of the idle construction worker has a clear basis in fact. The magnitude of the problem, though, varies over time and place, rendering it difficult to measure with precision. One study shows that only about 32 percent of the total time spent at the typical U.S. construction site involves actual direct work. The other 68 percent is wasted on equipment transportation delays, travel within the job site, late starts and early quits, personnel breaks, receiving instructions, and sundry other delays. Perhaps matters are not quite that bad, though. An important recent metasurvey (a survey of numerous studies) indicates that an average of 49.6 percent of time in construction is devoted to wasteful activities.[16] Whether two-thirds or "only" half of the time on construction sites is wasted, the industry apparently has succumbed to a deep-rooted illness. Many others concur. "This is a serious problem," argues Stanford civil engineering professor Paul Teicholz. "Over the past 40 years, construction projects have required significantly more field work hours per dollar of contract." Over that same period, productivity in other nonfarm industries has doubled. The

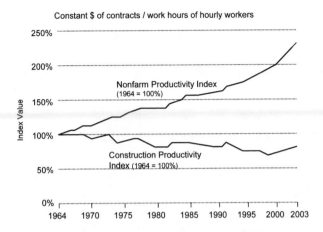

Constant $ of contracts / work hours of hourly workers

FIGURE 3. Construction and Nonfarm Labor Productivity Index, 1964–2003.
Source: U.S. Department of Commerce, Bureau of Labor Statistics.

headlines, we must conclude, are not aberrations.[17] Even if the industry's woes have been exaggerated, the stakes—for the national economy as well as owners' budgets—are simply too high to allow debate to trump action.[18]

Higher construction productivity would mean lower construction costs and hence more construction projects. Improving construction would lead to safer buildings and better infrastructure—bridges, highways, railroads, and tunnels. Similarly, lower housing construction costs would allow an even higher percentage of Americans to purchase their own homes and enjoy a true ownership stake in their country. Higher productivity would also mean more terrorism-resistant structures and the erection of more sustainable quality buildings. Perhaps most enticingly of all, lower construction costs would spell lower taxes.[19]

And those are simply the direct benefits. Indirectly, lower construction costs would ripple through the economy, and in a salubrious fashion. As the Business Roundtable pointed out in its study of the construction industry's ills, "the price of every factory, office building, hotel or power plant that is built affects the price that must be charged for the goods or services produced in it or by it."[20] Lower construction costs would mean lower rents, some of which would be passed onto consumers and some of which would swell corporate profits, never a bad thing in a country where most people own corporate securities, if not directly then through intermediaries like banks, insurers, or mutual funds.

The construction industry itself would of course also be a big winner if it could increase productivity. Lower prices stimulate demand for building, so there would be even more construction work to go around. The least efficient construction workers and firms might lose out, but the wages and profits of the rest would increase, perhaps dramatically. At least that is what happened when agricultural and manufacturing productivity soared in the eighteenth, nineteenth, and twentieth centuries. People shifted out of agriculture into manufacturing and out of manufacturing into services, boosting their productivity, real wages, and standard of living along the way. Construction should be no different.

Many believe that the industry's cyclical nature explains its inefficiency. Generally, the construction industry tracks, and even exaggerates, the nation's business cycle. Serious recessions, such as those experienced in the early 1980s and early 1990s, brought construction activity to a complete halt in some parts of the country. During brief periods of economic recession, construction firms fail, and workers are laid off for brief periods of time. During extended downturns, workers lose their jobs, move on, and the industry loses skilled workers.

The industry is cyclical, but the fluctuations are not a major cause of its structural problems. Three major pieces of evidence support that view. First, a survey showed that various contractors believe that management skills and manpower issues were the key drivers of construction productivity, ranking them far ahead of external forces like industry cyclicality. Second, the degree of construction industry cyclicality has changed over time; decreases or increases in cyclicality are not associated with higher or lower levels of productivity.[21] Third, cyclicality and firm size are also statistically unrelated, suggesting that fluctuations in demand are as likely to lead to the creation of larger companies as smaller ones. Contractors might stay small to avoid underutilizing capital during downturns or, as will be discussed later, to minimize risk. They could also respond to cyclicality as many other businesses have, by growing larger to diversify revenues during downturns, which typically strike certain regions and types of projects harder than others.[22] Contractors do not, however, take these measures because a dearth of competitive pressure drives industry fragmentation rather than concentration. In other words, industry structure renders construction firms vulnerable to the business cycle. Analysts who stress cyclicality are blaming effects rather than unearthing the causes.

THE UNDERLYING CAUSES OF LOW PRODUCTIVITY

So far we have discussed the *symptoms* of the productivity problems facing the construction industry. Construction is not competitive. On the face of it, this seems odd, given an industry that usually obtains its work through a closed bidding process, the vision of Adam Smith's competitive market. Those bids, however, do not get the job done by guaranteeing owners a fixed price. After work begins, construction contractors become de facto monopolies whose superior information and bargaining position enable them to take advantage of owners.

Not all contractors use their market power to exploit owners, but many do, and unfortunately they are the ones most likely to remain in the business. But the problem is not the contractors who, after all, are only responding to the incentives facing them. Rather, the industry's perennial productivity problem flows from the simple fact that one side has good information and leverage and the other doesn't. There is no reason to improve. In fact, when confronted with any suggestion for change, no matter how salutary, the standard retort of the industry is "This is how we have always done it."

Construction is a difficult business for sure. Much of the construction activity that supplies our indoor world takes place outdoors, exposing workers and equipment to the full range of Mother Nature's wrath. What looks like a nice site on a sunny June day turns into a caldron in August, a freezer in January, a mud hole in March. Everything needed to erect the building—workers, materials, and machines—must be brought in from elsewhere and in the right sequence. Whereas Michael Dell may have refined the concept of "just in time" manufacturing to speed computers to purchasers ordering online, nobody associated with a particular project is quite sure what surprises will ensue once excavation begins. Injury and death await the careless everywhere. Bricks fall; ground gives way; dump trucks slide off ramps onto occupied port-a-potties.

When the weather cooperates and nobody gets hurt, at least not hurt too badly, construction can move along *less slowly*. However, industry productivity rates in Canada and Sweden do not appreciably lag that of the American South, and storied northern construction firm Levitt and Sons worked "ten definite months . . . per year, more often eleven months, and if the weather was good, a full twelve months," so the main problem cannot be climatic.[23] The tradition that many of the employees of the building trades would not work in the winter months persisted long after the introduction of central heating systems made such strictures unnecessary. That was old news in 1924, when secretary of commerce and future president Herbert Hoover noted that "the seasonal character of the construction industries is to a considerable extent a matter of custom and habit, not of climatic necessity."[24]

Construction is also difficult because it is promoted by all concerned as a "custom" business; though undeniable, this does not explain much. One garage might be 20' × 10' × 15', another 18' × 12' × 14'. But they are both garages. One road might be 120 miles long and two lanes wide, another 65 miles long and eight lanes wide. But they are both roads. Each bridge, aqueduct, airport project is different literally, but the same fundamentally. Contractors know where the differences are and should be able to anticipate them. Many other types of professionals that provide custom services have little problem adjusting their skills and knowledge to particular circumstances. Each case an attorney or business consultant takes, each course that a professor teaches, each book that an author writes is a custom job, but not a major obstacle, except perhaps for neophytes. But few in the construction industry will acknowledge that for related building types, for example, hospitals, schools, or office buildings, 80–85 percent of the materials used are common to all.

AN INTERNATIONAL PROBLEM: GLOBAL COMPARISONS

The expansion of the global economy, which is especially evident in places like China, India, and the Middle East, is being led by unprecedented levels of construction. The volume of construction in China and Dubai alone makes the question of productivity and other industry-wide improvements an increasing concern for international investors and economists alike.

An old cold war one-liner, likely cribbed from Winston Churchill's memorable quip about democracy, went something like this: The United States of America has the worst government in the world . . . except for all the others. The same sad sentiment holds for the U.S. construction industry. It is the most productive in the world, or nearly so, but only because its competitors are so inept. We are in earnest here. The United States has long held the dubious distinction of leading the world in building. Immediately after World War II, when the unflattering views of the Temporary National Economic Committee on American construction were still fresh, the *Wall Street Journal* and *Fortune* ran articles like "Housing: Puny Giant" and "The Industry Capitalism Forgot," and books critical of the industry, like *The Crack in the Picture Window,* were widely discussed. But from afar we looked good: Europeans uniformly expressed admiration of American building methods.[25]

Just as most U.S. industries are among the world's leaders, the U.S. construction industry is still tops because of the institutional advantages of American society. America enjoys a stable, (relatively) nonpredatory government that protects property and civil rights. It does not destroy production incentives through the massive redistribution of wealth or provision of an overly generous social safety net. Moreover, it helps to support the infrastructure needed to transport workers, materials, power, and information, not to mention water and sewage, to where they are needed quickly and cheaply. Finally, and perhaps most importantly, it generally supports financial sector innovation and development. Given that solid foundation, still a relative rarity in today's world, it is difficult for U.S. construction businesses to be less efficient than their foreign counterparts.[26] A few countries are worth noting in particular:

In Brazil, construction labor productivity runs between a third to a half that of the United States. All other factors remaining the same, Brazilian construction workers and managers are no less intelligent, dutiful, or hard working than their American colleagues. Rather, they must contend with lower levels of competition, macroeconomic stability, infrastructure capacity, construction financing, and supply chain efficiency.

Brazil's construction sector, especially that part of it devoted to residential construction, is largely informal. In each locale, a few small inefficient firms use cheap casual labor, largely to avoid taxation. The firms almost exclusively use "craft" rather than "assembly" processes. In addition, there are few widely accepted standards for either material or workmanship. Brazilian construction firms rely much less on skilled subcontractors than U.S. construction firms, preferring instead to train and retain skilled workers. That preference may be due to the overall weakness of the Brazilian legal system. Simply put, firms cannot trust other firms, but they can control their workers because they are unsecured creditors.

Similarly, the paucity of good external financing makes Brazilian construction firms less efficient. They work on a smaller scale and buy materials only as needed, which often occasions delays. They also use less capital equipment than U.S. firms. Smaller Brazilian homes also means the construction of more walls, bathrooms, and kitchens per square meter than in America, and that is a big drag on productivity.

A dearth of competition also hurts Brazilian construction productivity. In the cement industry, collusive activity keeps prices artificially high. The twelve domestic producers, especially the two biggest ones, Votorantim and Group Joao Santos, which control 41 and 12 percent of the market, respectively, have essentially divided the country into near exclusive territories. (The ready-mix concrete industry in the

United States, by contrast, is apparently quite competitive.) Other barriers to entry, including prohibitively high start up costs, have kept the number of construction companies so low that Brazilian firms can insist on contracts that are explicitly mutable cost. Analysts and economists agree that mutable-cost contracts encourage contractor waste because they allow them to pass their inefficiencies onto owners. The result is a low level of market discipline.[27]

Brazil's prescriptive building codes are also extremely nettlesome as they are not at all performance driven. Walls, for instance, must be of a certain width rather than strength. Such laws of course reduce the incentive for adopting innovations leading to thinner, stronger walls. Macroeconomic instability, particularly high inflation rates, induced Brazilian companies to spend considerable effort timing markets and little effort improving productivity. In short, construction companies in Brazil have much less incentive to be efficient than those in the United States. That has prevented up- and down-stream industries from becoming more efficient as well. Brazil's prefabricated materials industry, for instance, is small, high cost, and highly concentrated.

India is also cursed with an inefficient construction sector, one that operates at just 8 percent of the U.S. productivity level. India's problems are similar to those of Brazil, with the added difficulty that it is especially costly and time consuming to secure clear title to land in rural India. In the cities, inadequate infrastructure limits developable land availability. Construction firms therefore compete on the basis of gaining access to land with clear titles or clear water rather than on the basis of construction practices.

The lack of price-based competition has prevented Indian construction firms from improving operational procedures. Poor organization of functions and tasks, inefficient design for manufacturing, and a dearth of large-scale projects keep Indian builders mired in the mud—literally. Mud homes are still being built in India, partly because of the low cost of rural labor, but partly because construction practices and materials are not standardized, or the standards remain unenforced. Rampant use of nonstandard materials invites contractors to source cheap, inferior materials, a source of profits that is much easier to tap than productivity increases. So, even brick home construction is often shoddy.

The difficulty of obtaining clear title to land has also stymied development of a mortgage market. That, in turn, reduces the number of new construction starts and also reduces the liquidity and hence value of commercial and residential real estate. It also induces owners to build slowly, room by room and even (mud) brick by brick, with very little use of even the simplest capital equipment, such as wheelbarrows. Everything from planning to painting is still done with hand tools, even when it would be economically justified to use circular saws or rollers. In a common scenario, one Indian man took twelve years to build his three-room home because his only financial resource was the savings from his farm income.[28]

The very long-term building process has stymied development of Indian project management skills. Foreign project managers working in India can finish buildings 15 percent faster than their Indian counterparts simply by implementing critical path scheduling. Further gains could be made by increasing supervision of workers, paying them by the task rather than hourly, and by increasing labor specialization. Today, it is not uncommon for the same Indian worker to both plaster and lay brick in the same room, on the same day. Adam Smith would weep, then point to the small "extent of the market" as the main culprit. The market remains small in part because contractors stay small to avoid taxes and burdensome regulations.[29]

The market also remains small because India's lack of a relatively cheap, transparent legal system impedes competition. The scarcity of competition, in turn, keeps costs high. Custom rather than standard contracts reign supreme. Most construction firms therefore prefer to create long-term relationships with subcontractors rather than to forge frequent, new arms-length contracts with untried firms. Most general contractors think nothing of paying, say, a 40 percent gross markup to a labor subcontractor in exchange for the relative assurance that he will procure the necessary number of unskilled labors.

In Poland, where productivity levels are about a quarter that of the United States, the two biggest problems are lack of demand and the unavailability of large land tracts. Both are related to the nation's recent emergence from communism. Many people pay low rents to former state-owned cooperative buildings and hence are uninterested in new housing at current prices. That will change as Poland's "baby boomers" mature and begin to seek homes. The lack of large tracts for new construction limits the scale of operations, keeping firms specializing in the construction of single family homes small and local. Firms specializing in multifamily homes in urban areas are much larger and rather more productive, in part due to competition from, and the employment of managers of, best practice international firms.

Polish workers are paid by the hour, with extra compensation for extra hours, and are poorly supervised, so they often slack during the day in order to earn overtime pay. Construction contracts are often poorly structured too. Contractors are often paid in installments as floors are completed. They therefore strive to get as many floors up as quickly possible, expending time and resources to build roads and other necessary infrastructural elements at suboptimal times. Winning bidders often are forced to start work before complete plans are in place.

A shortage of specialists also reduces the productivity of Polish construction. Instead of being performed in parallel by different specialized subcontractors, many tasks are undertaken in sequence by generalists who finish their jobs more slowly and at lower quality standards than specialists. Like India, Poland finds itself suffering from a nasty negative feedback cycle: high costs spur low demand, which means a small market, little division of labor, and hence a perpetuation of high costs.

Also like India, Poland suffers from government regulations that are overzealous when they impede productivity and ineffective when they could help it. For example, local authorities interpret building codes in idiosyncratic ways, making it difficult for nonlocals to enter. Unlike in Russia, however, widespread corruption is not found. Still, vestiges of the old communist bureaucratic infrastructure in Poland slow or even halt the construction process due to inconsequential paperwork discrepancies and delayed transmission of funds, and other administrative delays. Company employees are often idle as a result.

46 The small size of Polish construction sites limits the use of capital equipment. One contractor noted that on most of the jobs that he has worked on, excavators would not physically fit on the site. Finally, Polish workers, holding the *amount* of education and training constant, are less productive than U.S. workers. The *quality* of the education and training is partly to blame, as is the experience level of the average Polish construction worker.

Even some rich countries greatly lag the United States in construction productivity. The Japanese construction industry, for example, is only about half as productive as that in the United States.[30] Little wonder, then, that as late as 1980 half of Tokyo, the world's most populous city, was without a sewer system. The Japanese industry suffers from a lack of scale. In 2002, Japan was home to about 590,000 construction companies, employing some 6.5 million workers. Of those companies, 98.9 percent were capitalized at less than $1 million. The top six companies, however, are quite large and tied into keiretsu networks.[31] Japanese construction also suffers from a lack of standardized designs, methods, and materials. Moreover, most managers are architects or engineers not trained in effective construction management techniques. The result: poor compensation structures for workers, a dearth of scheduling expertise, misallocation of physical resources, which often have to be moved several times before being used, and other operational inefficiencies.

Price competition is very limited in Japan. *Dango* or collusion is common, as is *amakudari,* or the "descent from heaven" of retired government ministers into executive positions in construction firms. When they compete, Japanese construction companies tend to do so on customization and reputation, not price. They do because of the relative weakness of the Japanese legal system compared to that of the United States, and because of Japan's very limited secondary housing market. Taxes and other incentives discourage the Japanese from remodeling their homes and buildings; they prefer instead to scrap and rebuild. While that drives demand for new construction, it injures the secondary market, which is seventeen times smaller per dwelling than that of the United States. Of course, it is economically inefficient to scrap a building that could have been remodeled at less expense had the tax and other distortions not been in place.[32]

Japanese homes are much smaller than those in the United States and much more likely to be inadequately soundproofed, insulated, and air conditioned. Yet, due to the lack of standardization, they are usually custom designed, even at the low end of the scale. Moreover, they cost much more, so a smaller percentage of Japanese become homeowners and at a much later average age. Two by four construction, the U.S. standard, is still rare in Japan, where homes are built either in the traditional wood post and beam method by tiny family-owned firms or are prefabricated steel structures, likely built by one of three large firms that control three quarters of the prefab (prefabricated) market. Like other large Japanese corporations, those firms did not downsize when demand for their products slacked off in the 1990s, resulting in rampant overstaffing.

The Japanese are notoriously inefficient retailers. Many retail stores are tiny, yet are packed with salespeople, few of whom are actively engaged with customers at any one time. As it turns out, the Japanese are also very inefficient home sellers. The larger firms build very expensive model home parks. Rather than sell the model homes at some point, they tear them down and rebuild them every few years. Moreover, they employ numerous salespeople who spend most of their time cajoling Japanese families into having their perfectly functional existing homes torn down and replaced with new homes, of course overpriced and built to custom order. On average, each salesperson sells only eight homes per year. That means that the cost of maintaining the salesman is spread across only eight families per annum.

Barriers to foreign direct investment (FDI) have also kept the Japanese insulated from best practices. As mentioned above, the lack of a secondary market reduces competitive pressures on Japanese builders because they do not have to compete against renovators. It also reduces the amount of information available to Japanese purchasers regarding fair market prices. That is particularly troublesome because the Japanese government does not regularly report building transaction prices and appraisal standards are far from being as uniform as they are in the United States. Japanese banks assume that wood frame homes are worthless after a mere thirty-five years, so they regularly undervalue such structures, rendering it nearly impossible for anyone but the original owner to obtain mortgages for them.

The productivity level of the South Korean construction industry is much closer to that of the United States—about 70 percent of American productivity when measured by value added, and 93 percent when measured by square meters built. South Korean buildings tend to be of lower quality than those in the United States, partly from the use of lower quality materials and partly from the installation of fewer high margin extras. Both of those are largely due to price cap regulations in Korea. Most of the remaining productivity gap is explained by relative operational inefficiencies largely rooted in the lack of effective leadership at the design stage.

Construction productivity in Sweden is only about three quarters the U.S. level because the Swedes shackle their builders with myriad regulations regarding building quality, safety, and land use, each requiring government approval. In fact, Swedish construction firms spend as much time circumventing government red tape as they do trying to win in the market. Government subsidies for residential housing made customers insensitive to costs; firms were happy to oblige by engaging in joint pricing. Finally, strong labor unions make it difficult for managers to use their workforce in a flexible manner, decreasing teamwork and increasing costs. Reforms implemented in the 1990s decreased red tape and subsidies and increased competition. Productivity improved, but the industry is still trying to catch up. Swedish homes are of similar quality to those in similar climatic regions in the United States—they have to be—but they remain smaller or, holding size constant, more costly to produce.

If Australia is any guide, Sweden can catch up to the world leaders. In the 1980s, Australian construction groaned under the weight of union rules and labor disputes. Today, after a series of reforms, its productivity is 95 percent that of the United States, and almost identical to that of Germany and France. Holding quality constant, construction costs are also comparable to international benchmarks.

With U.S. ranking in the international league looking so good, why should we care that productivity in the U.S. construction industry is suboptimal? Who cares so long as most Americans can afford to own decent housing and megacorporations do not balk at the price of building or renting office buildings, factories, and other facilities? Any satisfaction in this situation is a dangerous and expensive delusion because as any construction economist will tell you, "the quality of the built environment affects all other aspects of the economy. A modern, durable, and flexible physical infrastructure is a necessary precondition for sustained innovation and competitive capacity; a decayed and unresponsive infrastructure will retard development throughout the economy."[33]

Simply put, laggard productivity inflates costs. Some are borne by private owners and developers and some are borne by the larger economy because huge amounts of capital are diverted into construction that could be put to other uses. In the case of public owners (the government, from the General Services Administration down to the local school board), the same problems result in the waste of billions of tax dollars every year. This is not a parochial "industry" problem, but a national policy concern. Construction in this regard keeps undistinguished company with health care and higher education where costs, holding quality constant, are skyrocketing far faster than inflation. Analysis of those industries we leave to others. But questions remain: Why are construction firms, from the neighborhood handyman to Halliburton, such lackluster performers? What can be done to improve the industry's productivity? Before we can answer these, we need to explore the other contributing factors.

INDUSTRY FRAGMENTATION AND SMALL FIRMS
Apart from its unproductive nature, the global construction industry shares just one other characteristic with the United States: its frag-

mented nature and the prevalence of numerous small sized firms. The United States has long been characterized by small firms, perhaps reflecting our nation's entrepreneurial spirit. In any case, by 1966, only 188 construction firms employed more than five hundred persons and only slightly more than 3,000 employed more than ninety-nine. Over 300,000 firms employed fewer than one hundred persons, and the vast bulk of those employed fewer than twenty. By 1985, the industry boasted 1.2 million firms and 5.5 million workers, an average of less than five people per firm. By 1993 the number of construction firms shrank to about 600,000, 83 percent of which employed fewer than ten people. For commercial construction firms, figure 4 illustrates not only the preponderance of small firms (for our purposes, less than fifty employees, i.e., the four tallest data bars), but also that this remained generally unchanged from 1998–2002. Only a dozen or so firms employed more than 1,000 people and not even 900 companies employed more than 250; this in an industry that in total employed over 4 million souls. After the construction boom of the past decade, the industry employs over 7.6 million today! Yet the industry continues to be extremely fragmented; the smaller firms so dwarf the large ones that the latter do not even appear on the charts.[34] Though the average construction firm today is larger than it has been in the past, consolidation of the industry has proceeded much more slowly than in the manufacturing and financial services sectors. To place the construction industry in perspective, Habitat for Humanity was actually the seventeenth largest homebuilder in the country in 2003 with its production of about 4,500 homes.[35]

Most construction firms are sole proprietorships or small business corporations, essentially individuals serving as subcontractors in order to enjoy business tax deductions and limited liability. Similarly, many small firms call their employees subcontractors simply to avoid the expense and responsibility of employees. The number of self-employed workers in construction more than doubled from 700,000 in 1970 to 1.6 million in 2000 compared with manufacturing, which increased less than 50 percent. By 2004, over 6.9 million work-

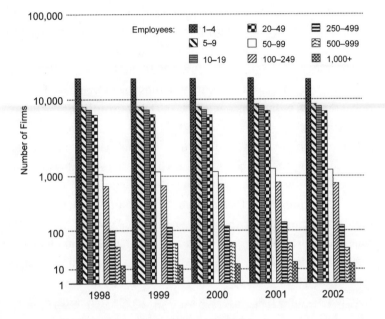

FIGURE 4. Commercial Construction Firms by Number of Employees, 1998–2002.
Source: U.S. Census Bureau, County Business Patterns.

ers were employed in the construction industry, and by February 2007, the industry employed approximately 7,650,000 workers.[36]

Small firms are especially prevalent in residential construction, where thousands of firms employ fewer than 100 people each and no single firm commands more than 1 percent of the market. The heavy construction sector that focuses on large-scale industrial, transportation, and utility projects, is dominated by large firms but is far from consolidated.[37] Both large and small firms routinely subcontract out specialized portions of the work. Small firms predominate across the U.S. construction industry as they do elsewhere in the world.[38] In fact, the smaller the firm, the less likely it is to have extensive available working capital, the less likely it will invest in research and development or new technology, and the more likely it is to subcontract any specialized work to even smaller firms.

The largest 400 U.S. construction firms are the ones engaged in the global market, but foreign contracts in most years make up less than a third of their total business on average.[39] The years with the highest percentages of foreign contracts were recession years in the United States. The figure also shows that the largest ten U.S. construction firms are, in most years, the most heavily engaged in the global market, prompting one scholar to label this slice of the industry oligopolistic.[40]

Overall, firm turnover in the industry is very high, about twice the national average for all businesses. Each year large numbers of new firms enter the field but approximately the same numbers leave it. Not all of the exiting firms officially go bankrupt, but clearly the owners found something better that they wanted to do. And undoubtedly some of the turnover represents firms merely changing their names.[41]

Why is the industry so fragmented? As contractor and author David Gerstel notes, "The unhappy fact is that the bar for entry into the construction business is set very low. Even California standards, reputed to be relatively tough, long have offered a contractor's license to anyone who can manage a couple of baby steps. All that is required is 'proof' (not closely checked, often fabricated) of several years' supervisory or journey-level experience in the trades and a low passing score on a superficial test about building codes, laws, and business practices."[42] The mere fact that there are books like Gerstel's with titles like *Running a Successful Construction Company* also point to the ease of entering the industry. There are no corresponding books called *Running a Successful Bank, Management Consulting for Dummies,* or *Surgical Hospital: A How-To Guide.*

A moment's reflection, however, will reveal that the causes of the construction industry's fragmentation must run deeper. After all, we would not patronize a restaurant that required us to buy food from one supplier, hire a different firm to cook it, a third to deliver it, and a fourth to bus the table, all while remaining uncertain of the meal's total price. And of course those businesses have become increasingly consolidated over the past few decades with the rise of national chains. People not only *can* form tiny construction firms they *actually do,* and in large numbers. Even in their heyday, storied construction firms like Levitt and Sons supplied only a small fraction of the market. The easy entry requirements therefore are a consequence and not a cause of a more fundamental problem. The fragmented nature of the construction industry has deep economic roots.[43]

A widely accepted theorem in economics holds that businesses expand until the cost of creating a product or a service within the firm and buying that product or service in the market are equalized. So if a firm finds that it is paying more to produce something internally than it could buy it in the market, it will divest. Conversely, if a firm finds that it could produce something at lower cost than it could buy it in the market, it will internalize its production. (Domestic "firms," a.k.a. households, behave in similar fashion, buying more products [clothes cleaning, restaurant meals, etc.] in the market as family income [i.e., the opportunity costs of producing in the home] increases.)[44]

Firms are interested in comparing costs, not prices, and total costs at that. So, for instance, suppose a firm produces some good A internally at $10.00 per foot but could buy A in the market at the quantities that it needs at $9.95 per foot. The firm would probably continue to produce A internally because the market price of A is only one component of its total cost. Other costs, usually termed transaction costs, might include: taxes, transportation fees, and uncertainty about the future price, quality, and availability of A. If A is a crucial component in the firm's business, the market price will have to be considerably lower than the firm's internal production cost before it will switch to the market.[45]

When a business expands by producing more of the same or similar products, it is said to engage in horizontal integration. When it grows larger by producing inputs or distribution services, it is said to engage in vertical integration. So a steel company that acquires another steel company is horizontally integrating. A steel company that acquires an iron ore mine or an automobile factory is vertically integrating. Business history is rife with examples of both vertical and horizontal integration.[46]

During the latter part of the nineteenth century and the first decades of the twentieth century a great deal of horizontal and vertical integration took place in American industry. Before World War I, it was not uncommon for large factories to be operated not by one firm, but by many small ones. Such inside contracting, as it was called, made a good deal of sense in the production of many industrial goods, including rifles and rifle cartridges. Important companies, like Winchester Repeating Arms Company, were little more than administrative and marketing shells. The vast bulk of the work was undertaken by contractors working within Winchester's building and even using its accountants and payroll clerks. In 1876, the production of rifles was divided among a dozen prime contractors, each of which hired several subcontractors that, in turn, hired the people who did the actual work. The inside contracting system produced many fine weapons, but productivity lagged over time because of high internal coordination and control costs. For example, contractors deliberately hid productivity improvements, or limited productivity to begin with, so that Winchester could not cut its piece rate. The tremendous demand for rifles during World War I provided the necessary impetus to integrate the contractors and their subcontractors, or, in other words, to put the entire operation of the plant under the control of Winchester's management.[47] Similarly in the early years of the steel industry, Carnegie Steel astutely reinvested large portions of its profits into developing state of the art technology, which allowed it to achieve substantial cost savings to the disadvantage of its competitors.[48]

As the Winchester case shows, it is often difficult to tell, before the fact, whether a firm should make or buy particular goods or services. Managers are people, too. They have often made the wrong call, either because of a miscalculation or, in some cases, greed. During the great conglomeration wave in the 1960s and 1970s, for example, managers threw together disparate companies to fatten their own salaries rather than to create value. In the 1980s, corporate takeovers by firms like Kohlberg Kravis Roberts dissected many of the conglomerates and other firms that had grown too large or that had vertically integrated too far.[49]

In the absence of market inefficiencies or distortions, firms should achieve the degree of vertical integration and scale (horizontal integration) appropriate to their particular lines of business. This will occur only if, through a process similar to natural selection, the firms that are appropriately integrated will have lower costs (and hence lower prices or higher profit margins) than firms that are too vertically integrated (and hence paying too much to make what they should instead buy), not vertically integrated enough (and hence paying too much to buy what they should instead make), too small (and hence not leveraging scale economies), or too large (and hence suffering from diseconomies of scale). The appropriately integrated firms will therefore be more likely to survive; the inappropriately integrated firms will adapt or wither and die.[50]

Construction firms are notoriously small and specialized. In 1970 vertical integration was, in the words of construction economist Peter Cassimatis, "nearly non-existent."[51] The trend since then has actually been away from integration and toward increased specialization. According to David Gerstel,

> As builders we work with an increasing array of subcontractors. Old trades subdivide into specialized new trades. Whole new trades spring up. A few decades ago, for example, foundation, frame, and finish were the province of general contractors. Now, we have specialty contractors in all three areas. Similarly, where we once just had plasterers, we now have stucco, veneer plaster, and drywall specialists. We used to automatically call the tile guy for a kitchen countertop. Now he competes with stone fabricators, cast concrete specialists, plastic laminate shops, and installers of a slew of other synthetic products. Meanwhile, the older trades have been joined by new specialties, including insulating contractors, waterproofing specialists, information technology installers, and solar-power guys, with more sure to come.[52]

Today, it is not unusual for fifty or more firms to take part in the design and construction of large projects like industrial facilities. Even tiny home renovation projects may require the input of half-a-dozen companies.[53] This increasing fragmentation directly increases the risk of miscommunication or miscoordination between the multiple parties involved, and thus directly increases the risk of additional costs and project delay.

Why the increased specialization and small size? Small, specialized firms can stay fully employed by moving nimbly from project to project as their specialties are required.[54] In addition, small firm size, which is to say the extensive use of subcontractors, is a response to the risks of construction contracting. Small contractors cannot afford to bid on more than a small number of projects—the risk of losing money on one or more is too great. Custom designed buildings represent unique specifications that pose unusual risks that they can ill afford to take. Many building sites pose risks of subsurface uncertainties that may not be apparent to a small contractor and thus not included in the bid. Finally, small contractors have little or no recourse to financing project anomalies that may affect cash flow and their ability to weather many of the problems that a larger contractor can absorb.[55]

The above risks are not inconsequential. Construction firms are more likely to fail than companies in most other sectors. Moreover, the construction industry is extremely cyclical and very sensitive to macroeconomic shocks. When construction slows, general contractors often retain monies due their subcontractors. This withholding can have a major impact on the smaller firms' cash flow. Many go out of business each year for just this reason.[56]

One reason for the industry's extremely cyclical nature is that the stock of buildings is immense compared to the stream of new buildings being constructed each year. Small fluctuations in demand for all buildings therefore have very large repercussions on the demand for new buildings. The risks noted above explain the wide dispersion of the results in studies on wasted time. According to a recent metastudy, construction workers have been observed wasting between 1.6 and 93.1 percent of their on-site time, quite a spread.[57]

SUBCONTRACTING THE RISK AWAY

As we learned in chapter 1, general contractors largely provide fixed-price contracts for a given scope of work (with drawings and specifications). The general contractor subsequently contracts with subcontractors, also often for a fixed price for a specific scope of work, and in doing so, partly shifts the risks of those portions of the work to the subcontractor. "You parcel the risk out to subcontractors," general contractor David Gerstel explains to his general-contractor-wannabe readers. The compelling need to spread or share risk explains why many construction firms find it cheaper to use subcontractors (buy in the market) than to grow larger (produce internally).[58] An early historian of Levitt and Sons stated the matter like this: "Sub-contracting, or the putting out system . . . enables the builder to use the capital of others, to split his risk and to delegate his responsibility. The system is also valuable for those who have limited managerial ability."[59] Of course subcontracting also raises the sticky issues of coordination and control. Will the subcontractor show up on time? Will the sub do the job correctly in the time allotted? For that matter, will the general contractor have the job ready? An electrical subcontractor prematurely called out to a job will lose a bundle. "I've wasted a good part of my day," one explains, "and I'm out hours of wages getting my crew out to the job. Then I have to move to a second job. But because we can't get it done . . . we have to return a second day, incurring more mobilization and travel time, all due to the contractor on the first job telling us he was ready when he wasn't."[60]

To minimize coordination and control costs, contractors and construction managers often employ carpenters and laborers directly, which combined account for about 40 percent of the man hours required on the average project. Workers in the other trades—plumbers, bricklayers, electricians, painters, roofers, and the like—make up the other 60 percent, but none of them on average is needed more than 10 percent of the time, so they are usually subcontracted. Members of some of the highly specialized trades—lathers, reinforced iron workers, ornamental iron workers, glaziers, and elevator mechanics—are needed less than 2 percent of the time on average and hence are almost always subcontracted.[61]

The cost of contracting is reduced by a hoary category of laws, quaintly still called mechanics' liens, that make it relatively easy and cheap for subcontractors to obtain relief should the general contractor default or the owner refuse to pay for questionable work. Mechanics' lien laws throughout the United States enable a general or trade contractor to place a lien—a claim for money due as a result of the work that improved the real property of the owner—against the title of the property itself. In so doing, the recording of the lien on the local property record serves notice to the owner, any mortgage lender or prospective purchaser that there is a "cloud on the title" that must be resolved before the owner can sell or mortgage the property in the future.[62]

Construction firms sometimes form what one researcher calls "quasi-firms," coalitions of construction companies analogous to Japanese *keiretsu,* Korean *chaebol,* and other networks of firms that leverage relational contracts. To minimize transaction costs, they move part way toward integration, creating a hybrid between outright ownership (make) and the arms-length market (buy). Owners usually contract with *keiretsu* styled general contractors on the basis of competitive bids. But these general contractors usually *do not* put out their subcontracting to bid. Instead, as how-to books suggest, once they find trustworthy subcontractors, they continue to work with them almost exclusively for extended periods. Doing so aligns the incentives of the parties and creates a mutually beneficial relationship to be replicated on future projects. The possibility of future interaction turns a "one-off" prisoners' dilemma, where both parties are better off if they defect (renege on payments, show up late, work too slowly, or do substandard work), into an "iterated" prisoners' dilemma, where both parties are better off if they cooperate. Most even dispense with written contracts after a short time. Says John Fitzwater of Clarksburg, West Virginia: "It's all verbal. . . . If our word isn't good enough for you, to hell with it."[63]

The relationship between the subcontractor and the general contractor benefits both parties because it minimizes the search and administrative costs of the GC while allowing the sub to achieve sufficient scale by working for several GCs simultaneously. Moreover, the general contractor need not worry about keeping specialists employed during slack times, nor must the specialists worry about having enough work to do for the general contractor.

In short, construction firms do not subcontract because they are small per se. Rather, empirical studies over a wide range of times and places show that general contractors subcontract because it is the most efficient way to do business given the realities of the building process. If it were to become apparent to the average contractor that it could be more profitable to grow and consolidate with complementary firms, would it take the risk? If such action resulted in increasingly profitable projects, would contractors begin to attract the necessary financing to grow larger still?

Another constraint on size appears to be the bidding process itself. To win bids without suffering the "winner's curse" (bidding too low and then potentially losing money if real costs turn out to be higher than bid), contractors often limit their geographic reach where they are knowledgeable of locally available materials, labor costs, and building types (where extensive experience improves productivity). A second constraint is that construction workers are more closely akin to craftsmen than to industrial assemblers. They therefore require, or at least desire, much less bureaucratic supervision. As a result, construction firms do not cultivate layers of middle managers around which expansion could take place. A third constraint is that even larger general contractors are unwilling to risk their limited capital or borrow on a large scale to acquire other large contractors.[64]

The network or quasi-firm organization of the construction industry has been in long-term equilibrium. That does not mean, however, that it will always remain so. Consider the experience of Winchester. Theoretically, the industry could see the extension of the use of arms-length subcontractors. In other words, it could move toward a pure market organization. The information revolution could make it easier, faster, and cheaper for general contractors to put work out to bid and to differentiate between quality and inferior subcontractors. Similarly, improvements in the legal system could also move general contractors away from relational contracting and toward the open market because it would lower the cost of enforcing one-off contracts.

But it is more likely that construction firms will become more integrated, that they will increasingly eschew the extensive use of subcontracting and instead acquire subcontractors outright. Construction projects, even small ones, are complex affairs, too complex to be left to the vagaries of the market.

Literally thousands of problems can arise on any given construction site, almost all related, directly or indirectly, to conflicts or poor coordination between disparate firms or small firm size.[65] Getting owners and just one firm onto the same page is difficult enough. Needing scores of firms and the owner, architects, and engineers to work together is a potential recipe for fiscal disaster. As it is currently constituted, the industry invites such disasters. Almost always, these problems result in additional project costs and delays that the owner will most likely absorb. Take for example the following hypothetical projects where it becomes painfully clear how the fragmentation and prevalence of small firms across the entire construction industry (including architects, engineers, contractors, and suppliers alike) cause or exacerbate significant project delays and unanticipated additional costs.[66]

On a complicated industrial and business park in Iowa, the city hired five different design firms, one from California, one from Chicago, one from St. Paul, and two local concerns. None of them was responsible for the entire project. They worked slowly, with frequent misunderstandings and miscommunications due to the physical distance between the firms, time zone discrepancies, and differences in regional practices. Unsurprisingly, poor overall design consistency dogged the project, which caused cost and time overruns.

A large chemical fluid waste storage farm required the use of paint that would not peel or discolor when it came into contact with corrosive petroleum waste products. Confusion arose because the engineer, the contractor, and the paint manufacturer did not communicate the precise product specifications with each other in a proper or timely fashion. As a result, the contractor applied the wrong paint at the wrong time. Assigning blame, and hence cost, spoiled relations between the parties, leading to additional difficulties as the project progressed.

A college building a hockey rink wanted the general contractor, a good-sized regional firm, to hire as many local subs as possible because they were team boosters. The general contractor had never worked in the community before and did not know any of the subs. The result was confusion, misunderstanding, delays, and of course cost overruns. The rink was not ready for the season and some of the work was shoddy because the local subs simply had no experience building hockey rinks.

An owner encouraged his architect to use cost-saving, innovative materials. The architect responded by designing a building clad using a prefabricated panel system composed of plywood covered by a thin stone veneer that was relatively new to market. The manufacturer of the panels was happy to fill a big order, not realizing that the intended use of its interior product was the exterior of a fifty-eight-story office building. After some unauthorized modification of the panels by the contractor, it figured out how to hang the panels. But when they were 90 percent done, the stone on the first installations began to crack and fall off. No one but the manufacturer knew that moisture and temperature changes made the product unsuitable as an exterior covering. The cost of the building nearly doubled because the stone panels had to be removed and replaced with a proven material.

A town put some public utility construction work out to bid. The general contractor was awarded the project in midsummer and promptly bought out subcontractors within a couple weeks. But the project's "notice to proceed" was delayed by bureaucratic red tape, changing the project start date from late summer to winter.

Many of the subcontractors backed out of their contracts or called for a renegotiation of terms given the later, and hence colder and more expensive, project start date.

A general contractor went out of business because the owner of a large project, a local developer, failed to pay. That, in turn, adversely impacted the cash flow of its subcontractors and the general contractors on other jobs. All of the firms were too small to obtain significant outside financing to help them over this liquidity hurdle.

A town working on a politically sensitive project lost out when protestors shut down several key subcontractors, small firms that could not withstand community pressures.

Strong Steel bid $7.5 million to build, deliver, and install a precipitator in an Ohio fossil fuel power plant. Due to delays by other contractors, it was not allowed on the site until July, almost four months late. Only then did its engineers learn that the center column pier on which all the measures were based was 1½ inches off. It might as well have been a mile. The work was delayed into the winter, which was unusually harsh, even for Ohio. The power plant fired Strong Steel for nonperformance. It was a bad move. Ten years and $29.4 million later, the power plant had its $7.5 million precipitator. Though long since bankrupt, Strong Steel received $18 million in compensatory and punitive damages. Had only a single firm been involved, the pier would have been positioned correctly (or had the steel division known of the change), the whole expensive mess would have been avoided and the power plant's customers would be paying less for each kilowatt of power than they now use.

An entrepreneur with no prior building experience developed a major luxury Las Vegas hotel and casino. Insistent on doing the construction his way, the developer forced the construction manager to sign a contract calling for completion five months sooner than experts advised, then insisted on a liquidated damages

clause of $350,000 per day, even though the construction man-
ager had also never managed a project in the Las Vegas area. The
result: a delay of several months in the opening of the hotel and a
ten month trial to ascertain the claims of the general and subcontractors, which totaled $140 million.

The fewer parties involved, the lower the chance disputes and miscommunication will arise. The larger and better capitalized the parties are, the more likely they are to increase their productivity and
profitability and weather the cash flow crunches and disputes that inevitably occur on projects.

There is one field in the industry where integration, consolidation,
and productivity increase is making headway: housing. How much
productivity improvement is possible? A UK builder, Sir Stuart Lipton,
recently claimed that a 25 percent reduction in costs and time to completion was possible. "House building techniques have not changed
much since Roman times," he rationalized.[67] Yale University professor
of architecture Phillip Bernstein puts the figure at a whopping 30 percent. "It's not just the consumption of energy," he explains, "it's the
use of materials, the waste of water, the incredibly inefficient strategies we use for choosing the subsystems of our buildings. It's a scary
thing."[68] Regardless of the ultimate improvement to be obtained, it is
clear that there is much that can be done to improve productivity.
Even a 10 percent improvement would represent a noticeable, though
initial, step in the right direction.

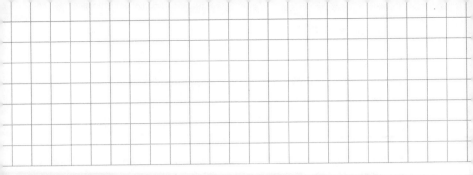

False Starts and Frustrated Beginnings

A HISTORY OF THE INDUSTRY

History sheds some light on the difficulties and possibilities of better
performance. The most promising starts have been seen in the housing sector where standardization of design and construction method-
ologies were viewed as easier to achieve. In 1947, for example, *Fortune*
wrote that "House building . . . is the one great sector of modern society that has remained largely unaffected by the industrial revolution.
Recognition of the feudal character of the housing industry is essential for understanding its sorry performance in the past and assessing
its chances for improvement in the future."[1]

Early Attempts at Cooperative Ownership

The housing construction industry is littered with good intentions
and creative efforts that fell by the wayside. In late nineteenth century
Britain, for instance, a group of well-meaning souls tried to create a
construction cooperative called General Builders, Ltd. An early ad-
herent thought the project would prove a smashing success due to the
fact that the ownership structure, which was similar to that of a joint
stock company, would reduce waste because the workers were also the
owners. He was wrong. General Builders went nowhere. Cooperative

workers' ventures like that established by the Amalgamated Clothing Workers in New York City managed to create some fine apartment houses in the early twentieth century, but they did not blossom into major producers. Some, thinking the profit motive would spur improvements, created limited-profit construction companies, firms that returned rents once profit thresholds had been achieved. They fared no better than the full-fledged co-ops.[2]

For-profit corporations could in fact generate profits but not much growth. While there were some corporate success stories in the New York City region before World War II—City and Suburban Homes' capitalization, for example, grew from $489,300 to $4,255,690 over the forty years between 1898 and 1938 while it paid dividends averaging 4.2 percent—no true giants emerged as they did in railroads, steel, oil, electricity, or a host of other industries.[3]

That fact was not lost on contemporaries. Over the decades numerous schemes have called for the integration and consolidation of the construction industry. In 1931, George Hull claimed that the main barrier to industry consolidation was the Sherman Antitrust Act. If that act were modified to allow for the creation of huge construction firms, he argued, building construction costs would plummet, new home prices would drop, additional demand would appear, employment would improve, and the construction of new buildings would pull America out of the Depression. None of that happened, of course, probably because laws are not as important to economic outcomes as people think. The Sherman act was not the barrier to integration, it was the prevalence of mutable-cost contracting.[4]

But that did not stop perennial attempts to rationalize the housing construction industry, most of which centered around mass production in one of two forms: huge tracts and prefabricated homes (prefabs). The basic ideas behind both were sound. By building 100 or 1,000 houses at a time, economies of scale could be tapped. By moving as much construction off-site as possible, builders could use more productive, factory-like procedures immune to the vagaries of weather and construction unions. After completion, the prefabricated parts are trucked to the home site, where they are relatively quickly and easily assembled, or, in the limit, the entire house is built in a factory and delivered to its site. Prefabrication sounds easy, but it isn't, or at least it traditionally has not been; it has a long history and was quite advanced in nineteenth century Britain. But British prefabs, mostly ugly corrugated iron structures destined for the colonies, did not win much acclaim or attention and high transportation costs ensured that even relatively inefficient traditional on-site construction was soon preferred. Twentieth-century American prefabricators would face similar problems.[5]

Original American Prefab

In 1917, storied inventor Thomas Edison and Charles H. Ingersoll, a watch manufacturer, planned to build mass-produced affordable concrete houses in Union, New Jersey. Edison sent machinery to a limestone quarry to begin making concrete to pour into molds to prefabricate affordable houses, but they ended up costing three times his estimates because of unforeseen difficulties pouring the concrete. Eventually, Edison obtained a patent for a single pour concrete house, but only a few score of them were built. Most stand to this day, testament to a good idea that not even Edison could make work on a large scale.[6]

In 1932, General Houses tried to become a "center firm" along the lines of General Electric, General Motors, and the like by introducing America to prefab steel homes through a franchised dealer distribution system and extremely generous mortgages for the day: fifteen years at 5 percent interest with no or low down payments. Unable to find distributors, General Houses sought help from Sears-Roebuck, which already had failed to sell many of its own Crafton homes. It sold fewer than 200 units before dissolving. Similar schemes also fizzled, all because they could not provide homes at prices low enough to induce people to buy them in large quantities. In 1936 a company in Jersey Homesteads (now Roosevelt), New Jersey, proclaimed that it was going to revolutionize home construction by casting complete homes, electrical lines and all, out of concrete in a factory. There was only one problem—the structures quickly collapsed. Not surprisingly, sales did as well.[7]

68   The Roosevelt administration did not embrace prefab housing as part of its anti-Depression housing program. Calls for local public housing authorities to aggregate the market went unheeded. World War II, however, spurred the prefab industry enough to induce U.S. Steel to purchase Gunnison Homes in 1944. As the war wound down, and pent-up demand for homes led many analysts to call for the conversion of military factories into prefab housing production sites.[8]

The housing shortage was so bad in the immediate postwar period that the Truman administration felt compelled to appoint William Wyatt as "Housing Expeditor." Wyatt, who was new to the construction industry, set forth an ambitious plan to use the War Powers Act, the War Mobilization and Reconversion Act, the Federal Public Housing Authority, the War Assets Administration, the Federal Home Loan Bank, and a host of other government entities to help build 2.7 million homes in 1946 and 1947 with an industry that had never before built even a million new homes in a year. He failed miserably, partly because he could not get the sundry federal agencies to work together and partly because the building industry and the public demanded an immediate end to price controls and materials rationing.

To help meet the demand, Paul Litchfield of Goodyear proposed building homes out of rubber and gunite, a type of concrete blown out of the end of a pump hose. Other firms took a more traditional approach but enjoyed no more success. Having failed to obtain FHA certification as "standard," prefab homes made by the likes of Dymaxion and Lustron could not obtain government subsidized mortgages. Predictably, demand for them lagged. That was ironic given that another part of the government in 1946 had induced Lustron to form in the first place and had even provided it with low-interest loans from the Reconstruction Finance Corporation.[9]

Lustron and others also found it difficult to manage overhead and other costs. In Lustron's case this was probably not due to bad management, as its head, engineer inventor Carl Strandlund, had managed to increase the gross income of Oliver Farm Equipment Company from $20 to $120 million per year *during the Great Depression.* Strandlund's 1,025 square foot steel-frame prefabs were put together on an assembly line, prompting Architectural Forum to note that Lustron's factory, a former Curtiss-Wright fighter plane factory near Columbus, Ohio, was "the first real demonstration of the seductive theory that houses can be turned out like automobiles." To reduce on-site assembly time, the parts of the house were carefully loaded onto a large truck in the opposite order that they would be needed on site. Experienced crews could assemble the thing in just 350 man hours. But Lustron made some strategic marketing and "make or buy" blunders that cost it big. The silliest was its purchase of a 1,800-ton press to build its own bathtubs when bathtub manufacturers could supply them at a much lower cost. Buyer financing was also a problem. Some banks wouldn't lend at all, while others wanted to make payments in little dribs and drabs as was customary with traditional building techniques.[10]

Many prefab designs also ran afoul of local building codes. Lustron was again a typical case. Obtaining variances for its copper plumbing and other unusual features was time consuming and expensive. Some markets, like Chicago and Detroit, barred Lustron houses entirely. "Acorn" houses that could be shipped to sites and quickly "expanded" to five times their shipping size also made an appearance before dying. Almost 200 prefab companies bit the dust in the early postwar years. Lustron expired when the Korean War broke out and the government wanted its factory to again produce fighter aircraft.[11]

As the industry's postwar woes worsened, *Fortune* magazine proclaimed the worst housing crisis "since the James River landing." Things looked very ugly indeed in 1947, when, just like after World War I, prices spiked but production volume remained relatively flat. "The slight gain in 'starts' in 1947 as compared with 1946 was the result," *Fortune* claimed, "not of the heroic efforts of the industry, but of a heroic revision of the figures by the U.S. Government." *Fortune's* biting critique of the postwar construction industry still rings true today in many ways: "Any industry that functions as badly as the house building business must have some really distinguished ailment. It has often been called a monopoly, which it is not. Every town, village, and hamlet in the U.S. has at least one house builder who is beholden to no one except God and an unbelievably inefficient system for building houses. . . . But while the housing industry is subject to no general monopoly control, neither is it competitive. . . . The price, more often than not, is cost plus what the market will bear."[12]

Builders did eventually ramp up production, but homebuyers clamored for yet more units.[13] High birth, net family formation, and migration rates, combined with increased demand for single family homes from minority groups, the increased rate of destruction of older houses, rising incomes, and mounting savings all conspired to keep total demand high for over a decade.[14] Construction looked so profitable that two big life insurers, Metropolitan Life and New York Life Insurance, decided to get into the game, building Parkchester, Stuyvesant Town, Peter Cooper, Riverton, Parkfairfax, Parkmerced, Parklabrea, Lake Meadows, Manhattan House, and Fresh Meadows. They found neither profit nor praise in the endeavors and exited.[15] Former head of the National Association of Home Builders Nat Rogg once remarked that big builders "are like the dinosaurs whose bodies were too big for their brains to control."[16]

Trailers and other types of mobile homes, developed in the 1930s as vacation homes, gained acceptance as primary housing after their extensive emergency use during World War II. Due in part to the postwar housing crunch, they grew in popularity, size (from 8' × 30' to 14' × 60'), and complexity in the 1940s, '50s, and '60s. Sales volume more than doubled between 1951 and 1957, from $248.3 to $579 million; the number of units shipped grew from 1,300 in 1930 to over 400,000 in 1970.[17]

Mobile homes were rarely actually moved after their initial placement. Their main niche was as convenient, compact homes for younger and older couples and lower income groups. In 1973, 40 percent of owners were thirty-four or younger, 25 percent were fifty-five or older and fully half had incomes less than $6,000 per year. Such customers were relatively unconcerned with the fact that their homes depreciated rather than appreciated over time. (In fact, they were financed over three to eleven years, like automobiles or other items such as equipment, with large down payments or trade-ins required.) Interestingly, even trailer manufacturers tended to be small, with even the largest ones producing only 100 units per week and many turning out only 100 or 150 per year.[18]

71

Out of the trailer industry grew sectionalized house manufacturers. Rather than a single structure, sectionalized houses are two or more prefab sections designed to fit together on site. Because they face fewer size limitations, sectionalized house manufacturers can make homes that closely resemble traditionally built structures in factories.[19]

Techniques, Technologies, and the Emergence of the New Town Movement

Mass production of homes using more traditional on-site construction techniques also held some promise. In the late 1940s and 1950s, speculative builder Levitt and Sons made a big impression on the home construction industry with its mammoth, mass-produced Levittowns. The Levitts—Abraham, Alfred, and William—got the idea, and ironed out some of the kinks, while building huge housing projects for the navy in Norfolk and Portsmouth during World War II. Levitt and Sons did not do much prefabrication. In fact, William Levitt once claimed, "prefabrication is a dirty word to us." Rather, most of the work was done on-site but in an assembly-line fashion. "We tried to copy the automobile industry," Levitt recalled. "A fellow would come to one house and go bang, bang, bang, and then go over to the next one."[20]

Though not a licensed architect, Alfred Levitt influenced the design of the company's homes. As the largest builder in the country with 7,000 starts, the company enjoyed enough monopsony power (purchasing clout) not only to cut great deals, but also to spur materials manufacturers to produce new products, including closet doors made of split bamboo. The company also built apartment and office complexes, schools, and other public buildings for its towns.[21]

About the same time in Glen Burnie, south of Baltimore, Jack Byrne combined mass production and prefabrication by building his prefab factory close to a big development of steel-framed homes that he was putting up. The factory—a series of Quonset huts that he learned to build while in the Seabees during World War II—was supposed to cut down on transportation costs by being mobile and movable from development to development and state to state as needed. Byrne grew large enough to dispense with subcontractors. Byrne's system, like that of the Levitts, allowed for the completion of numerous small homes thousands of dollars below what small competitors could profitably offer.[22]

The successes of Levitt and Byrne spurred a "new town" movement, the construction of entire towns by a single firm. Over the next few decades, new towns sprang up in California, Arizona, New York, and elsewhere. Their commercial success, however, was limited at best. The biggest new town was Columbia, Maryland. James Rouse started the town in 1962, after secretively buying up twenty-two square miles of Howard County from some 328 different owners. Income contouring, the gradual change in house value from street to street, family life counseling centers, a community concert center, indoor tennis courts and subsidized bus service attest to the socialist leanings of the planning committee, which was chaired by a member of Mark Raskin's New Left think tank, the Institute of Policy Studies. As a community, Columbia was a smashing success. As a business, however, it was a dismal failure. Connecticut General Life Insurance, which bankrolled the project, ended up writing off $21 million on a project that Rouse originally claimed would double its money every five years.[23]

Most other new town projects also floundered, even those with substantial backing from HUD. The most complete flop was Gananda, New York, about twelve miles from Rochester. Only two of the projected 17,700 houses were built and one of those burned. Before it failed in 1974, the Gananda Development Corporation blew $45 million creating amenities, like an artificial lake (a silly idea given that the splendor of the Finger Lakes was a short drive away), valued at only $10 million. Chase Manhattan and several other banks lost millions, as did

HUD and area farmers. Newfields, Ohio; Jonathan and Riverton, Minnesota; Shenandoah, Georgia; and Flower Mound, Texas, faired little better. Easy government money, small and inexperienced developers, exorbitant costs due to the Davis-Bacon Act and outright greed were among the most outstanding causes of failure.[24]

73

Midcentury Visions of Conglomeration

In 1959, amidst this chaos, MIT professor Burnham Kelly called for the creation of "a special subsidiary to operate all the way from land development to building." Such a firm, he noted, would bring to construction "a range of management skills and fiscal resources not usually available." "The combined impact of a group of publicly financed and well-managed organizations operating on an integrated basis across the entire production process," he argued, "would be almost certain to lead to the elimination of conventional restrictions."[25] In 1964, Charles Foster similarly argued that the construction industry lagged in innovation largely because of the small number of large firms. He went so far as to suggest the vertical integration of contractors and manufacturers of building materials, but the failure of construction forays by Union Carbide and Koppers put a damper on his enthusiasm. He conceded that consolidation did not make economic sense. Yet just a few years later, HUD announced its In Cities program, which was designed to test home building innovations and identify constraints on housing production. HUD awarded a contract to Kaiser Engineers but little was accomplished before the new Nixon administration shuttered the program.[26]

By the early 1970s, enough large corporations were testing the waters of the construction industry to spur HUD secretary George W. Romney (1907–1995) to assert, a little heatedly, that the United States was engulfed in "a revolution in housing construction unmatched *since men came out of the caves and started building dwellings with their hands.*" By the end of the 1970s, Romney envisioned, "industrialized housing will dominate the market."[27] Romney, a former auto industry executive and governor of Michigan, was wrong. But he was not alone.

In 1969, the executive vice president of Boise-Cascade, then the nation's largest housing and construction company, predicted that by the mid-1970s, "nearly all housing produced for the mass market will bear the trademark of a major national corporation." Merrill Lynch, the Institute for the Future, and academics also missed the mark.[28]

The problem was that the increased corporatization of construction in the 1960s and 1970s was motivated by management empire-building and the prospect of government subsidies, not economic efficiency and standalone profitability. It was, in other words, part of the failed wave of corporate conglomeration, not a structural change in the underlying economics of the industry. Corporate behemoths in aerospace (AVCO, Boeing, Lear Siegler, TRW), aluminum (ALCOA, Kaiser, Reynolds), appliances (American Standard, GE, Tappan, Westinghouse Electric), chemicals (American Cyanamid, Dow, Hercules), conglomerates (CBS, ITT, 3M, and Singer), finance (City Investing, CNA Financial, Dreyfus), oil (Gulf, Occidental, Shell, Standard), steel (Bethlehem, Inland, Republic, U.S. Steel), transportation (Ford, Freuhauf), and utilities (Eastern Gas and Fuel, American National Gas) all purported to have the expertise necessary to successfully enter the construction industry. "There is hardly a major industrial organization without an iron in the fire," Richard Bender proudly proclaimed in 1973. Most of those companies, though, got burnt. These companies lacked expertise, but many also entered the market imprudently. This was partly because they wanted to make sure that forecasts of a huge increase in the demand for new homes would pan out, and partly because they saw home construction as a means to dispose of real estate assets, excess inventory, and the like, and not as an end in itself.[29]

The late 1960s and early 1970s *did* witness successful horizontal and vertical growth of large construction firms like Boise-Cascade, Behring, Centex, Fleetwood, Kaufman and Broad, National Homes, Redman Industries, Ryan Homes, Skyline, Stirling Homex, Toll Brothers, and U.S. Home. Some even went public. Stirling Homex, which built big, plastic, stackable rooms, was quickly shuttered for fraudulent accounting practices. Despite the fact it created a much vaunted "volumetric housing system," Boise-Cascade diversified into office product manufacturing and distribution. It eventually spun off Office Max and sold its construction businesses. Others, however, including Skyline, Centex, Toll Brothers, and Fleetwood, continue to thrive. To this day, none conduct a truly national business, though Centex is a Fortune 250 company traded on the NYSE. Kaufman and Broad, now KB Home, has penetrated only thirteen states and, interestingly enough, France. Toll Brothers owns land and builds in eighteen states. Ryan Homes is still limited to a dozen mid-Atlantic states. U.S. Home is in only fifteen states, but it is widely dispersed geographically and its parent, Lennar Corporation, owns builders in a few other states. Redman is now part of Champion Enterprise, which purports to be the world's largest homebuilder because it has installed 1.5 million manufactured and modular homes in the United States and western Canada.[30]

Sales of prefab homes have waxed and waned over the years, mostly in response to interest rates and the prices of traditionally constructed homes. Prefab home sales have inversely followed economic real estate cycles. But they were never *popular*. Vernon Swaback put it best: "While offering immediately available, low-cost shelter, the mobile home, with few exceptions, is a jarring intrusion on the landscape." Aesthetics aside, quality was often wanting. Prefabs, mobile, and modular homes were built in much the same way as regular homes, after all, only with less skilled labor and often to inferior standards. As Swaback eloquently puts it: "Mobile home assembly lines are caricatures of the automobile industry."[31] Most importantly of all, holding quality constant, big price advantages were fleeting. The average price of manufactured housing, both singles and doubles, declined in real (inflation-adjusted) terms in the early 1990s, reaching their nadir in 1992. Prices have since risen but are still below their 1980 levels. Since about 1995, buyers have increasingly eschewed singles for doubles, so the total average price approaches the average price of doubles alone.[32]

To this day, the prefabrication of components like wall panels, roof trusses, and duct work is arguably more important than complete prefabrication of homes, but even it has faced worker resistance from those accustomed to building traditionally, that is, on site, by those who view factory fabrication as a potential threat to their job security. As late as 1969 an industry analyst argued that "the extent of prefabrication in construction has been limited thus far."[33] Nevertheless, by the early 1970s some observers, like Richard Bender, were convinced that America was in the midst of a construction revolution, or rather evolution. "There has been no sudden change, no single invention, or technical innovation," Bender argued, "which can be pointed to as industrializing building, but certainly the industry today has a very different look from that of a generation ago." He interpreted the industry's evolution as similar to that experienced by the consumer electronics industry after the proliferation of the printed circuit board. He especially pushed the idea of a "building system." Building systems, he argued, were "analogous to the early printing press. Once the alphabet and rules are invented there is no limit to what can be written with the system." Like so many before him, however, Bender was wrong, or at least decades ahead of his time, because Lego-like buildings are still quite rare. Bender himself pointed to one reason—transportation costs often exceeded factory savings.[34]

Bender urged American construction firms to pay close attention to developments in Europe, especially the so-called industrialized systems like the Malmstrom-Jespersen system and the closely related Finnish B-E-S system, which used standardized precast, steel-reinforced concrete slabs that came in thirty-nine sizes and configurations. The failure of those systems in America is telling. Despite federal government subsidies, the technology could not be imported into the United States because of local inspection codes, union work rules, worker inexperience with the techniques and materials, and possibly even sabotage. The closest we got was a plant in Rochester, New York, which set up in the old Penn Central boxcar factory. After a serious of mishaps, including repeated electrical fires due to the incompetent use of aluminum wiring combined with conventional lugs instead of compression clamps, the plant manager one day simply walked off the job, an equipment payment was missed, and the crude experiment ended.

Five of the eleven apartments built in Rochester using the system experienced serious fires before the end of the 1970s.[35]

Fragmentation and the Origins of the Construction Manager

The 1970s also witnessed for the first time projects overseen by construction managers using fast-track project delivery, as described in chapter 1. By 1983, a third of large owners employed construction managers using the fast-track method. *Harvard Business Review* touted the change as the Next Big Thing. The use of the construction manager, however, is stymied by the fact that the CM has little incentive to keep projects on budget since its fee, based on a percentage of the cost of the work, increases as the cost of work rises.[36] Moreover, the CM's work can be difficult to bond depending on the availability and profitability of the insurance market. The bond is a kind of insurance guarantee for the owner by a surety that the CM will complete the work if the CM or any of its subcontractors fail. Bonding is often the requirement of lenders and the CM actually adds variability to outcomes. As one observer puts it, "Good construction management is great; bad construction management is awful."[37] Especially in the early 1970s, construction managers had little or no formal education. They were former craftsmen turned foremen turned general foremen, learning their management skills, in the words of one study, "by trial and error, with many trials and lots of errors."[38]

Exacerbating the problem in the early era of the CM was the thorny question of whether the construction manager was an agent of the owner or an independent contractor to the owner. The difference is critical to how the parties apportion risk for the project. As an agent, the construction manager bears little or no risk managing the project because it operates under the aegis of the owner, in effect serving as the equivalent of an owner's employee, even when signing subcontractor agreements on behalf of the owner. As an independent contractor, however, the construction manager is "at risk" and bears full responsibility for all the attendant problems that may be encountered during its management of the construction process, including responsibility for the subcontractors who it contracts with directly. However, there remains a real danger for the agent construction manager if it acts outside the scope of its agency. For example, by improperly handling trust funds due subcontractors, an agent can be deemed at risk to the owner and its subcontractors. In such an instance, the courts could rule that the construction manager is not immune from liability for such actions. By acting at risk, the agent opens itself up to liability, and the owner has someone to sue.

Strong construction environments such as the current boom of the past few years sometimes see construction managers successfully leveraging the high demand for their services to decrease their risk by seeking agent agreements with owners. By assuming the agent role, a construction manager effectively precludes itself from any substantial financial exposure if a project is delayed or suffers cost overruns. In other words, they expect to be rewarded equally whether the project finishes on time and on budget or not. Many owners do not understand until it is too late or choose to overlook that a construction manager who is serving as an agent is not at risk except for actions outside the scope of the agreement.[39] *Caveat emptor,* owners.

Whether employing a construction manager at risk or as agent, problems often plague fast-track projects. Fast-track encourages mutable-cost contracting, since the essence of the fast-track process mandates that construction begins before the architects and engineers have completed the total building design. Therefore, it is impossible for the owner to secure a fixed-price contract where the costs of the yet-to-be-designed building are still unknown.[40]

In 1983, the Business Roundtable published an ambitious report on the state of the construction industry titled *More Construction for the Money.* "This Project," it began, "is a long-range, four-phase effort to develop a comprehensive definition of the fundamental problems in the construction industry and an accompanying program for resolution of those problems leading to an improvement of cost effectiveness in the industry." Like similar efforts before and since, the study failed to achieve its aims, largely because it took a scattergun approach. Its impact was reduced by the fact that it did not identify mutable contracts as construction's core cancer. Instead, it castigated the usual symptoms: weak management, lack of technology, poor education, union meddling, and overbearing government regulations. As a result, the book's recommendations, which numbered 220, were doomed from the start. With competition weakened by mutable contracts, construction firms in the 1980s continued to function in largely traditional ways, with only a few striving to make big productivity gains. Emcor, for example, made a serious bid to become a full-service construction company. The early 1990s recession, however, forced Emcor into bankruptcy. It has since re-emerged but hasn't regained its early momentum.[41]

Other recent attempts to transform the construction industry are doing better. One of the nation's largest home construction firms, Pulte Homes, Inc., has thrived building upper-middle-class houses, which are prefabricated in sections in its factory in northern Virginia. By building everything, even the foundation, in a factory controlled environment, Pulte rarely faces weather-related delays. Its homes are not completely customized, but homebuyers can make numerous choices regarding size and layout. Pulte thinks that it will be able to run a profitable business because its radical departure from the traditional process has given it one major advantage, control of production from start to finish. Pulte and other large contractors, like Holiday Builders and Adams Homes, have moved into hot zones, like Florida's Ocala region. Pulte made its move by buying Arizona-based Del Webb for $1.7 billion in 2001. By late 2004 it was busy building a 1,300-home community.[42] Companies like competitor, Toll Brothers, found themselves in 2004 and 2005 building luxury homes that were deceptively standardized in design and breaking all previous sales records. Within a two-year period, homes in the New York region that were selling for $560,000 were selling for at least $935,000.[43] Overall, the home construction industry has constructed over 13.5 million single-family homes since the mid-1990s, exceeding 1.6 million alone in 2005.

In recent years highly integrated companies, like Fluor Daniels and Bechtel, have evolved out of basic primary contractors. Given the huge size of the industry, such behemoths are rare, but change may be afoot. Since 1994, *Fortune* magazine has listed the construction and engineering companies in its list of the top 1,000 U.S. businesses as measured by annual revenue. The absolute levels demonstrate the overall weakness of the sector. Given the immense importance of the industry, construction firms are comprehensively underrepresented in numbers, in revenues, and in employment. Year-to-year comparisons are more heartening. Over the last decade, the number of construction and engineering companies in the Fortune 1000 has increased significantly. The average list position has dropped over 100 places, suggesting that construction and engineering firms' revenues were growing faster than those of other large companies. Company size as measured by the number of employees has also increased markedly.[44]

Is the problem the process or the participants?[45] Those who think it is the process blame design-build, fast-track, and the like. Those who think it is participants call for more education (of owners, contractors, architects), more regulation, more of this, and more of that. The real problem, argued here, is both process and participants are hostage to market failure caused by asymmetric information and incentive incompatibility. This is where we must look for a solution, for a way to reverse the industry's drift downward. Once incentives are aligned and asymmetric information reduced, all of the players will behave differently, and processes will be reformed.[46]

FOUR

Asymmetric Information

THE BIG BARRIER TO CHANGE

Why have we not witnessed the successful consolidation or industri- 81
alization of the construction industry? Why do builders continue to
make such extensive use of subcontractors? How could economically
inefficient practices persist for years or even decades? Market inefficiencies in construction arise from the existence and persistence of
asymmetric information: the contractor has more knowledge than
the owner. That, in turn, allows for the perpetuation of mutable cost
contracting, which essentially destroys competition and allows numerous other problems, some major and some minor, to arise and
thrive. As Nobel Laureate in economics Douglass C. North put it,
"When competition is 'muted' (for whatever reasons) organizations
will have little incentive to invest in new knowledge and in consequence will not induce rapid institutional change. Stable institutional
structures will be the result."[1] No one has the incentive to substan-
tially improve. The industry all but says, "We're doing just fine with
the status quo, thank you very much."

The doctrine of *caveat emptor* (buyer beware) has lost much of
its force in recent decades, and it is not clear why it should be upheld
in construction, where information asymmetries are so large. Other
markets characterized by high levels of asymmetric information—
legal advice, finance, medicine, education—are highly regulated, pro-
fessionalized, and/or intermediated, in large part to protect consumers

from unscrupulous producers. There is no reason why property owners who contract to build buildings for millions of dollars should be
held to a higher standard than purchasers of other complex, big-
ticket, customizable services.[2] There is no doubt that asymmetric information leads to mutable cost contracting. But it also creates a host
of other problems that stem from the resulting lack of effective competition in construction: weak and short-sighted management, inadequate education of industry professionals and meager investment in
research and development.

Mutable Costs

Markets run on information and do not run at all without it. Markets
run best when both buyer and seller have equal access to information,
but in the construction industry, they do not. The fact that owners do
not have near equal knowledge is *the* major reason why inefficiency
and mutable costs persist in construction. For a number of reasons peculiar to construction, building owners cannot easily compare building price or quality—at the start, during construction, or even after
the job is done. Most owners cannot even read blueprints, much less
fathom the complex process of transforming the prints into usable
structures. In most instances, the construction team pre-sets the project budget by reviewing the design documents prepared by the architect and the engineers. There is rarely anyone equally knowledgeable
about material or labor costs to effectively challenge the budget set by
the contractor. Most inexperienced owners cannot readily distinguish
between reasonable and unreasonable contractor bids. Even when
they can, their only real alternative if the price comes in higher than
the project budget is to reduce or eliminate features since the contractor will be unlikely to reduce its overall price without a commensurate scope reduction. Even then, the contractor will maintain the
same degree of profitability.[3]

Moreover, sundry difficulties—real or imagined—can necessitate
numerous change orders, which are always presented after any real

threat of competition has passed.[4] As construction economist Patricia Hillebrandt explains, "The monopoly power of the negotiating contractor will be greater, the greater the time and money already invested by the client in these negotiations."[5]

Though nominally fixed, traditional U.S. construction contracts are in fact disguised mutable-cost contracts because contractors find it so easy to raise the price *during* the construction process. This is "change order artistry" at its finest: "Competitive bidding . . . often leads to the owner getting nailed during construction for numerous extra charges by a builder intent on making up for the too low price he had to submit to win the job in the first place."[6] Another guru says that he always tells prospects that "it would be *very easy* to 'low-ball' a figure, get his name on the dotted line, and then start with the added costs. . . . It puts him on notice to watch out for this maneuver from the competition."[7] Yet another states matter-of-factly, "Some contractors may bid low with the intent of garnering profits from change orders."[8] Such low bidding is notoriously common because the bidding process encourages it.[9]

Change orders present a very knotty problem. Sometimes change orders are necessary, for example if the owner orders a change in the design after a prior approval or if the architect omitted an important detail. But they can also be gouging mechanisms. "Often," one study recently noted, "contract change proposals are the result of contractor errors or omissions unrelated to the contract specifications."[10] One industry text instructs prospective contractors to build a "'slush fund' into every project, to be used if a disgruntled owner insists on not paying for a change and 'you felt you had to give.' Cheer up; maybe the owner will ask for a legitimate change order *and you can get your money back*."[11] Such advice only inflames a dysfunctional relationship and perpetuates the root causes of industry malaise.

Contractors have devised many techniques to ensure a profit. "Prospects have a way of thinking site work will cost what it will cost and there's nothing to do but pay," one contractor advises, "so capitalize on this attitude and stress building cost and places to save."

"Chances are," the contractor continues, "that the numbers you give the prospect [for the site cost] will be more than what he has in mind. . . . Keep quiet. He'll speak when he has his breath back."[12]

84   Is it any wonder that cost overruns became an ever more prevalent fact of life on construction projects across the nation? Consider the following recent examples that received wide publicity in construction circles:

> The owner, architect and builder of the $419-million Miami Performing Arts Center have reached a $44-million settlement that is expected to put the high-profile project on positive footing after years of delays and big cost overruns. The two-building complex is 600 days over its original schedule and more than $67 million over budget.[13]

> The press has widely reported the disastrous experiences of school districts throughout New York State and the country in constructing and renovating schools. Studies such as the 1999 study by PricewaterhouseCoopers LLP for the New York City School Construction Authority confirmed a consistent pattern of delays and cost overruns in school construction and examine proposed reforms.[14]

> The Romney administration [Massachusetts] was unhappy . . . about . . . Arthur Winn's campaign to pry loose $20 million in no-interest or low-interest state loans for his over budget Columbus Center, the mega condo and hotel project that will straddle the Massachusetts Turnpike. . . . Winn's co-developer, Roger Cassin, has been the front man for the $450 million (and counting) monster, with Winn doing his best to stay out of sight.[15]

> A minor league baseball stadium in Little Rock was initially projected to cost $28 million, but by opening day in April 2007, the stadium will have cost an additional $5.6 million due to increased construction material costs and additional scope. Taxpayers helped finance the stadium's original cost, but the developers and

fans will pay for the overruns in additional proceeds from tickets, parking, and concessions.[16]

According to one study, over 90 percent of transportation construction jobs overshoot their budgets. Worse, the study found no improvement over the last seventy years! Other studies, though, suggest that "only" about a quarter of construction jobs are over budget and about the same percentage are finished late.[17] Everyone admits, "it is not unusual for large and unique projects to run over budget."[18] How-to guides caution owners to keep their guard up lest cost overruns overwhelm their budgets. But that is difficult to do when the contractor holds the trump cards: better information and monopoly power.[19]

Ineffective Intermediaries

Traditionally, architects acted on behalf of owners to mitigate predatory contractor behavior, but increasingly they have shown themselves unsuited to the task. Architect software developer Larry Rocha warns that "buildings have become much more complex," inducing architects to push technical responsibility and liability onto other parties. "Designers," he notes, "have become less interested in how the building actually goes together, which causes a disparity between design and construction cost." That raises the trillion-dollar question: "Who is responsible for the cost effective constructability of the building?"[20]

In the 1970s the American Institute of Architects also aided the retreat by regularly revising its standard form agreements to reduce the architect's scope of services during the construction phase from "full time" on-site availability where it "oversaw" the construction to "periodic" site availability where it simply "observed" the construction. While seeking to limit the liability of the architect for construction and safety problems, the change in services caused irreparable harm to the profession by removing architects from an active role during the construction phase.

Into this vacuum the construction manager rode, selling new services to owners in the face of the architects' retreat. While ostensibly acting in the interest of their new owner clients, these construction managers were, as many industry insiders say, simply contractors with suits and ties. With no true intermediary protecting owners, predatory change orders became common. Without a knowledgeable intermediary to serve its interests, the owner was now in a predicament: the sole party with the knowledge of construction costs was the same party who was in charge of construction. The competitive bidding process now merely allowed the owner to choose his poison: general contractor fixed price or construction manager guaranteed maximum price.[21] With either one, the end result was likely to be the same.

Quality, or rather the lack of it, compounds the problem. It is not uncommon for contractors to offer an owner a false choice: "Price, quality, or schedule—pick two, forget about the third." Construction projects may come in on time and on budget because quality was sacrificed, but that still does not mean the owner will have gotten what he paid for. According to Joseph Ciskowski, research director of Jim Walter Corporation, basic walls and ceilings in American houses are not acceptably plumb or level. Floors squeak because carpenters used moist lumber. Concrete is poured when it is too cold or dry to permit proper hydration so it cracks or spalls. If a corner can be cut, figuratively, it often is. A man who makes his living selling bathroom fixtures to builders notes, "Quality doesn't get you anything with these [contractors]: they'll cut your throat for a quarter."[22] Unsurprisingly, serious disputes, and hence lawsuits and arbitration cases, are commonplace.[23] Often, however, owners find it difficult to "push back" on change orders for a variety of reasons. Without an independent method of determining whether the price increase is legitimate or not, an owner cannot capably challenge a price shown on a change order. The fact that delaying the approval of a change order will clearly lead to a construction delay that will cost them even more than the contractor's extra charge puts an owner at a severe disadvantage. Further, the fear that denying the request for a change order will jeopardize quality is, in many instances, a legitimate concern.[24]

As a consequence of their limited ability to contest change orders owners often create "contingency allocations" at the outset of a project to cover the extra charges. In some instances, even these contingent funds fail to cover the number of change orders on a project.

Some suggest that the best owners can do is to see problems far enough ahead of time to duck. One recent study listed twenty-three "of the more visible telltale features" that indicate trouble is on the horizon. The list includes incomplete and highly customized bid documents; a wide spread in bids; a bid list reflecting inexperienced general, prime, or specialty contractor(s) for the specific project in question; and important parties in agent or not-at-risk positions.[25]

Others suggest that alternate construction delivery such as fast-track or design-build methods can mitigate problems. Perhaps, but they are remedial only and miss the root problem of asymmetric information between owners and contractors, and they largely do not ensure a fixed contract price, although design-build can come close. Recall from chapter 1 that design-build projects align the economic interests of the architect and the contractor. In so doing, it removes the architect from whatever limited role it might have played as the intermediary, or owner's representative, during construction. "Everyone at this table," a contractor told a group of his peers at one association meeting, "would admit they've been in a situation where without the (architect) on the other side of the table, they might have been able to get away with something." The trade-off for owners in design-build is that while they benefit from holding a single source responsible for the design and construction of the project, they give up control of much of the process. For example, the design-builder has great leeway to make final decisions on materials and quality that might otherwise be at odds with those of the owner in a design-bid-build process. Without a doubt, an owner who engages a design-build team must hire an independent owner's representative to ensure that its design intent and quality expectations are properly executed.[26]

Effective owner intermediaries are lacking throughout the industry, perpetuating asymmetric conditions that result in mutable-cost contracting. This is the disease that infects the body of the construction industry from head to toe. Consider the head: what should be the brain of the industry? What is wrong with management?

Wanted: Better Management

That management in construction is suboptimal is widely recognized and not a problem unique to the United States. As a report for the World Bank pointed out, "diagnoses of the problems affecting construction enterprises—and often the entire construction industry of a country—often take the form of encyclopedic listings of ailments including corruption. As a rule, they miss the important point that many of those ailments are only symptoms of the underlying problem of weak enterprise management."[27] But before improvements to management in the construction industry can be made, we need to identify the problem underlying the weaknesses of management. Recall that over 90 percent of all contractors are composed of firms of less than twenty people.

The implications of asymmetric information for the general structure of the industry (many small firms, the competitive incentive to underbid, the monopolistic nature of the relationship with the owner) provide very little incentive for management training. Training is a cost that is difficult to bear for small firms with low profit margins and little assurance of future income, and the additional costs of employing managers whose contribution to production may not be immediately apparent are also difficult to maintain. Even owners of construction firms have little time to devote to project management, spending most of their time securing the next project or overseeing the all-important cash flow.

Construction is inherently difficult. In *Blake Construction Co. v. J. C. Coakley Co.*, Associate Judge Kern likened the construction site to a battlefield, replete with its own fog of war. "Except in the middle of a battlefield," Kean wrote, "nowhere must men coordinate the movement of other men and all materials in the midst of such chaos and with such limited certainty of present facts and future occurrences as in a huge construction project."[28] The moving parts can seem nearly countless, their management little short of miraculous when one considers the myriad reasons, both within and outside the contractor's control, for failure: flawed overexpansion strategies, obsession with volume work, poor project selection, insufficient capital, unproductive field performance, problem owners, macroeconomic volatility, credit market changes, and the list goes on.[29]

The unfortunate truth of the matter, however, is that many construction firms are, and traditionally have been, poorly run businesses.[30] One study found that "more than half the time wasted during construction" was directly "attributable to poor management practices."[31] As construction consultant Leslie M. Kusek recently lamented,

> Construction firms, engineers, architects, and the myriad of other professional service providers that serve the built environment—we're getting beaten up badly. And we blame the economy, stiffer competition and those blasted clients that don't understand anything about the value of our services—only the bottom line price. Folks, look in the mirror. We are traveling down this spiraling road by our own choice! . . . We are not strategically directing the destiny of our companies. Many of us unconsciously bid on work, not fully understanding what revenue base nourishes our firms, or what weakens them. What types of clients deliver the most profitable projects? What types of projects do we want to position ourselves for, for future business trends? Where should we be investing our business development and marketing dollars to grow? Where are we going?[32]

These are questions of management. Others agree. According to Mark Dancer, vice president of Pembroke Consulting, "Contractors are pragmatic, down-to-earth business people, slow to adopt new practices and slower to invest in new technologies."[33] Much of what contractors have to say about change doesn't even make sense. One builder told his colleagues, apparently with a straight face, "You have to be a little *in-*

novative. Look around and see what *other people* are doing."[34] It is probably a good thing, then, that such "managers" as these give general directions but allow lower-level supervisors, foremen, and even the laborers themselves to decide precisely how to complete assigned tasks.[35] It is these individuals who are in most instances the front line problem solvers on a project. But these workers cannot be expected to see the larger picture.

How competent, or incompetent, are the leaders of construction firms? Performance varies, of course, but some neglected fundamentals raise doubts. Construction site managers, one study showed, are often selected on the basis of folkloric stereotypes rather than scientific evidence of characteristics that lead to success. It is also known that many construction managers neglect to cover themselves from personal, property, and liability risks. As most firms are preponderantly small, they do not have access to high-quality legal, accounting, and business advice. They also rarely hedge against changes in interest rates, weather conditions, or materials prices. Academic studies have successfully predicted construction cost overruns, so construction managers could do likewise, if they had the expertise and incentive to do so. And, of course, as identified above, if overruns can be predicted, they can be prevented.[36]

Risk arises when the assessment of the probability of an event is statistically possible. Uncertainty arises when the probability is indeterminate. Risk is therefore insurable but uncertainty is not. Good managers know the difference between the two; great ones help to change uncertainties into insurable risks. For example, it is uncertain whether an architect will supply drawings on time. A good manager, however, will change that uncertainty to a risk with a probability of default near zero by informing the architect of the large costs he will bear if he does not produce the drawings on schedule (backcharges, lawsuit, whatever it takes).[37]

But that is not all. Many of the smallest construction firms begin business without a plan. The seat-of-the-pants approach quickly leads many of them into deep financial trouble. One who bid too low on a new custom house had to mortgage her own home in order to com-

plete the project. Another took on too many small jobs at once and had
to get a big loan from his mother to continue in business.[38]

Some larger contractors do have a plan, but lack a strategy. The distinction is an important one. A plan is merely a logical set of steps. A
strategy, by contrast, takes account of what other relevant parties—
like competitors—will likely do. So when a feasibility study says that
there is a demand for 200 units of townhouses near a certain golf
course, a contractor with a plan may construct only 100 units, just to
be on the safe side. Unfortunately—for the contractors and for non-
townhouse owners—there were five such contractors in the area, so
the market was soon glutted with 500 units. A contractor with some
understanding of strategy would have given consideration to the fact
that his competitors were also likely to react aggressively to the per-
ceived opportunity.[39]

Construction firms may stay small simply because their owners
and managers do not know how to run bigger, more integrated concerns. Most contractors find it difficult to complete even simple administrative tasks like accounting and hiring. Others may not feel
comfortable or capable of affording skilled advisors such as accountants and lawyers. Contractors often hire low-skilled workers because
they confuse labor rate with labor cost. In other words, they do not understand that productivity is the key, not wages. A contractor could
pay a new, unskilled worker $5 an hour but only get $3 an hour of
work from him. Or the contractor could pay an experienced, skilled
worker $30 an hour but get $50 or $100 an hour of work from him.
Or the contractor could hire a guy for $15 an hour who usually pro-
duces $20 an hour of work but through effective people skills start
to get $25 an hour out of him, just because the worker likes the con-
tractor and enjoys his job. Of course calculating labor productivity is
a good deal more difficult than asking an applicant how much he
needs per hour.[40]

Small and even some large contractors find themselves cash-
strapped on occasion and need to borrow cash from Project A to fund
Project B, a dangerous expedient, especially given that they rarely run
credit checks on clients.[41]

Given such limited business skills, contractors naturally find that it is better to buy a needed good than to make it internally. For their money, smaller and simpler is better. The expectation seems to be that companies will never grow to be huge, so why bother even to get big?

Geographic and regional regulatory differences along with construction market segmentation have conspired to keep firms small. For example, some rather sizable construction companies that tried to expand into new states or markets ran into difficulties. Kitchell Corporations's expansion into Texas, for example, failed miserably when the owner went bankrupt with millions in unpaid change orders due. Kitchell admitted that the company expanded too quickly, forcing it to put inexperienced people in charge of projects that they couldn't handle.[42] Many a builder has sought to expand geographically only to learn that house designs differ fundamentally in different parts of the country and that there are good reasons for the distinctiveness. Some of the reasons are physical. A Yankee outfit once entered the Dallas market hard by building homes with full basements, a novelty in the area. After the first rainstorm his customers had full basements all right, full of water! In some low-lying and humid areas of the South, houses are built on piers, with a skirt of siding masking the crawl space underneath, to mitigate flooding and promote ventilation. Other reasons are more cultural. In Philadelphia carports are acceptable, but in balmy autocentric California they are not. "You buy property in an area you don't know," Robert Levenstein, president of Kaufman & Broad, once remarked, "it's with you a *long* time."[43]

Other firms have foundered because the local tradesmen simply did not know how to use certain materials or technologies. In Connecticut, radiators continued to be installed in new homes instead of the central forced air systems that were so popular in the Midwest merely because the local building tradesmen didn't know how to properly fabricate the sheet metal for the necessary duct work, but the plumbers knew all about radiators.[44]

It is understood throughout the industry that the management of the average construction firm is not very good. Larger, better capitalized firms could attract better managers, people with the human capital skills and knowledge needed to deal with tax, insurance, and legal advisors who routinely advise large corporations. With such a team in place, larger contractors could, for example, devise a program to offer extended warranties and cost-effectively protect themselves from future lawsuits by forming "captives," limited liability corporations designed to receive, hold, and invest warranty payments and pay from such affiliated companies any claims that may arise. Larger firms would also find it easier and cheaper to purchase protective insurance coverages and procure external financing. By selling commercial paper, bonds, or even equity rather than relying on credit cards, mortgages, personal and bank loans, or client advances, larger firms might find it easier to market their services to Fortune 500 companies.[45]

Larger firms would also find it easier to hire men like Kenneth Neumann, CEO of Neumann Homes, a Warrenville, Illinois, homebuilder who gets 6 new houses out of each employee per year instead of the 3.5 to 5 prevalent in the industry. He also sells houses to 8 out of every 100 candidates, twice the national average. Neumann gets this productivity the new-fashioned way: by forging a strong corporate culture that demands excellence. He built a corporate university, Neumann University, where he teaches three classes a week. Neumann also leads by example in action, word, and deed. The privately held company cracked the half-billion revenue mark in 2006 and hopes to be the world's largest homebuilder by 2020. While it still has a long way to go (it was ranked fifty-eighth in the United States by housing revenue in 2006, up from sixty-sixth in 2005), this goal is a bit different from most other contractors who, by 2020, might hope to have retired on fat change orders.[46]

Larger firms could also begin to see their businesses as portfolios of construction projects, much the way that financial institutions see themselves as portfolios of assets with different risk/return, liquidity, and maturity characteristics. Today, construction firms tend to impose higher markups on jobs poorly matched to their capacity. In other words, they attempt to earn higher profit rates on smaller jobs that they see as nuisances (high fixed costs), and on larger jobs that they see as risky. A large, well-managed construction firm would never bid on a job larger than it could comfortably handle since it would never permit more than a reasonable amount of its resources to be committed to such a project. Small jobs would be treated in the aggregate, not as independent projects. Some architects and designers have proven the economic viability of doing small jobs at high volume, for example, nationwide rollouts of large retail stores. Builders could do the same, if they had the requisite management skills. For the moment, they do not. As we will learn in the next chapter, many do not even have control over their own labor force.[47]

Education: Unsurprisingly Inadequate

Back in 1959, MIT professor Kelly Burnham lamented that "the combination of genuine design ability and a sensitive understanding of the housing industry is rare, and almost nowhere is it being taught."[48] There has been little improvement since.

There are a fair number of baccalaureate and associate degree programs in construction management accredited by the American Council for Construction Education.[49] The programs look good, on paper (or rather in the ether), but what is really needed in this era of specialization are more interdisciplinary professional graduate programs in construction management. As early as the 1980s a major study recognized that "improving the education of tomorrow's construction executives in universities and colleges can make an extremely important contribution to increasing cost-effectiveness in construction." That same study noted, "university-level education, to be truly effective, should combine academic and on-the-job training."[50]

Construction professionals often obtain degrees in civil engineering or architecture. Engineering programs stress math, science, and engineering courses. Architecture programs stress design studio courses informed by art and architectural history, architectural theory, and the social sciences. But the two rarely mix, though they ought to. As one government study noted, to drive the construction industry's productivity higher "architects will need to know more about engineering, and engineers will need to learn more about design." And all construction professionals need better interpersonal skills and team problem solving experience.[51]

Perhaps worse, both types of programs are severely deficient in coursework related to business, economics, cost estimating, real estate, and management. Most instruction is in the classroom, not on actual construction sites. As a result, in an ultimate irony, students learn how to analyze (take apart) but not to synthesize (put together). In other words, students learn to think of construction as a series of discrete sub-processes rather than the erection of efficient, economical edifices. Construction is therefore seen as many discrete physical tasks rather than as a process with user-satisfaction as the end result.

Architectural education also remains dim in this regard. For literally millennia, one learned the art of architects by apprenticing to a master. Such a system ensured that student apprentices learned all aspects of the field, including the proper methods for building what it had designed. "Thus," writes storied architect James Marston Fitch, "the vast majority of building was in the hands of those whose origins were closer to the craftsmanship of millwright and mason than to academic scholarship."[52]

By World War II, however, the architectural apprenticeship system had given way to formal university education as had other professions. The university system retained the worst features of apprenticeship while jettisoning its core strengths, its links to the real world and the low student to teacher ratio. Today, ten to twenty architectural students in a "design studio" are taught by one "critic," a professor who critiques their work. When the critic is skilled and engaged, the format is superb. But all too often, the critic has limited professional practice experience and is not terribly interested in integrating the fundamentals of how buildings are really constructed with design instruction. "The price paid for this new professionalism," Fitch laments, "was high. . . . Few contemporary architects have firsthand knowledge of actual construction methods and techniques." One of the biggest problems contractors voice is the poor and incomplete preparation of architectural drawings. While they reflect the design aesthetic desired by the architect, they do so without clearly depicting a corresponding understanding of how the particular design element is to be physically built in the field.[53]

In engineering and architecture programs alike, students learn how to conceive and design projects, not to manage them. They often do not learn how to properly integrate the technical necessities of a building (HVAC, lighting, or life safety systems) or how to successfully coordinate their consultants' designs for such systems with their design concept. Yet this is what the world demands in its buildings. Little wonder that by the early 1970s architects designed only 2 percent of single-family dwellings and led only 5 percent of all construction projects in the United States. Their typical product was not the built building but its paper facsimile.[54]

To a surprising degree, designs still rely on paper, rather than digital, processes. From the first days of architectural and engineering school, design professionals learn that the accurate reflection of the professional's design intent on behalf of the owner must be evidenced in a drawing. As a result, the design team, which often includes twenty or more consultants, assembles from a host of sources drawings and other depictions of their ideas that, when fully assembled and coordinated by the architect, typically total hundreds of large format drawings. Ironically, even this cumbrous set of materials does not include the detailed written specification book that minutely identifies thousands of other pieces of information to be assimilated by the construction team as it prepares to bid or build.

Research and teaching resources devoted to creating an understanding of how buildings are actually built would be especially useful.[55] Today, architects readily admit that they are not "aware of the cost implications of many common construction practices and procedures."[56] Contractors, even carpenters, quickly learn to correct for architects' mistakes. "There aren't many architects around," Dallas contractor Jesse Harris says, "who know you can't get a four-inch stack in a four-inch wall." As Gil Wolf of the National Plastering Institute notes, "A building is not built the way it is on paper—the architects' lines always measure out [on the drawing], but it's not going to be that way when you start to build."[57]

If only architects were the only problem. A spate of studies suggests that engineers are far from blameless. According to one recent study, "engineering activity is a real bottleneck in constructing industrial facilities. This activity has far reaching impact on several aspects of the project and it significantly contributes to its successful or unsuccessful implementation." The absence of a common system for assessing engineering performance, however, stymies efforts to measure the impact of poor engineering more precisely.[58] Again, an educational system that values abstract theoretical thinking over field experience is a key problem. A study published in the early 1980s rings true even today: "Too many engineers, separated from field experience, are not up to date about how to build what they design, or how to design so structures and equipment can be erected most efficiently."[59]

In the 1990s, attempts to reform engineering education were attempted because some professors realized that they were delivering stale material in a stale way. Engineering education contained too little synthesis and exposure to actual industrial conditions. As a consequence, engineers could handle only narrowly defined problems, communicated poorly, and did not work well in teams, especially those composed of non-engineers.[60] Some progress was made but ultimately foundered on the fact that most engineering professors did not wish to mend their ways. Even the American Society of Engineering Education argues that engineering education is lacking. The engineering student of the future, one of its former presidents argues, "must be just as interested in cost and ability to manufacture as in product performance, because engineering achievement is measured not only by now well something is done, but by how soon and for how little."[61]

A reasonable reader may very well wonder why architectural and engineering schools do not improve their performance or, lacking that, why new, better architecture and/or engineering schools do not arise and supplant the existing ones. The answer is far from simple, but it can be summed up in a few words here—U.S. higher education is also an inefficient sector, one characterized by high barriers to entry, significant market distortions due to high government involvement in higher education, and the use of sub-optimal ownership structures. Almost all U.S. colleges and universities are nonprofits or joint-stock corporations; the theoretically superior form, the professional partnership, is almost never used. Government subsidies and endowments make nonprofit schools fat and complacent, while concern for stockholder interests render corporate schools perpetually under gunned in the brainpower department.

The advent of larger construction firms would help because they could pressure governments to reform state-run schools and could endow more professorships and construction research programs. If those efforts proved unsuccessful, large integrated construction firms could start corporate research and training centers as other large corporations have done.[62]

Anemic R&D

Larger construction firms could also do more to encourage improvements in industry research and development, which has traditionally been lackluster since the status quo hardly rewards it. By about 1900, American construction firms employed the world's most sophisticated building technologies because they were at the forefront of the installation of the most modern building features: steel frames, elevators, electrical, plumbing, telephone systems, and central heating. They gained more expertise in the 1920s and 1930s building national highways, dams, and other major infrastructure projects. During World War II, they learned how to build airports, bridges, and other crucial infrastructure fast and strong. After the war, they helped to rebuild the world's shattered cities. When the cold war grew chilly, they built U.S. military installations around the globe. In the 1970s, American construction companies built technologically advanced buildings for the Saudis and other newly rich oil kingdoms, among others.[63]

During the 1980s, however, U.S. construction firms lost their near global monopoly on advanced building skills. Predictably, the rate at which these firms gained experience on these sophisticated projects has declined. Like companies in most other industries, and like construction firms in other nations, the U.S. construction industry should have invested in research and development projects. But they didn't, and they have paid the price. In the 1980s, U.S. construction firms spent about 0.4 percent of sales on R&D, about the same amount they spent in the early 1960s and far less than Japanese construction companies and firms in other U.S. industries like appliances (1.4 percent), automobiles (1.7 percent), even textiles (0.8 percent). Materials manufacturers conduct some R&D, but they tend to concentrate on their narrow product lines rather than improving the overall construction process. Some industry analysts don't even seem to understand what research meant. One has asked, in all seriousness, "which comes first, the investment or the market?"[64] The answer depends on one's vision for the industry. Is it willing to invest in transformative behavior now, or wait until an external influence demands it?

Most construction-related R&D, therefore, is not, and never has been, conducted by companies, but rather by professional organizations and universities. For example, the Construction Industry Institute, a research institute for engineering and construction associated with the University of Texas at Austin, is composed of over ninety member organizations. With the motto "Best Practices for the Construction Industry," it disseminates research findings and implementation aid to the entire industry, including owners, contractors, and suppliers via conferences, Web site links, continuing education courses, and publications. The Structural Clay Products Institute and the Douglas Fir Plywood Association have conducted beneficial research programs, as have the National Association of Homes, the American Society of Heating and Air-Conditioning Engineers, the American Institute of Architects, and the Home Manufacturers Association. The electrical utilities industry invests hundreds of millions of dollars in R&D each year, but only a small percentage of that goes for "ideas applicable to construction."[65]

Since 2000, a collaborative research and development organization, FIATECH (Fully Integrated and Automated Technology) has been "bringing the benefits of technology throughout the life cycle of all types of capital projects." Supported by some major owners (Dow, DuPont, Intel, Procter and Gamble), contractors (Bechtel, CH2M Hill, Fluor, Jacobs Engineering), and product and material manufacturers, FIATECH is trying to help all participants in the construction process to gain access to practical new technologies that can streamline processes, improve information accessibility, reduce supply chain barriers, and decrease engineering, construction, and operational costs.[66]

Government also helps out in limited ways. The National Science Foundation and the Pennsylvania Infrastructure Technology Alliance (PITA), for example, help fund the Center for Advanced Technology for Large Structural Systems (ATLSS) at Lehigh University in Bethlehem, Pennsylvania. "The role of ATLSS," proclaims its Web site, "is to conduct research and educate students on technology issues affecting these industries in design, fabrication, construction, inspection, and protection." Federal laboratories, including three civil engineering laboratories for the armed forces, and the National Bureau of Standards' Centers for Building Technology and Fire Research conduct research on a range of topics with civil applications. Compared to other countries, government support of construction in the United States is, like the industry itself, extremely fragmented.[67]

To combat that fragmentation, in 1993 President Bill Clinton established the National Science and Technology Council (NSTC), a cabinet-level entity that was to coordinate the federal government's science, space, and technology programs. The following year the NSTC organized a committee to coordinate and focus the construction-related research activities of fourteen federal agencies. The committee established very aggressive long-term (ten-year) goals, including 50 percent reductions in delivery time, operating costs, worker safety measures, pollution, and building durability. Unfortunately, the industry did not even come close to reaching those targets despite an average investment of $500 million per year in construction R&D activities through a spate of initiatives (PATH, NESBIC, HITEC, EvTEC, CEITEC, NCSBCS, CONMAT, PAIR) that would make admirers of the New Deal's "alphabet soup" programs proud.[68]

That outcome would not surprise anyone conversant with the history of government construction subsidies, which have ranged from complete disasters to big disappointments.[69] The Civilian Industrial Technology Program (CITP) is a telling case. Formed in 1962 at the behest of J. Herbert Hollomon, an assistant secretary in the U.S. Department of Commerce, the CITP called for "a national coordinated research program, interdisciplinary in nature and industry-wide in scope." It had three primary goals: (1) to foster innovation in lagging industries, including construction; (2) to study the information and technology needs of those industries; (3) to help to diffuse information and technical aid between those industries and universities. Due to vehement opposition from the construction industry and free-market ideologues in Congress, support for CITP, which was never fully funded, soon disappeared.[70]

The Department of Commerce considered the construction industry a laggard because, though undoubtedly a large part of the economy, its productivity growth, at 2 to 2.9 percent per year, was quite low compared to productivity growth in chemicals, airlines, electric utilities, and even agriculture and textiles. The department attributed its slow growth to "technological lag." Indeed, a study by Arthur D. Little, Inc., published in 1963 declared that "during the last thirty years there has been no major technological change of major economic significance for the building industry. . . . Technological change has been primarily evolutionary in small increments. . . . It can hardly be called 'innovation.'"[71]

One problem with government and university research is that because construction firms do not pay for it directly, they feel no pressing need to make use of it to recoup costs. As a result, many innovations are made not by the construction industry but by materials manufacturers who hope to bring new products to market. Take, for instance, the common garbage disposal, which, of course, was once not so common. General Electric spent well over $1 million in the early 1950s to develop and market the product, considered a lot of money at the time. Where in the industry might something like this have happened? Likely nowhere.[72] Even today, most construction advancements remain limited to product manufacturers, whose products can in fact

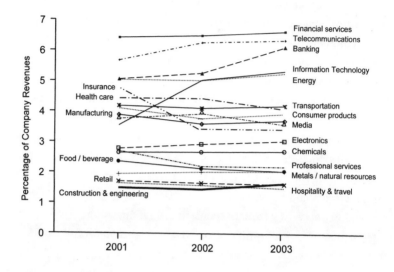

FIGURE 5. U.S. IT Spending by Industry, 2001–2003. Source: e-Marketer, 2003.

improve contractor productivity. The Simpson Strongtie product line of specialty engineered connectors is one example that has made wood framing, among other things, more productive for contractors than ever. For many construction firms, however, merely staying abreast of recent product developments is taxing and continuing education is altogether unappealing.

In 1987, the Department of Commerce noted that "over the next twenty years it is totally reasonable to expect that we will see widespread application of the following technologies: advanced materials, microelectronics, automation, biotechnology, computing, membrane technology, superconductivity, and lasers." About the same time, the Office of Technology Assessment made similar claims. Almost twenty years have elapsed and none of those technologies are widely used in construction. As figure 5 shows, construction and engineering companies are far behind firms in most other sectors in terms of information technology (IT) spending.

Figure 6 confirms that the construction industry is the last thing from a major employer of scientists, engineers, IT professionals, or technicians. In fact, it never has been.[73]

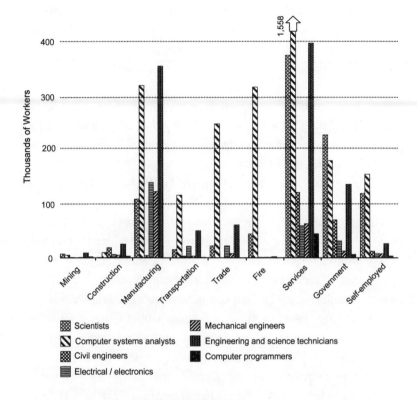

FIGURE 6. Employment of Scientists and Engineers by Industry, 2000. Source: U.S. Bureau of Labor Statistics, National Industry-Occupation.

The industry is so backward that it recently *boasted* that 27 percent of contractors currently have a functional Web site. Most in the industry approach IT with skepticism. Criticism of the industry on this point also comes from abroad. Sir John Egan, former chair of the Strategic Forum of the Confederation of British Industry recently stated, "The industry doesn't use computers enough. The car industry could not deliver its incredible annual improvements without computers. With widespread use of computers, everyone in construction could practice on them, rather than on their customer."[74] Surprisingly, even larger construction companies have been slow to join the telecommunication and digital revolutions. The adoption of Web-based project management and cost estimating software has been painfully slow, though experts agree that it considerably boosts productivity, especially on more complex jobs by enabling all team players to share project information faster and with greater clarity. Four out of five construction firms do not use this kind of collaboration software at all. Only companies with annual revenues greater than $250 million per year are likely to own an advanced project management software package, but even then one in three of that group still has not invested in this basic productivity tool.

According to a recent report prepared for the National Institute of Standards and Technology, inadequate interoperability—that is, the inability to manage and communicate electronic project data both internally and between collaborating firms—costs architects and engineers working on capital facilities almost $1.2 billion annually in lost productivity. According to the report, inefficient business process management is the second greatest cost of inadequate interoperability.[75]

Unlike firms in competitive industries, construction companies still have not learned that computers are not overhead expenses. They are tools as much as jackhammers and front-end loaders. In skilled hands, they increase productivity many times over. Readily available software can help construction teams to coordinate on-site activities, assign the proper liabilities and costs to the proper parties, and track everything from workers to I-beams in real-time. When not properly carried out, a failure to coordinate the trades results in delays and finger-pointing between the contractors, designers, and owner over who will pay for the costly change orders that ensue. Yet a recent study estimated that construction companies waste at least $15.8 billion per year on inefficient communication systems alone.[76]

According to Ric Johnson, a vice president of Constructware, a supplier of software that facilitates collaboration for large construction projects, the pressures on project executives to achieve greater efficiency and shorter construction schedules demands new responses designed to reduce costs, improve quality, increase business responsiveness, and evaluate life cycle costs and emerging sustainable products and technologies. A sales executive for a company trying to introduce a technology wonderfully called "intelliRock" (implanted computer chips that provide real time data on the strength and maturity of new pours of concrete) grows impatient: "Builders and engineers welcome change to their industry in much the same way that buggy whip manufacturers helped usher in the era of the horseless carriage."[77] Disdain for technology is nothing new for construction. A study completed in the early 1980s created a list, "long familiar to most construction executives" of "major impediments" that "tether construction to the past."[78]

Why this near-Luddite attitude? Industry fragmentation is a big part of the answer. There are no dominant firms. Small firms across many different industries have traditionally found it difficult to allocate resources for development. Most U.S. construction companies concern themselves with short-term survival rather than long-run productivity gains. Few prepare either short- or long-term business plans. Moreover, companies hesitate to spend resources developing processes that cannot be patented or otherwise protected from free riders.[79] Technology is the most important aspect of productivity after human labor costs on a project. It is also the most neglected. Excuses abound. And because the industry is devoid of the competitive pressures that transformed the automobile, aircraft, and numerous other industries, the excuses win, the industry stagnates, and the owners lose.

Promising Technology: Building Information Modeling (BIM)

Clearly, there are exceptions. Some firms have begun to invest a substantial amount of their own profits in technology and R&D, for their own benefit and that of the profession. Notably, they are not the better capitalized large contractors and construction managers, but design professionals. In projects such as the Guggenheim Bilbao in Spain and the Walt Disney Concert Hall in Los Angeles, Frank O. Gehry, along with a small number of other progressive architects across the country, have eclipsed many other firms in their use of advanced design software technology. Gehry has excelled because he breaks all the molds, not just design ones. For example, he and his partners make extensive use of CATIA software, a program originally developed for the aerospace industry by Dassault Systems of France. The Gehry firm, frustrated by the fact that contractors needed better information than that provided by two dimensional standard architectural and engineering drawings, saw CATIA as a better way to represent to contractors Gehry's complex designs, though in principle the tool is as useful in simpler designs. Gehry's architects design curved roofs and walls (signature Gehry design elements) using CATIA's three dimensional parametric modeling capability. Parametric modeling represents a huge productivity gain over standard 2D, and most 3D, drafting software because changes made to the 3D model not only change the model, but simultaneously change all the drawings and databases linked to the model.

The firm's extensive use of CATIA inspired it to form a separate company, Gehry Technologies, to create and market a more industry-friendly version of the software to its fellow design professionals. Digital Project is its advanced architectural and engineering 3D-modeling software using the CATIA engine, all for a relatively affordable price. Some would say a small price, given the potential return on investment that can be realized utilizing this software and other similar packages. Digital Project was used on Gehry's highly acclaimed Ray and Maria Stata Center at the Massachusetts Institute of Technology, leading its dean of the school of architecture to state that Gehry Technologies "have reconceived the process of construction." By using its specialized software, Gehry included much greater and more precise amounts of detailed information about its complex designs to the contractors than it could have had it used traditional drafting software. The payoff? The project remained within its $300 million budget and earned praise from the project's steel fabricator despite the many highly customized pieces required by Gehry's design. Former Gehry Technologies CEO Jim Glymph notes, "we very much believe that the technology has arrived at the stage where it can have an impact in the industry." Yet, according to Glymph, "What Gehry . . . does is process change; this is where it starts. Software is simply an enabler."[80]

The utilization of sophisticated software technology in design and construction is by no means limited to the megamillion dollar Frank Gehrys of the world. An example of where smart, sophisticated thinking along these lines is also being conducted is in the work of younger firms like Sharples Holden Pasquarelli (SHoP). From its inception ten years ago, the firm has designed fully digitized projects where every piece of wood, steel, and glass is designed and constructed using 3-D modeling software. The purpose is surprising but simple: to lower project costs. Says partner Gregg Pasquarelli, "Gehry is more shape-driven. We're more process driven. We would never build an elaborate framework to support a curve. We'd let the curve be determined by information from our materials suppliers or by the parameters of the fabrication techniques." Using design software called Rhino, those parameters are input to the digitized design model. The software then knows to restrict SHoP's designers from cutting or bending the curve beyond its real-world limitations. If SHoP designs a curved panel that conflicts with its fabrication limitations, the software alerts the designer or modifies it automatically, with SHoP's approval. In one project, SHoP used the software to optimize custom zinc wall panel shapes to the standard, raw zinc panel size to reduce unusable scrap and thereby save costs. Although Rhino is a more modest 3-D program than Gehry's Digital Project, SHoP enjoys many of the same benefits—as do its clients.

Digital Project, Rhino, and similar packages offered by Autodesk, Bentley, and other modeling and analytical software makers are collectively known as Building Information Modeling (BIM) software. BIM is a collaborative digital process, using one or many of these leading software packages, to model and analyze detailed data covering a multitude of building characteristics, such as air flow, heat gain, structural analysis, and costs, among others. The architect embeds data and digitized information into a 3D model that can be shared with the owner, contractors, and project engineers.[81]

For example, imagine that the architect is in the process of designing an office building that will include a two-story atrium. After constructing the basic 3D model of the building, it shares the model with

107

its structural and mechanical engineers. The structural engineer layers in the structural grid and the mechanical engineer layers in the ductwork and plumbing mains and risers. The software alerts the architect to a potential conflict between a beam and a riser. While the architect coordinates a solution with the engineers, the mechanical engineer runs an energy analysis of the atrium, simulating several seasonal and daily variations and calculating lifecycle costs over the next twenty years. This information will be saved and downloaded to the owner's building management system for use after the building is constructed. The energy analysis predicts that the glass and aluminum panel curtain wall needs to be modified to reduce solar gain. By inputting the desired solar gain data into the model, the software automatically modifies design elements of the curtain wall with the architect's approval. The revised design is shared directly with the curtain wall manufacturer, who can directly fabricate the custom shaped panels from the 3D model and the detailed 2D drawings automatically created from the model. These enhanced deliverables—to owners and contractors—are potentially more valuable than the traditional 2D drawings and specifications most architects currently crank out.

There are other several major advantages of BIM for the design team. BIM increases coordination and can significantly reduce conflicts between the architect's, structural engineer's, and mechanical engineer's designs before the bid drawings are issued rather than discovering the conflicts during construction when they instantly become change orders. BIM also accelerates the design process, allowing multiple design schemes to be tested and analyzed in real time. And it improves the design process by reducing errors and optimizing every aspect of the building. The higher quality of these design documents produced with this software has been widely heralded by owners, and as a result is leading to higher fees for design professionals.

BIM yields significant benefits to the construction team as well. Fabricators and installation contractors can download exact measurements of the design specified by the architect without having to produce the time-consuming shop drawings typically required for review by the architect. A single software platform directly linking the design team to the contractors and suppliers transforms the once daunting shop-drawing and coordination-drawing reviews into a series of more manageable and efficient processes, reducing time spent on requests for information and costly change orders. BIM produces detailed data enabling the contractor to more accurately estimate quantities and costs. The more reliable design information reduces the number of requests for information about the design and thus enables the contractor to feel less at risk. The software has also become a favorite contractor tool for creating a strategic day-to-day construction sequence. For example, a contractor can create a 3D model to illustrate the sequence in which it will erect the steel framing and coordinate it with the other subcontractors' work schedules.

For the owner, the advantages of BIM cannot be overstated. It quantifies lifecycle costs of the building in the years following completion of construction. It reduces uncertainties for the owner, who may not otherwise be clear about what precisely is being designed. With BIM, owners can understand how long it will take to build and how much it will cost. More good news for owners: Gehry claims that this technology has reduced dreaded change orders on his projects by at least half. More accuracy in the design creates more accuracy in cost and schedule estimates, streamlined procurement, and better communication and coordination. According to Gehry, "You know where you are going before you start construction, so you minimize the surprise from the owner's standpoint. You get all the bad news up front."[82]

What does the future hold? According to Philip Bernstein, vice president of the Building Solutions Division at Autodesk, a leading design software company, "we're never going back" to the age of the master builder/architect because "the world's just too complicated." "The replacement of the master builder," according to Bernstein, "is going to have to be somebody who orchestrates the process and all the information that technology creates. And who's going to do that?" he asks.[83]

Frank Gehry would be a good answer but, needless to say, most architects are not Frank Gehry. While BIM is here to stay, it will likely be several more years before it is widely adopted and affordable enough for the average architectural firm. If the transition is to happen sooner, other players will need to step forward and drive the process. Owners are in a position to do just that by making BIM a requirement on their large, complex projects. This has already started happening—and from a surprising place: the U.S. government. To cut down on rampant cost overruns and delays, the General Services Administration, which is responsible for over $12 billion in active construction projects across the country, now requires a BIM 3D model from its architects and engineers.[84] Public and private owners alike may also drive mainstream BIM usage as they adopt in ever greater numbers sustainable green design building practices. The BIM process is critical in helping the design team develop energy optimization models and analyses that are the cornerstone of green building. Owners will also flock to BIM when they realize it can be used as a predictive business and financial model as well as a design model. For example, traffic flow analyses for a parking garage will reveal the optimal mix of spaces and the revenue generated for each. Similarly, assigning a revenue value to each seat in a stadium design will allow owners to project in real time revenue forecasts for multiple seating plans. On another level, life-cycle cost analyses of mechanical equipment can be linked to the day-to-day management of those systems to ensure that they are optimally maintained and operated. There is an enormous opportunity for owners to benefit from BIM.

Until owners step up to the plate, leading design firms like Gehry and SHoP must combat the architectural profession by ignoring the cry of the AIA and the professional liability carriers to sidestep accountability in the construction process. "If we want the profession to try new methods we have to be willing to take responsibility for the risk of what we are proposing," Pasquarelli asserts. "We have to break down the conventions of the profession."

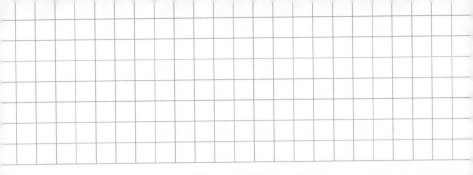

Minor Blemishes

UNIONS, WORKERS, AND GOVERNMENT

The effect of many small firms in the construction business is not limited to inadequate management skills and general lack of strategic
planning. The effects seep down to the workers, those most directly
involved in the building of houses, office buildings, and our crucial infrastructure. The inclination of construction workers to value independence and fraternity impacts productivity, raises prices, and increases rates of avoidable accidents. Only when the larger problems of
asymmetries and mutable cost contracts are resolved will the construction industry be able to improve labor relations and insist on beneficial government reforms.

As we have shown, the root problem with the American construction industry today is a high degree of asymmetric information
and its role in perpetuating mutable cost contracting. Because construction companies can pass the cost of inefficient practices onto
owners, the construction industry is not highly competitive, despite
the large number of small firms that inhabit it. As argued in the previous chapter, mutable cost contracting allows construction firms
with weak management to survive and even thrive. Those managers
often do not hedge risks or even differentiate between insurable risks
and uninsurable uncertainties. Many do not even plan, let alone strate-
gize. They neglect to invest in R&D and education. Those are very se-

rious problems that go a long way toward explaining why the construction industry is broken.

Labor Unions: The Good, the Bad, and the Indifferent

The productivity of the construction industry rests on the productivity of its laborers as well as on its management. Labor issues are where the hammer hits the nail, the arc hits the metal, and the shovel hits the dirt. The role of labor unions in the construction industry's woes, and its few successes, is poorly understood. Unions have been repeatedly bashed over the years. Some of the bruises are deserved, but many are not. Without a doubt, unions have improved the wages, working conditions, and lives of millions of construction workers. By providing training and good wages they probably also increased worker productivity somewhat. But unions have also at times limited innovation in construction.[1]

Economists have long understood that unions can raise wages by restricting labor supply and increasing labor demand by preventing the introduction of labor-saving technologies and prefabricated materials. In Southern California, for example, unions bar the use of roof trusses. So through at least the 1970s the area's peculiar, steeply sloped roofs had to be built up from rafters by carpenters, the old-fashioned (expensive) way.[2]

In the construction industry the interest of the employees (workers) are more closely aligned with their employers (contractors) than with owners (buyers). In many industries, employers are huge, so they can overpower or overawe workers. The tables are turned in construction. Labor unions have a long tradition of strength in the building trades because they often outsize and outwit employers, which traditionally are small firms with little expertise or training in labor matters. Historically, this created the impression that union wages were more a function of negotiating skills than productivity. By the 1940s, unions were so much bigger than most contractors that, according to *Fortune*, they rode roughshod over them, dictating "wages and working rules with little hindrance." In the 1950s, unions insisted on increasing the geographical size of collective bargaining agreements from cities to entire regions in response to increased contractor mobility. In the 1960s, unions helped to spread the payment of fringe benefits to construction workers. In the 1970s, unions were widely blamed for exacerbating the "housing crisis." A study in the 1980s showed that union construction workers earned 58 percent more than nonunion workers. (They worked 4 percent fewer hours, too.) Another study of office building construction showed that union work rules raised costs by 2 percent and higher union wages raised costs by 9 percent. Other studies were also highly critical of unions, especially their intricate rules and chronic jurisdictional disputes. Labor unions, though, are not at the heart of the industry's ills—industry fragmentation is.[3]

Labor-management relations in the construction industry are shaped by several unique realities. The high degree of seasonality, the cyclicality of the industry so dependent on the economy, the short duration of each project, the dangerous nature of the work, and the size of the average employer help explain the historic attraction of unions to construction workers.[4] Construction work can be both debilitating and deadly. Construction workers suffer work-related injuries and illnesses at a rate about 50 percent higher than the all-industry average, adding about 6 percent to construction costs.

Most contractors cannot offer regular employment. Instead, they hire workers on an as-needed basis. Unions are therefore organized along craft lines and serve as both bargaining agents and clearinghouses, assigning workers to contractors on a per-project basis, sometimes even recalling and reassigning them to another contractor and project before the original one is completed. Usually only larger contractors have enough clout with the unions to keep a "crew" together for extended periods of time. One problem with the splintering of unions by trade is that a labor dispute in a single trade can hold up all construction activity. Rarely will different unions cross each other's picket lines. Another problem is job demarcation lines between trades.

As early as 1792, building-craft unions emerged in Philadelphia, but they were little more than loose associations of independent craftsmen. In the antebellum period, craft organizations began to distinguish between masters (owners of construction firms) and journeymen (skilled laborers), but there was no distinct labor movement because entry into the business as a master was relatively easy. An apprenticeship, a little experience as a journeyman, and a small capital endowment were all that one needed. Shortly after the Civil War, the National Labor Union and the Knights of Labor tried and failed to obtain consistent support from the ranks of the skilled building trades. Only with the rise of the American Federation of Labor (AFL) in 1886 did unionization take hold.[5]

Modern labor unions in the building trades arose late in the nineteenth century soon after the traditional apprentice system began to break down. That was not coincidence. Contractors, like one in Buffalo, New York, put large numbers of cheap apprentices to work and thereby won numerous bids, much to the detriment of the local journeymen. Unions arose to stop such practices. One of their first orders of business was to limit employment of apprentices.[6]

Construction unions, especially in big cities like Chicago and New York, have long been identified with graft. The fact that "off the books" payments could not be readily identified by owners in the contracts for a project made it easy for union "bagmen" to protect the steady payments they received during the course of a project. It is still all too common today for unions to staff a project with "no show" jobs or family members who could sit in a construction trailer each day while drawing regular worker salaries. Such payments are easily disguised within the project's general condition costs charged to the owner, especially on large projects.

Contractors frequently found it prudent to buy "strike insurance," or in other words to bribe prominent union leaders to keep workers on the job. Such bribes were often disguised as payments for violations of labor contracts. Union rules were so intricate and changed so frequently, and the use of subcontractors was so extensive, that it was nearly impossible to ensure that no union rules had been broken on a site. Powerful union "business agents" or "walking delegates" could always find cause to threaten to strike unless the matter was adjusted to their satisfaction. When contractors failed to make side payments, unions physically threatened them or attacked their businesses with "stench bombs." Through the better part of the twentieth century, project disruptions, violence, or the threat of it, remained an important component of the construction industry in New York, and even in otherwise staid places like Quebec.[7]

In nineteenth-century New York, each trade promulgated "trade agreements" with industry employers. Strikes were rare, except after the termination date of agreements, but their impact was heightened by the commonplace use of "sympathy" strikes. (In Chicago in 1887, sympathy strikers numbered 30,000.) In June 1903, after a succession of strikes, lockouts, and criminal prosecutions, employers federated under the banner of the Building Trades Employers' Association. After much cajoling, that association managed to convince building trade unions to agree to an arbitration plan. After reforms were put in place in early 1905, an arbitration board composed of 120 members, 2 from each employers' association and union, reduced the amount of labor strife, but the construction industry remained a hotbed of union activity.[8]

From World War I through the Korean conflict, labor union growth in the building trades was strong. Until the passage of Taft-Hartley in 1947, labor unions controlled a large segment of the industry, over 80 percent, almost always in closed shops. Although Taft-Hartley itself did not ban closed shops, it allowed state legislatures to do so by enacting what came to be known as a "right-to-work" provision.[9]

If anything, Taft-Hartley increased labor strife in the construction industry. While strikes decreased in most sectors after World War II, they actually increased in construction. By the late 1960s the construction industry was the most strike-prone industry in America, responsible for about 25,000 postwar strikes, or approximately 20 percent of strike activity, as measured by both the number of strikes and the number of lost days. Apparently, unions learned that they could defeat contractors at least in part because "any construction worker with an automobile can hunt down work in a nearby area when a strike shuts down building in his city."[10]

Strikes moderated in the early 1970s partly in response to govern-ment wage controls and to the establishment of the Construction In-dustry Stabilization Committee (CISC) by Executive Order 11588 on March 29, 1971. Unions, management, and the public each enjoyed equal representation on the CISC, which was chaired by Harvard Uni-versity dean John T. Dunlop. In general, CISC granted wage increases only where productivity gains warranted it. The CISC staunchly op-posed work rules and informal practices that added to costs, such as late starts, early quits, excessive time allotment for set up and break down, guaranteed hours, extended lunches and breaks, productivity restrictions (e.g., number of welds per day), "featherbedding" of crews (unnecessary helpers), and so forth. The CISC also sought to iron out wage inequities that had arisen due to the rampant inflation of the pe-riod. For instance, by early 1971 a skilled carpenter might earn $5.00 an hour while an unskilled worker made $6.50 simply because the car-penters had last negotiated in 1968 and the laborers in 1970. The CISC was dismantled after the Nixon administration implemented general price controls.[11]

In the early 1970s, some 40 percent of construction workers were unionized. The figure today is much lower, around 15 percent, due to the increased prevalence of open shops. The causes of the dra-matic shift are unclear. Some argue that jobs simply shifted away from areas of union strength, namely commercial projects in the North, to areas of union weakness, namely home construction in the West and the South. Others suggest that union workers simply became too expensive to hire on most jobs. Union advocates, how-ever, describe a successful all-out political and business "assault" on union prerogatives during the 1970s and 1980s. Unions have held their ground recently, thanks to "salting" and public relations initiatives, but a recent international analysis of labor union decline suggests that continued economic growth and globalization will likely thwart any significant union growth. One thing is clear: construction firms were not responsible for the decreased significance of labor unions. Some combination of politics, ideology, big business, economics, and demography were.[12]

Membership decline from 1975 to 1995 in some unions, like the plasterers union, was simply a function of decreased demand for plastering. But the declines, averaging 30 percent over many trades, reflect a sea change in labor relations, especially in home construction. Yet, as we have seen, the construction industry, though productive by world standards, has experienced a long lull in productivity growth coterminous with the decline in union strength. That strongly suggests that unions were not the big problem that they were once thought to be.[13]

There can be no doubt that where unions are still strong they have a profound effect on construction wages. Union weekly wages in construction are higher than in any other industry. Nonunion wages are much lower, dragging the construction average down considerably. Complicating matters, however, is the very real possibility that union workers are more productive than nonunion laborers. Union workers are better trained and educated on average, need less supervision, and have incentives to work hard to maintain their high wages. They are also easier to hire because search and remuneration negotiation costs are low, and they are less likely to quit, even when *holding wages constant*. Although rigid union work rules limit work-site flexibility, on net they may help productivity by maintaining an efficient and intact Smithian division of labor. On a dollar basis, therefore, union labor may be competitive with lower-paid, but less productive nonunion labor. "The only reason we go to union bricklayers is efficiency," says John Fitzwater of Clarksburg, West Virginia. "A union bricklayer," he explains, "can lay four times as many bricks, and he does it properly."[14]

Union training programs and apprenticeships teach workers these skills. Most construction firms are too small, and too impermanent, to invest much in training their own workers. Because companies do not want to pay to train a worker who will probably soon move to another firm anyway, nonunion workers receive very little formal educational assistance and no training aside from what they can pick up on the job.[15]

Since the end of the old apprenticeship system in the late nineteenth century, unions, not employers, have assumed the role of worker training. Unions used the opportunity, however, to restrict entry into trades and hence keep wages up. As a result, workers tend to never receive enough training, some not more than entry-level. Big, integrated construction firms, in contrast, would, like firms in most other industries, find it profitable to train and even educate its workforce to an optimal level.[16]

Despite the training, unions often discourage the use of incentive-based compensation such as piecework. Where allowed, piecework is a powerful tool for increasing productivity. David Gerstel relates the following: "The two-person system reached its pinnacle with the advent of production framing in California during the 1960s and '70s. Carpenters framing on a piecework basis, and motivated by it to pump out work as rapidly as possible, winnowed every unnecessary move out of the framing process. A team of two seasoned production framers could nail up, stand, plumb, and line the walls of a three-bedroom, two-bath house *in a single day*."[17] William Levitt also used piece rates. "If a fellow was smarter than another fellow, or if he worked harder, he made more money," Levitt recalled.[18] Performance-based bonuses abounded.[19]

Generally speaking, though, laborers or labor teams are not allowed to compete head-to-head through a piece-rate mechanism. Sheetrock installers, for instance, get paid by the hour rather than by the number of properly installed drywall boards. The rationale for hourly payment is that some installations are more difficult than others. For example, a cathedral-style ceiling is more difficult and expensive to sheetrock than a flat, eight-foot high ceiling. Similarly, fixed setup costs render bigger jobs more lucrative than small ones.[20]

Of course, those measurement problems loom much larger because the industry is so fragmented. Workers on the clock have no problem waiting for another firm to finish up before they can get started. It is a good time to get a coffee and enjoy a smoke while making a nice wage. Piece-rate workers, on the other hand, would wage war against any other firms standing in their way. A single, integrated construction firm could reduce conflicts and increase efficiency through better coordination of work and direct disciplinary controls. It could also weight different types of jobs fairly, or at least internally consistently, allowing them to move many of their workers to piece rates. The days of construction workers standing around doing nothing or moving like snails would soon end.[21]

Construction Worker Culture: Autonomous and Unruly

During the long nineteenth century, which is to say from the early days of the Republic until World War I, factory owners and workers struggled for control of the industrial workplace. At the beginning, workers in all fields enjoyed a great deal of autonomy. They consumed alcohol on the job and often got employers to pay for it! They worked their own hours, more or less, and worked in their own way, at a customary pace. Workers were loosely monitored. Punishments, when administered, could be physically severe, but journeymen and other free laborers would not suffer much before moving on. By the end of that period, the industrial factory was an alcohol-free zone where the clock told workers when to begin and end work. Time study experts tried to turn workers into appendages of machines, directing their every repetitive movement down to the smallest detail. After World War II, factory owners realized that they had pushed too far. Trying to turn people into machines led to worker dissatisfaction that manifested itself in absenteeism and low quality output. Following Japanese models, U.S. factory owners began to allow workers more autonomy on the job, flexible working schedules, and the like. That sea change, however, did not return industry to the loose working conditions of the pre-industrial era. Managers, not workers, retain ultimate control.[22]

The same cannot be said of the construction industry, where management-worker relations remain very much in the spirit of the pre-industrial workplace no matter the scale of the project. Construction workers have a culture of their own, a very colorful if thoroughly inefficient one. The contrast between construction worker and modern factory worker culture is starkest in the realm of drugs and alcohol. Factory workers have long since given up any pretense to drinking alcohol on the job; they submitted relatively easily to drug screening.

Not so construction workers. According to a 1997 study by the U.S. Department of Health and Human Services, construction workers are more likely to abuse drugs and alcohol than any other employee group. In the worst categories, about one in four is a substance abuser. "If we have a slab to pour on Saturday morning, we do not pay the boys on Friday," says one Southwest builder. "If we do," he explains, "half of them will show up hung over and the other half won't show up at all."[23]

The abuse stems partly from the physical rigors of the job, and its intense seasonality and cyclicality, but perhaps mostly from the very social nature of the business, which many take to be a "way of life" rather than a mere occupation. Construction workers are often enmeshed in a large circle of friends and family who are also construction workers. Such connections come in handy when looking for work or trying to obtain a lucrative but rare union slot. Almost no one walks onto a site and gets a job without knowing someone already employed there. And that is how most men are hired: right on site. The office is rarely involved, except to process the decisions made in the field. Construction workers' trucks, toolboxes, hard hats, and tool belts signal their experience and ability better than any paper résumé could.[24]

Construction workers are more independent and flexible than the typical factory "hand." In fact, according to Gil Wolf of the National Plastering Institute, "the tradesman considers himself in an artistic field. He takes a bunch of nothing and he builds something from it."[25] Construction workers can (but may not) work with less supervision, and are more likely to work together in teams, or with "helpers." Some workers join crews that stay together for long periods, moving from job to job as a unit. These crews can become very efficient as they know everyone's strengths, weaknesses, moves, and moods. But they will all quit if one of them is fired and, of course, it is more difficult to find work for five or ten guys at once than one.

Autonomy brings job satisfaction but it also tends to perpetuate inefficiencies and minimize the role of management. Workers, sometimes in conjunction with union reps, decide if weather conditions are acceptable or not. They also decide if a work situation is too dangerous. At many a site, an otherwise unshakeable construction worker who feels uncomfortable going into an unsupported trench, onto a rickety scaffold, or up an icy steel beam would have elicited immediate support from co-workers, each of whom knows that construction is intrinsically dangerous. At any time, a truck could slip out of gear, a wall can give way, or a million and one other things can go wrong, and they will all lose a day for the funeral service.

Workers also decide the best method for completing assigned tasks. Generally, as one plumber related, "the foreman lays out the day's work in the morning, and unless we run into trouble we might not see him again all day." A good worker resents close supervision as a reflection on his competence, or rather lack thereof. Construction workers react strongly to any encroachments on their independence. In many ways, they are more like white-collar service professionals than factory operatives. In fact, construction workers have been known to pity factory workers. "I see that auto workers in Detroit want early retirement," one commented. "I don't blame the poor bastards. I would want to retire at thirty-five if I had to stand in one place and put left fenders on all day." At the same time, though, absenteeism and turnover in construction is higher than in many other industries. Some absenteeism occurs when workers take more lucrative side jobs. Some happens because workers feel they need a day off to hunt or attend a ball game. Some is to exact a form of retribution against bosses.[26]

The mix of intense physical labor and worker autonomy can be frightening if you have a guy, who may be stoned wielding a hammer, or, God forbid, a guy with a nail gun who thinks that he knows best. At the very least, the combination creates a good deal of labor unrest, open shop or not. As one construction worker put it, "If the boss wants a thing done one way which the worker thinks should be done another, or if the worker thinks the boss has spoken to him in an unacceptable tone of voice, or if the man simply disapproves of the way the captain runs the ship, he is likely to make a 'shove it up your ass' speech and leave." That is no mere anecdote. According to one study, a poor relationship with a boss is the number one reason that construction workers quit jobs, ranking just ahead of unsafe conditions.[27]

Given the close familial and friendship ties between workers on most sites, a clueless authoritarian boss could soon find himself crewless as well, especially in the peak months. That is why construction supervision is often described as "democratic." Rather than ordering the workers around, the crew chief asks what they think about a particular issue. Then he issues general directives rather than specific orders. Because supervisors and foremen were once workers themselves, this style comes naturally to them.[28] According to one study, only 13 percent of foremen receive "*any* training in the art of supervision," so it isn't surprising that supervision remains loose.[29] The cost of ineffective supervision is an unmotivated workforce that consistently complains about major site problems such as material or tool unavailability, on-site management confusion, incompetent and disrespectful supervision, communication breakdowns, and lack of recognition.[30]

Personal relationships, rather than impersonal rules and procedures, predominate on many work sites. Given the informality of the culture, it is not surprising that when there are more workers than slots, the rationing process can be a personal one. Explained one superintendent: "I'm going to choose men who know the work but who are not prima donnas. I'm not interested in superstars. Maybe they'll give you 200 feet of pipe in one day. The next day maybe some dust will blow in their face and they'll take off on you. I'd rather have guys who are steady." Fair enough. But decisions can also come down to ethnicity, religion, or other economically irrelevant characteristics. Many workers become drinking buddies with foremen in order to enhance their job prospects. Foremen do not hire incompetent men—they can ill afford to do so because their personal safety is at stake—but when there are four openings and sixteen qualified applicants, those known to buy their share of "rounds" tend to get the nod. It also helps to have good social skills, which in this context means being able to bowl, play pool, cards, darts, and, perhaps most importantly, to "shoot the shit" about sports, women, or whatever.

The problem that arises, of course, is the problem of merit: exceptional workers may stay at home idle while others, with more penchant for beer and baseball, work. (Even in something as seemingly straightforward as bricklaying, some workers outshine others. The most efficient bricklayers, it turns out, have good math skills.) Many a good man has left the field due to job insecurity.

Many construction workers, to their great credit, see themselves as craftsmen. They take pride in their work and are embarrassed when it is not up to snuff. Getting it done right is certainly better than doing it wrong. But it isn't as good as what we need now—getting it done right and right quick. Worker autonomy stands in the way to the extent that it shackles managers from using fairly simple planning tools like "crew balancing," which maximizes their performance at specific tasks.[31]

Construction firms can afford to allow workers to be autonomous and to get paid by the hour because they simply pass costs onto owners. If the construction industry ever becomes truly competitive, firms will no longer be able to afford to do so. Construction workers will then be paid by the hour and accept managerial direction, or they will remain autonomous and be paid by the piece. Large construction firms paying piece rates could help leverage the fiercely independent culture of construction workers, since one of the things that unions do well, labor scholars have found, is to protect or enhance worker autonomy. Workers paid for their time rather than their work really ought to follow their employer's directions. Workers paid for their work rather than their time, on the other hand, deserve to be left alone. Currently, due to weak management, construction workers usually get paid by the hour *and* tell their bosses how they are going to spend that hour.[32] Demographics may be on the side of change here. Robert Gasperow of the Construction Labor Research Council says that the industry's current demographic structure is "just unprecedented." A large percentage of construction workers will be retiring soon. That will force the industry to introduce new young blood that will not be as deeply acculturated to traditional practices and attitudes.[33]

Government Rules and Regulations: Big Headaches in Small Packages

Government regulations at the local, state, and federal levels have historically impeded change in the construction industry and continue to do so to this day. In other industries with big powerful firms, economically inefficient government restrictions have been swept aside by intensive lobbying efforts. Not so in construction, where small firm size leads to a free rider problem that makes it difficult for the industry, big as it is in the aggregate, to apply sufficient reform pressure in Washington, or even in state capitals.[34]

The problem intensified in the postwar period as state and federal laws and regulations increasingly affected construction. By 1980, one study included a chapter called "The Stultifying Role of Government," which asked readers to "consider the range of regulatory areas that affect construction": accessibility for the handicapped, aesthetics, boilers, consumer protection, demolition, environmental protection, explosives, financing, flood plains and wetlands, food handling, fuel storage, historic districts, liability, material and equipment acceptance, sanitary and storm sewers, streets and roads, signage, soil conservation, wages, and more.[35]

Everyone associated with the process of purchasing land and building on it over the last twenty-five years knows that regulation has grown exponentially. Though benign relative to other places, there is little doubt that the current system of government regulation of construction is repressive enough to impede U.S. productivity growth. According to construction economists, "many current regulations are superfluous or redundant, and regularly stifle the entrepreneur's incentives to develop systems and build infrastructure that is cheaper, safer, or quicker to construct and maintain."[36] Entrepreneurs are too busy filling out forms to implement good ideas. A recent study found that small construction firms spend twenty-one weeks per year to complete government paperwork. That is twice the national average for small firms.[37]

Still unconvinced? Consider the following, written by a *government* task force: "New York City's byzantine building code makes the required permit processes lengthy and frustrating. Permits for building plans, demolition, construction, hoisting, etc., require inspections and approvals from a large number of agencies, including the City Planning Commission, the Department of Environmental Protection, the Buildings Department, the Fire Department, the Department of Transportation, the Landmarks Commission and the Bureau of Highways."[38]

Ever stay in a New York hotel? In addition to the city's explicit hotel tax, guests in every Manhattan hotel pays hidden taxes that recoup the extra costs of erecting buildings in an over-regulated jurisdiction. Though the magnitude varies over time and place, every American—every time he or she uses a building or a road (bridge, tunnel, etc.) or electricity or factory-made products—pays this implicit tax.[39] As builder Sam Lefrak has said, "The legislators have legislated us into the ground."[40]

Local building codes, which number in the thousands across the country, create a patchwork of regulations that, in effect, prevent construction firms from expanding, because they are afraid to risk working in jurisdictions where they are unfamiliar with the intricacies of the codes and the code inspectors. The latter is an important consideration because even where the codes are identical, their interpretations can vary widely. Richard Mettler of the Home Builders Association of Phoenix notes that the five communities in the greater Phoenix area "have a uniform building code, but the interpretations aren't uniform. You complain to Phoenix, they say Tempe or Mesa doesn't know what it's doing." Because of chronic staffing problems, weak management, and other obstacles, different people *in the same municipality* have been known to make contradictory recommendations and rulings. "One of the most pervasive problems in building-code enforcement," one study concluded, "is a widespread lack of qualifications among building officials at all levels: administrators, plans examiners and inspectors." That, of course, led to "delays and inconsistent enforcement."[41]

Unsurprisingly, many local codes are not so much concerned with the safety of a building's occupants as it is with providing employment for members of various construction crafts. In Arizona, special interests managed to mandate the installation of water softener attachments (but not the softeners themselves as they would damage the environment) in each new home, a $70 plus loss to homeowners.

Inspectors merely attest to basic safety, not overall quality, and they certainly do not do cost-benefit analyses. So they offer very little economic protection. Fire codes also have safety in mind, but they rarely attend to cost/safety trade-offs, and unfortunately, in many places they are an additional set of codes.[42]

Calls for code standardization are not new. In 1959, MIT professor Kelly Burnham called for "national acceptance of a standard code for plumbing." In the 1960s, one prefab manufacturer suggested that the creation of a single, rational building code would allow him to cut his production costs at least 25 percent. The situation has not noticeably improved since. As construction economist Peter Cassimatis explained, "changes in building codes are infrequent and, when they occur, of limited scope." And then one may have to wait until the inspectors retire before there are any de facto changes. Britain abandoned local codes in 1965, but local building inspectors continued to insist on adherence to the old regulations anyway.[43]

Other laws and regulations, including set-back ordinances, housing codes, zoning ordinances, health codes, multiple dwelling laws, and minimum housing standards can also impede innovation and raise contractor costs unnecessarily.[44] "Land use decisions," asserts UCLA law school professor Donald Hagman, "provide the main opportunity for local government corruption." Even if the zoning commissioners are honest, they can inadvertently increase land prices by restricting the supply of land that can be turned to specific uses. Of course such decisions are sometimes quite purposeful. In large portions of Connecticut, the minimum lot size is one acre in order to exclude lower income groups.[45]

The classic historical case of minimum housing standards going awry was New York City's "new law" of 1901, which outlawed the notoriously ugly, crowded, and unsanitary dumbbell tenements (so-called because the tenements looked like dumbbells in plan, and, some jest, because the designer was one). These buildings grew like weeds throughout the five boroughs in the latter part of the nineteenth century. Much to the horror of Jacob Riis, Theodore Roosevelt, and other progressive advocates of the stricter law, contractors responded to the law by ceasing to build low-end apartments at all. The living conditions of the working poor deteriorated as ever larger numbers of them crowded into the same old dumbbells.[46]

Such scenes have been repeated, in different areas and to different degrees, ever since. For example in 1976 in Prince George's County, Maryland, the zoning commission decided that 10 percent of all new multifamily units had to have double-wide doors, ramps, and special bathroom amenities for the handicapped. The added cost halted the construction of new units.[47]

Each new wave of legislators, it seems, has to relearn one of the most important lessons of the past, namely, that economic improvements cannot be directly legislated. As Martin Mayer explains: "The energy in the system is that of the builder, the buyer, and the lender [he could add insurer here too], not that of the government." Laws can enable or disable but they cannot construct buildings. And, unfortunately, they mostly disable.[48]

Laws also impede construction industry consolidation. Mechanics' lien laws, for example, vary greatly even between contiguous jurisdictions such as New York and Pennsylvania. Fundamental differences in these laws increase the costs of operating in multiple jurisdictions by influencing everything from builder-subcontractor contracts to capital and external financing needs. In some instances, the filing of liens can limit an owner's ability to fund the project or secure long term financing. In New York, for example, the law permits subcontractors who work for a construction manager to file mechanics' liens against an owner's property if they have an unpaid claim for work. In addition, the construction manager has the legal right to file its own mechanics' lien for the total amount of all subcontractor claims, effectively doubling the amount the owner will have to bond, as required by agreement with its lender.[49]

Laws may impede construction industry innovation by forcing owners to coordinate work by not allowing them to delegate the tasks to others, like construction managers. They sometimes force public entities to accept the lowest bid even if the bidder is thought to be too inexperienced for the job. And they often force public owners to follow the traditional design-bid-build method of construction rather than the newer design-build or fast-track methods. According to PricewaterhouseCoopers, the Wicks Law, a law mandating the use of four different independent prime contractors on public contracts, adds $30 per square foot to the cost of public buildings in New York City. By preventing the use of the single contract system used by the federal government, most states, and almost all private developers, the Wicks Law runs counter to established best practices. It also helps to breed corruption and a noticeable lack of contractor coordination in New York's construction industry.[50] Wick's Law projects are notorious for ending in complex litigation.

Many locales and states require contractors to be licensed. Such regulations, however, are de facto revenue devices rather than bona fide screening mechanisms because the license issuers rarely ask for updated firm information and because the licensing periods are much too long to provide effective monitoring anyway.

Insurance regulations vary from state to state. They can be quite nettlesome, especially for smaller contractors.[51] Title insurance is another irritant that adds up to big bucks—hundreds of millions of dollars a year. In the United States, no matter how recently a property has been purchased, its title must again be searched for defects, encumbrances, liens, and the like. The process can get ridiculous. As one story goes, a New York lawyer questioned a New Orleans lawyer whose search went back "only" to 1803. The New Orleans lawyer purportedly replied:

> Please be advised that in the year 1803 the United States of America acquired the territory of Louisiana from the Republic of France by purchase. The Republic of France acquired title from the Spanish Crown by conquest. The Spanish Crown had originally acquired title by virtue of the discoveries of one Christopher Columbus, sailor, who had been duly authorized to embark upon the voyage of discovery by Isabella, Queen of Spain. Isabella, before granting such authority, had obtained the sanction of His Holiness, the Pope; the Pope is the Vicar of Earth of Jesus Christ; Jesus Christ is the Son and Heir Apparent of God. God made Louisiana.[52]

Federal laws and agencies have also impeded builders. In the 1950s, a homebuilder had to abandon the use of Federal Housing Authority (FHA) financing because the agency's inspection rules slowed down his building process too much. Though he could physically put together a home in two weeks if left unfettered, waiting for FHA inspectors increased his construction time considerably. To avoid red tape, contractors rehashed sub-optimal designs that had previously received FHA approval.[53]

Other federal laws that have impeded the construction industry include the Davis-Bacon Act, the Copeland Anti-Kickback Act, and the Eight-Hour Law,[54] all of which forced contractors to increase compensation for their workers on federal construction projects. When the size and number of federal projects are large enough in proportion to other construction projects underway in the same region, the acts serve to increase the wages of all construction workers. Costs may not increase, though, if the higher-paid workers are proportionally more efficient than lower-paid ones. (Also, the laws may have societal benefits that we do not consider here because our focus is on improving the construction industry's productivity and not on using the industry to increase social justice.[55]) According to a recent study, though, the laws also "petrif[y] the outcome of competing views of how construction work should be staffed and paid on public works projects." They are also the reasons why "unions representing less than 20 percent of the private construction work force consistently set the parameters controlling most of public construction." All three laws are enforced by blacklisting noncompliant contractors, and forty-one states have adopted "little Davis-Bacon Acts." Executive Order 11246, the 1965 order that created the Office of Federal Contract Compliance to enforce federal "affirmative action" policies, also distorted costs because there were no established quotas and guidelines remained vague. What satisfied one inspector another found grounds for contract revocation.[56]

Unsurprisingly, tax codes also disrupt the construction business. Since the 1960s, federal and state governments continued to legislate in ways favorable to real estate owners. Many apartment buildings got built simply to help owners gain tax advantages, big tax advantages, via accelerated depreciation schedules. As Martin Mayer explains, "Assuming an investor in the 70 percent bracket and a 90 percent mortgage, double-declining-balance depreciation on the whole building yields an average tax reduction of $31,600 a year for five years for every $100,000 invested—a yield of 31.6 percent per year tax free to a very rich and heavily taxed investor even if the apartment house makes no money at all."[57] Bully for them, but it meant many apartment buildings went up that the American people really didn't need. That money would have been better spent on single family homes or consumption goods.

Government has also hurt even when it has tried to help. Many of its programs, especially those purportedly designed to aid "urban renewal," turned into multimillion dollar boondoggles. "This is the essential fact," New York senator Daniel Patrick Moynihan once admitted, referring to urban housing programs: "The government did not know what it was doing."[58] Section 236 housing erected during the Nixon administration, for example, was not really needed.[59] Worse, it cost 20 percent more to build than comparable private apartment buildings in the same city. And the quality was substandard. Sam Parnas, associate of a firm that managed Section 236 housing in the Los Angeles area, decried, "They threw this shit at us like you'd throw water out the window. Where were the inspectors?" Almost half of the 236 apartment complexes had defaulted by 1975; a sizable percentage turned into slums.[60]

The Metropolitan Detroit Citizens' Development Authority (MDCDA) was another government failure. Formed in 1966 in response to President Lyndon Johnson's call for private enterprise support of the Model Cities program, the MDCDA received funding from the New Detroit Committee after the July 1967 riots. In 1968, MDCDA announced an industrialized housing competition that promised contracts on 1,000 sites scattered across Detroit. A dark-horse bidder, a prefab outfit called Peerless Manufacturing, won but immediately went bankrupt. A successor company called Prebuilt arose from its ashes but was later discovered to have connections to organized crime. Unable to obtain financing, it too failed before delivering a single home.[61]

Finally, many government regulatory barriers are intimately intertwined with labor union restrictions. Unions regularly resort to building codes to prevent the use of prefab components and other labor-saving devices. To protect union plumbing jobs, for example, New York long prohibited prefabricated plumbing trees and insisted that each pipe joint had to be hand-wiped on site. More fundamentally, the power of labor unions, which are essentially worker price-fixing cartels, is largely a function of government policies.[62]

While government regulation of construction is generally accepted as necessary for the public good, it has often stymied innovation by reinforcing what experts call "the industry's conservative inclination." Government need not champion cutting-edge innovation, but it should not stand in the way either. Again, larger firms would help here. Levitt and Sons, for example, found government restrictions but a minor nuisance. In some cases the firm simply bullied local government into making changes or exceptions. In other cases, as when the state of Pennsylvania insisted that floor tile could not be run up to the fireplace, it simply went hunting for the cheapest loophole, which turned out to be running the tile up to the last row, then giving the homeowner the requisite materials and information to finish the job. We have the same basic goal in the next chapter, to provide the industry and owners with the last row of information needed to protect their buildings and budgets from a badly broken industry.[63]

SIX

Fixing the Construction Industry

CONSOLIDATION, INTERMEDIARIES, AND INNOVATION

People respond more vigorously to personal incentives than to fuzzy programs that promote "partnering" or the creation of "more trust and faith" between planners, architects, engineers, contractors, and owners. That is why only one overarching recommendation is viewed as the cornerstone of this book—consolidate and integrate. Large, vertically integrated firms will solve most of the industry's internal problems and reduce or hedge against a good many of its external ones as well. In contrast with figure 1, which summarized the industry's reasons for failure resulting from mutable costs and asymmetric information, figure 7 presents a chain of reform that could mitigate those primary problems and lead to the industry's future success.[1]

133

The construction industry will rapidly consolidate once it becomes less expensive for construction firms to internalize competitors, suppliers, and distributors than to treat with them through the market. In other words, problems of fragmentation will be addressed when it becomes cheaper to make rather than to buy. That will happen when owners, especially governments, insist on true fixed-price contracts. By weighing true risk against higher profitability, smaller firms will no longer remain the norm. When contractors can no longer wiggle out of bid terms after all credible threat of competition has ended, construction firms will finally feel the full brunt of market competition. This will occur whether the projects are traditionally bid, fast-tracked

FIGURE 7. The Equation for Industry Reform. Source: Barry B. LePatner.

or negotiated as a design-build contract. The key is putting the contractor (or its surety) at risk, not taking what may turn out to be purely nominal bids.[2]

The resulting shakeout will be rapid. Many firms will fail, but remember, many fail already. Instead of being replaced by swarms of new tiny firms, however, bigger firms will form because of frenzied merger activity. Where it will end, no one knows. But we surmise that a decade after the introduction of fixed-price contracting there will remain from a few score to a few hundred construction firms, a dozen to a score in each of the major subcategories. Those big firms, which will come to have a significant presence in the Fortune 1000, will do everything from manufacture and stockpile construction materials to maintain structures they erected years and even decades before. Construction sites will resemble modern automobile factories more than pre-industrial artisanal playgrounds. Buildings of all types will cost less than they do now, and/or there will be more of them, and/or they will be of higher quality. Broken buildings and busted budgets will be "fixed" by fixing the contract price.

Many of those involved in the construction industry—from the lowliest laborer to the loftiest lawyer—are finger pointers. It isn't my fault, but his or her fault. "Full of motes in other people's eyes" as Martin Mayer put it. But the simple fact is this: the construction industry's problems are not the fault of anyone in particular. It is the plethora of asymmetric information and the dearth of intermediaries that is the heart of the industry's productivity problems.[3]

Construction is complex, no doubt about that. But lots of things are, and yet they still get done, and for less expense (holding quality constant) than in construction. Why? As Martin Mayer explains, businessmen can fail to resolve the complexities of construction and yet still survive because "the costs incurred can be loaded onto the mortgage and paid by the customer slowly." The reason for that, we argue, is that de facto mutable-cost contracting reigns supreme because of high levels of asymmetric information. Contractors bid too low but make up for it through change orders. Sometimes owners fight back, but all too often they do not, or cannot. They end up paying for the contractor's inefficiency and incompetence and for the industry's waste and low productivity.[4]

The construction industry needs one or more intermediaries, firms that will reduce the amount of asymmetric information between owners and contractors and enforce fixed-price contracts. Once those institutions are in place, construction firms can begin to compete on the basis of price, quality, and time. Firms made inefficient by poor managers, union shackles (to the extent that they exist), unproductive workers, corrupt connections, and overzealous local regulations will fade. Efficient firms, those with relatively good managers, productive workers, and good environments, will grow bigger. Where appropriate, they will integrate vertically and horizontally. After achieving critical mass, they will begin to invest in R&D, industry education, and lobbying efforts. Some may use design-build, fast-track, or lean construction methods. Some may continue to use more traditional methods. But one thing is certain: each will use the method or methods, including the latest available hi-tech building management system that makes it the most competitive in its chosen markets.

How Will an Intermediary Arise?

The underlying mechanism may already exist. Three possibilities—not mutually exclusive—appear to be present. First, construction managers—assuming they are willing to accept a total commitment to the interests of the owner, not their subcontractors—working cooperatively with architects could become the industry's most important intermediary. Alternatively, guaranty companies might be induced to expand their current role and provide oversight of the construction manager. Finally, given the crucial importance of maintaining truly hard money contracts, hard-nosed, independent owner representatives or project managers with extensive practical construction experience *working on the side of owners* to oversee the construction manager and design team could significantly reduce the information asymmetry.

Before addressing how an intermediary might arise, it is important to understand the dynamics of the bidding process. Owners typically expect contractors to offer bids for free. Most contractors comply, or at least appear to. Working up a real bid, however, is serious work that can cost anywhere from hundreds to tens of thousands of dollars depending on the size and complexity of the job. Contractors cannot afford to expend such large sums for the mere chance of losing a bid. So, most of them most of the time base their bids on experience. They "whip up" a bid "with no trouble" by comparing the proposed job to similar ones they recently completed. They put down some rough figures, then adjust them to circumstances. If they are hard up for work and the owner looks strapped for cash, they adjust downward. If they are flush and the owner appears wealthy, they adjust upward. If they know the owner has a history of paying late or is experiencing financial difficulty they tack on a premium. If they win the bid and it turns out too low they skimp or look for excuses to make changes. If they win and the bid turns out too high they reap the profits.[5]

How might a contractor or construction manager align its allegiance squarely with the owner? If it acts more like a professional than an opportunist. Some charge owners for what many of them call cost planning or "pre-construction" services. Basically, they sit down with the owner and an architect and attempt to hash out a complete, realistic budget and scheduling plan. A couple of thousand (or tens of thousands depending on the project's scale and complexity) dollars in fees later, the owner has the needed information, down to the nail and putty type, to get the project done right. Essentially, the owner has paid the contractor and the architect to decrease the information asymmetry inherent in the project. Then, the owner can put the design out to bid with confidence or, as usually happens, hire the estimating contractor to complete the work. The best thing about the cost planning arrangement is if a change (exclusive of scope increases) becomes necessary, the original contractor, not the owner, is responsible for it. The contractor and the architect cannot play the blame game on each other because both were involved. By paying for the bid, the owner has essentially purchased a guarantee that the work will be completed as budgeted. As will be discussed later, a tightly drafted contract defining the final price as truly "final" provides an added layer of protection, should any difficulties arise.

Large owners that need many buildings of similar type can approximate cost planning by repeatedly using the same battle-tested plans. One large bank, in fact, uses identical plans for all of its branches. Costs vary somewhat due to the condition of the site, the state of the local labor market, and changes in raw material prices, but there can be no major surprises. And their branches go up fast. Unfortunately, most owners do not build enough to have the luxury of learning from their own past mistakes. But others could learn on their behalf.

Alternatively, construction work could also be guaranteed by third parties. To some extent, they already are. Most large construction firms are bonded. Should a contractor default or go bankrupt, the bonding company will step in and complete the job or pay another firm to do so for the amount of the contract. There is no economic reason why bonding companies could not expand their role and guarantee the completion of projects for a fixed price and quality. Bonding companies, rather than owners, would pay for any cost overruns. Of course they could quickly raise the rates of contractors that frequently underbid on projects and make unwarranted change order and delay claims. They could refuse to provide a bond for those who prove inept at establishing a proper fixed price. That would encourage contractors to make realistic bids, ones near the true cost of project. (Again, with normal profits. Nobody expects contractors to continue building if they cannot make a commensurate profit.) Cost-planning contractors would have lower guaranty bond premiums than their guesstimating counterparts because they would be much less likely to go over budget.[6]

How could this work in real life? An owner would agree to a set project budget. As the design progressed, the architect, the construction manager, and an independent cost-estimating company would provide budget estimates. Once the design is 80 percent complete and most, if not all, unknown design issues are accounted for by set allowances (for example, $X for yet unspecified kitchen equipment), the construction manager would be required to enter into a fixed-price contract for the total project. With these assurances, a project bonding company or lender would enter into an agreement with the owner as follows: For a premium, the owner agrees to pay the full cost of the contract plus no more than 5 percent of any cost overruns or additions. In return, the premium paid to the bonding company or lender would cover any claims by the construction team in excess of the bonded cost plus 5 percent. Successful contractors who meet the project budget and schedule will have a successful track record that could be used when bidding on future jobs. Those who repeatedly cannot meet performance requirements will suffer increased bonding costs. In other words, contractors will need to make more accurate bids, or they will find they are no longer bondable.

The third possibility for an effective intermediary is a construction savvy, independent consultant with extensive practical experience as a project manager for owners. Seasoned architects, facilities directors, and in some cases, retired construction executives would fit the bill, provided they did not lapse into a contractor entitlement mindset. These individuals, or teams of individuals for more complex projects, would serve as the project leader, maintain coordination between the design and construction team, and be capable of resolving complex problems fairly and expeditiously—all while standing guard over the project budget and schedule. While independent owner's representatives can be found on many projects, they are often akin to a "clerk of the works," or project administrator without real construction-cost experience and therefore have little authority over the contractor. Or they are often ex-contractors who represent owners as if they were still contractors always acquiescing to excessive contractor claims because "that's how it's always been done." What is needed, however, is an owner's representative who is as capable micromanaging the coordination effort as they are negotiating hardball with subcontractors and number crunching financial statements and project schedules.

However intermediaries may evolve, they will stand or fall on the bedrock of the construction contract. A true fixed-cost contract, in contrast to today's highly mutable deals, is imperative if construction industry productivity is to improve. Only by fixing the cost can owners force contractors to improve. Basically, once a construction project begins the contractor becomes a monopolist and begins to behave as such. "Unlike lump-sum contracts," a recent study notes, "the contractor is often not motivated to control costs; indeed the higher the cost, the greater the contractor's profit in poorly constructed cost-plus-fee contracts."[7] Mutable-cost contracts may be appropriate for complex projects entailing a high degree of uncertainty, but economists have demonstrated mathematically that fixed-price contracts are superior for most projects.[8]

Once fixed-cost contracts are the norm, contractors who cannot make accurate estimates will find themselves eating the cost themselves instead of passing it on to owners via change orders. Suddenly, it will make sense for contractors to introduce more capital equipment, innovative procedures, new materials, and the latest technology to keep costs down. When this happens, as it has in many other industries, a shakeout will occur. For the first time in a very long time, perhaps in the industry's history, inefficient construction firms will be forced out not to be replaced by equally inefficient firms the next day. Efficient firms will find themselves attracting more business. They will grow larger. Soon, they will find that they can acquire smaller competitors rather than suffering them. Waste Management, here we come.[9]

With bigger companies will come bigger salaries and more perks. That will draw better managerial talent, which will find ways to reduce costs further. Big firms will also find it easier and cheaper to borrow from banks and, at a certain size, directly from the money and capital markets. More business schools might team up with engineering and architecture schools to offer programs in construction management. Someday professional construction schools could rival architecture schools in prestige. Construction companies may begin to get serious about research and development, an area they have traditionally approached with timidity. They might also consolidate vertically by purchasing suppliers and/or distributors and pressure governments to reform antiquated zoning laws, building codes, and other regulatory entanglements. Before you know it, construction industry productivity might begin to resemble that of the manufacturing or telecommunications sectors in their heydays rather than the anemic healthcare and education sectors.[10]

We do not oversimplify. It is amazing how important a seemingly little thing like a contract can be. One study found that "owners could save ... 5%, and perhaps more, through more astute contractual arrangements."[11] If even this minimal amount were achieved, every local school board raising a $50 million bond issue for new schools would see savings of $2.5 million, which could be used for teacher salaries and new computers or textbooks. If contract terms are endlessly mutable and allow producers to push costs onto buyers, as they do today across most of the construction industry, then we can expect profligacy and little innovation. If contract terms are fixed and make producers suffer for cost overruns that the owner isn't directly responsible for under the agreement, then producers will be forced to look for better, less expensive materials and processes. Productivity is high where contracts are fixed price: airplanes, automobiles, computers, consumer appliances and electronics, food processing, and the like. It sags where contracts are mutable: education, healthcare, legal services—and construction.

Architect James Marston Fitch suggests that the layperson should be educated to be more architecturally astute. "This should be a structural part of a primary and secondary education," he argues, "like physical education." Mr. Fitch may wish to observe America's waistline after fifty years of public school mandated "phys-ed." Educating potential owners, or even just actual owners, would be a waste of precious resources. Most of us will never order the construction of a new building. Even if we do, we could never learn enough without becoming contractors ourselves. And perhaps not even then would we be able to stop change order artistry in its tracks. Even if we could learn enough, most owners have little market power, accounting for only a tiny part of the market, so contractors would let the matter go to court. Of course this analysis means that most owners have little incentive to improve the construction process. But they have a tremendous incentive to improve the construction contracts that they sign.[12]

Private owners have no professional association and hence no standard contract comparable to those promulgated by the American Institute of Architects (AIA) or the Associated General Contractors (AGC), which predictably favor their members. Moreover, no private owner orders the construction of enough buildings to induce builders to adopt a true fixed-price contract. Government, however, does and it is not unaccustomed to using its market power to exert social control. Between 1993 and 2004, government has accounted for slightly over 20 percent of the total construction market in the United States by value.[13] "No institution," asserts Michael Ceschini of Ceschini CPA in Port Jefferson, New York, "plays a more dynamic role in the construction industry than does the United States government."[14]

So perhaps only a consortium of public entities would have the pull necessary to change the direction of industry development. In addition to removing barriers to innovation, governments could help to spur industry change by taking the lead in reforming construction contracts. Through "aggregation," government can create demand large, stable, and long-lived enough to attract significant entry.[15]

Governments and other owners can also compile data on contractors for use in-house, or for sale to third party databases that track contractor performance. The state of Hawaii, for example, was able to get more bang for its construction buck by compiling data on its roofing contractors. Instead of going with the low bid, the state began to contract with the "best value," the best combination of bid and expected performance based on the contractor's track record. (Empirical evidence supports the notion that contractors who do poorly on one job are more likely to do poorly on subsequent jobs.) So Roofer A who bid $100,000 on a job might lose to Roofer B's bid of $150,000 if Roofer B had a superior record of completing work on time, on budget, and at the specified quality (nonleaking roofs). The system works because it creates an incentive for roofers to do what the owners want. "The contractors were no longer bidding to install roofing materials," the authors of an academic study of the system noted, "but they were bidding to waterproof the building." Successes like those of Hawaii have prompted calls for the federal government to eschew low bids in favor of accepting best-value bids. (Interestingly, the Japanese government has long had a contractor rating system in place.)[16]

Hitherto, however, government attempts to create monopsony (monopoly buyer) power have proved ineffective. In the early 1960s, for example, the Department of Defense turned to prefab housing for military personnel, a throwback to the Quonset huts of World War II and the military's brief flirtations with Lustron homes. Only about 2,000 units were produced because neither the prefab companies nor the military profited from the deal.[17]

In the late 1960s HUD implemented Operation Breakthrough in an attempt to reduce housing costs by introducing mass production techniques to the U.S. construction industry. "Operation Breakthrough" was supposed to reduce the need for high wage skilled workers, to introduce new, nonwood building materials, to rationalize building codes and zoning laws, to aggregate market demand, and to stimulate the domestic economy after America's draw down from the Vietnam conflict. It did none of those things. On half of the sites chosen—Houston, Macon, St. Louis, Wilmington, and Seattle—various forms of opposition to experimental construction arose. In some places local agencies would not waive building code restrictions. At other sites, locals feared living in unproven buildings. At others, residents complained about eyesores, property value reductions, and the like. Budget cuts led to the cancellation of 375 units in Wilmington and

Houston. Fearful that high profits would never materialize, builders complained, slowed down, and the program flopped.[18]

The governments of other countries have not fared much better. In Malaysia, for example, the government recently gave tax breaks to firms employing the prefabricated Industrialized Building System method. "Instead of building the whole project," one government official asserted, "contractors should just assemble the components at construction sites to build projects." A few years ago Thailand initiated a similar program. It is too soon to tell if the programs will be successful. In the 1970s the French government initiated a program called Qualitel, a standardized system for rating apartments. The idea was simple—help reduce asymmetric information between renters and owners by making it easy to compare the rental prices of properties with different characteristics. The problem was that the system was voluntary and nobody much cared for it. It is still around though.[19]

As a Rand Corporation study pointed out, "technological change in housing requires substantial institutional change which a demonstration program alone cannot accomplish."[20] True enough, but to transform the industry the government does not need to induce contractors to construct fancy buildings. Contractors will do that when there is a demand for fancy buildings. Rather, the government should direct its efforts toward the creation of viable intermediaries. Remember, what the industry needs is a truly fixed, fixed-price contract, a contract that builders cannot jigger to "hold up" owners. Such a contract would guarantee to owners a fixed price and a fixed quality. The guarantor should be an independent company, to wit not captive to either the owner or the builder.[21] Such an arrangement would throw the risks of construction off owners and onto contractors and their guarantors, the parties best able to bear it, the ones with the construction experience and superior information. Under the proposed system, contractors would have a clear incentive to foresee potential problems and to mitigate any that might arise. Guarantors would employ people who understand the building process—a cadre of private inspectors similar to those long used during the construction of power and petrochemical plants. By protecting the guarantor's interests, those professional monitors would also shield the owner from the contractor's mistakes.[22]

144 Under such a system, contractors with the best business plans and the best reputations for quality, on-time, on-budget work would have the lowest guarantee charges from the best guarantors and hence, other things being equal, the best chance of winning contracts. Owners would face higher initial bids, but none of the uncertainties that pervade the current quasi-mutable-cost system. They would, after all, essentially be hiring the guarantor to monitor the builder and to guarantee his work.

By having the contractor acquire such coverage, instead of the owner purchasing the services of a monitor (like an architect or a construction manager) and guarantor directly, owners ensure that they will receive monitoring services at a competitive price and quality. The problem with direct hire, of course, is the old principal-agent problem inherent in all owner-agent and employer-employee relationships.[23] Namely, the employee or agent (architect or construction manager, both of which receive fees) has an incentive to do the minimum amount and quality of work necessary to maintain his job, not to work in the best interests of the owner (employer).[24] The problem is particularly acute in construction because most owners do not construct enough buildings to provide hired monitors sufficient incentive to work diligently in their interests as there is little chance of repeat business.

Hired monitors have some reputation capital at stake—owners might bad mouth them to other potential owners—but of course owners cannot readily ascertain the quality of the monitoring services provided. So even if they suspected that the hired monitor had done a subpar job, their opinions would not bear much weight. Moreover, construction managers, like other professionals, undoubtedly manage their public client list to their advantage, providing the names of only the best references. Finally, entry into construction management, like entry into most construction roles, is easy, so the markets are glutted with managers, and reputations lose strength in such situations.[25]

Readers conversant with current construction practice will immediately perceive that the proposed guarantor system is merely an extension of the current one based on performance or surety bonds.[26] Traditionally, various types of bonds protect subcontractors and owners in the event of a contractor's insolvency through the agency of a third party that promise to pay damages and/or to see to the completion of the contract. (Such bonds should not be confused with professional liability insurance, which cover, often only partially, the defalcations or negligence of construction managers and design professionals.) The proposal here is to extend the bond system to contractor "soft defaults," or in other words, to instances where the builder remains solvent but seeks to renegotiate the contract price through change orders not initiated by the owner. Surety companies in recent years have indeed begun to tighten their underwriting, to the point that some analysts believe that "bondability is now a true barrier to entry" for smaller, weaker construction companies.[27]

Readers might also recognize that the contract-bonding system proposed here would mimic the incentives of the most efficient part of the U.S. construction industry—the speculative building segment. Speculative builders (acting as developer, contractor or both) design and construct homes and standard office buildings, which they then hope to sell. Because prospective owners (buyers) enter the process at the tail end, the economics of speculative building are radically different than under traditional owner-specified construction. Speculative building is the ultimate fixed-price contract because there is no one to pass cost overruns onto. The market dictates success or failure. If a builder is inefficient, it will not be able to sell its houses, apartment complexes, or office buildings for a profit. The more efficient it is, the higher its profit.[28]

The shortcoming of speculative building is financing. Speculative builders must have the cash to buy all the land, materials, and labor requisite for the project and, if necessary, to hold completed buildings for a favorable market. Except for speculative savings and loan associations that have long since failed, banks and other lenders generally do not relish making such loans unless the builder is heavily capitalized. Under the proposed system, owners are obligated to pay the fixed contract sum, making financing much easier to obtain because a buyer is already committed to the purchase. Fixed-price contracting in a sense takes the speculation out of speculative building.

Other types of intermediary arrangements are also possible. Britain has an extremely interesting system, one based on inspections by the National House-Building Council (NHBC). Hundreds of NHBC inspectors scour building sites. Builders welcome them because they want to retain their NHBC registration, which most mortgage lenders require. The NHBC also monitors complaints after the home is completed. Unlike the Better Business Bureau, however, its bite has real teeth, so builders bend over backwards to rectify problems. Most claims are quickly settled, without escalation to arbitration. The NHBC, it should be noted, is not a government agency, so it appears to do a much better job than the FHA or local building inspectors. The system is superior to that employed in Finland, where lenders withhold the last 10 percent of payments. A year after completion, an inspection is conducted and the problems get fixed before the final invoice is paid, which is usually roughly equal to the contractor's profit. Problems that crop up after the final payment, however, become the owner's problem.[29]

In the 1970s, an attempt to create an American version of NHBC got off to a good start. The Home Owners Warranty (HOW) monitored 100,000 homes, and oversaw only twenty arbitration cases. The program faltered, however, because the Federal Trade Commission interpreted the Magnuson-Moss act—which stiffened requirements for "warranties"—in such a way as to render HOW illegal. That might have been the worst thing to ever happen to the U.S. construction industry.[30]

Another approach to the problems of contracting and asymmetric information is the "negotiated bidding" or "cost planning" system, briefly mentioned above. In that system, a contractor, an owner, and an architect/designer work together to create fieldwork-quality plans and a budget that is construction-cost savvy. The contractor and the architect serve to check each other while at the same time earning a guaranteed payment for providing a valuable service for the owner—the completion of a full set of plans for a building that the owner *can afford to build.* At the end of the cost planning and design phase, the owner can hire the contractor to do the job at a negotiated rate or he can put very precise, contractor-ready plans out to bid. Armed with those precise plans and detailed, realistic cost documents, owners can greatly reduce the threat of change order artistry if they decide to use another contractor. If they use the one who helped with the cost planning, the risk of the change order game is almost completely eliminated.[31]

Richard Bender has suggested yet another type of intermediary, a "building center" that would analyze an owner's plans, adjust the dimensions to fit standard subassemblies (bathrooms, kitchens, HVAC units), and generate accurate cost and time projections. Building center staff would put the prefabricated subassemblies together on-site, guaranteeing proper assembly. The manufacturer of each subassembly would guarantee its work, much like auto or washing machine manufacturers do.[32] IKEA and Home Depot offer these services at a smaller scale for kitchen and bath design, but no one provides these kinds of services at the macro scale.

Any intermediary that successfully eliminates mutable-cost contracting is likely to provoke the industry consolidation that analysts and pundits have called for and erroneously predicted so often in the past. Recall that firms seek to enlarge themselves vertically and horizontally until the costs of internalizing production of goods and purchasing those goods in the market are equalized. Under the mutable-cost contract system that has long prevailed in the construction industry, contractors were able to impose the costs of their small size and lack of integration onto owners. If a subcontractor failed to show, or plans had to be changed, or workers walked off the job, or the price of cement increased, or the weather was unexpectedly bad, an experienced contractor could deftly shirk responsibility and get owners to pay for it.[33]

Under a truly fixed-price contract, contractors would have to eat those costs, indirectly through higher future fees if they chose to resort to the guarantor, directly otherwise. Suddenly, it would be more efficient to internalize subcontractors, architects, materials suppliers, and the like in order to exert more control over costs. Several key values would soon result: rapid consolidation and integration, perhaps combined with design-build or lean construction processes, the embrace of innovation in general, and closer attention to industry best practices.[34] Diseconomies of scale might militate against the emergence of a handful of megafirms. For example, single and multi-family housing complexes reach efficient scale on projects of about 200 homes. Many of the problems associated with the industry's current fragmentation, however, including the lack of R&D, seasonal unemployment, poor management, and lopsided labor relations, would evaporate.[35]

In short, a much more productive construction industry could emerge by merely contractually aligning the economic incentives of contractors and owners. The increased productivity would lead to a combination of lower prices and higher quality that, in the end, will leave all parties better off. None of this means, however, that owners cannot continue to benefit from skilled legal counsel, architects, construction managers, or professional dispute settlers. Owners especially need internal auditors who understand the construction business beyond adding up the amounts shown in the contractor's monthly requisitions. Those auditors need to be well placed in the organization and they have to work hard to ensure that the owner is not being taken advantage of by change order artists.[36]

The government can relatively easily adjust statutes and regulations to ensure the smooth functioning of this system. For instance, it can allow insurers to replace public building inspectors. Government courts can ensure that the contracts maintain their fixed-price bite. Governments have a fairly good record here. They were, for example, the first owners to insist that builders post performance bonds. Under the federal Miller Act (1935), contractors have to supply a performance bond (and a closely related type of bond known as a payment bond) that is satisfactory to the governmental entity letting the contract. Most states passed equivalent legislation applicable to state and municipal construction projects. Private parties followed their lead, albeit slowly and with some prodding from legal analysts.[37]

On the other hand, government projects are notorious for allowing contractor cost overruns. The major expansion of Miami's International Airport, originally budgeted at $500 million fourteen years ago is now expected to cost more than four times that amount—over $2 billion—before it is completed.[38] Productivity on government construction projects lags that on private projects by a significant margin, likely because public officials have less incentive to keep caps on costs since they can often simply appropriate additional funding or, if a local municipality, float another bond issue to the taxpayers. Most Americans want low taxes, but plenty of public goods, including nice schools, parks, municipal parking lots, stadiums, roads, and bridges. Such seemingly incompatible goals can be reconciled only by making the construction industry more productive, capable of producing more built space with fewer dollars than in the past. The real impetus for fixed price contracts may ultimately come from taxpayers at the polls.[39]

Contracts: Ensuring That Prices Stay Fixed

At the heart of the design and construction process are the contractual agreements between owners, contractors, and designers. Given that construction is a trillion dollar-a-year industry, it would be easy to imagine that those in the business spend a great deal of time and money negotiating and drafting construction contracts. In fact, relative to most fields in the business world, construction contracts are inadequate. More often than not, work begins well before finalization of the critical contractual documentation governing the relationship between the parties. Even when complete, construction contracts, especially those used on projects involving $1 million or more, are generally faulty, in large part because construction firms, even large ones, rarely employ more than one senior lawyer and architectural firms usually have no in-house counsel at all. By now it is obvious who reaps the benefit and who bears the burden of ineffective agreements, as well as what contractual solutions might create leaner and more productive projects. As the Athenian lawmaker Solon has purportedly said, "Men keep agreements when it is to the advantage of neither of them to break them."

150

One set of agreements that today govern the movement of hundreds of billions of dollars annually arose from the British form agreements of the nineteenth century. In the late nineteenth and early twentieth centuries, the nascent AIA extended them into a series of standard agreements (e.g., A201 and B141) for all types of projects. In the 1960s, increasing litigiousness saw an increase in the number of claims for malpractice brought against architects. In 1960, only 12.5 percent of firms had malpractice claims brought against them. By 1969 it was 20 percent and by 1979 it was 35 percent. Not only was this a drain on productivity, but it greatly increased insurance expenses. The increase in claims resulted in an insurance market that failed to offer higher levels of coverage even as project costs soared and liability correspondingly increased. With greater exposure came less protection. Architects sought relief by changing words, not actions.[40] In response over the past forty years, the AIA has repeatedly revised its standard form contracts in an attempt to further isolate the architect from potential liability associated with the construction process. The architect would now be "the representative" of the owner during construction; would only "visit the site at intervals appropriate to the stage of the Contractor's operations," but only to "become generally familiar with and to keep the Owner informed about the progress and quality of the work," to "endeavor to guard the Owner against defects and deficiencies in the work," but "not be required to make exhaustive or continuous on-site inspections to check the quality or quantity of the work," nor "have control over or charge of, nor be responsible for the construction means, methods, techniques, sequences or procedures, or for safety precautions or programs in connection with the work, since these are *solely* the Contractor's rights and responsibilities."[41]

The standardized AIA contracts make broad and potentially dangerous assumptions regarding the scope of work and other crucial variables. Worse, they look after the interests of contractors first, then architects, with owners' interests coming in a distant third. Moreover, they are sadly out of touch with most of the more complex projects and are totally inapplicable for many projects where they do not define adequately the particular processes of highly technical projects.

For example, the renowned architect Frank Gehry, whose work and BIM innovations we introduced in chapter 4, is one of many architects who refuse to define their services in terms of the AIA's standard owner-architect agreement.[42]

Despite their hoary roots and severe limitations, the standard agreements serve as the basic contractual template for tens of millions of square feet of corporate office space built annually and untold lesser projects. Though ubiquitous, they are quite simply inadequate to the task because they do not pay enough heed to Solon's reminder that a superior contract aligns the interest of all parties to it. Gehry put it best when he noted that it had always been his "fantasy to try and find a way to become the responsible part of the *team* with the client and become a *partner* with the construction company instead of an *adversary*."

Owner-generated contracts also tend to be lopsided. Sometimes owners—usually governments or large organizations—seek to use contracts they have developed over time. When they send out requests for proposals to architects, engineers, and contractors, they attach their form agreements and note that any party that wishes to submit a proposal is expected to sign the standard agreement with little or no change. In these cases owners benefit: the contract plays to their interests and negotiating time and costs are reduced. To the extent that the contract is skewed in their favor, however, they undoubtedly receive higher bids on their projects.

Ideally, architects and engineers work assiduously to prepare a set of "construction documents," the detailed design drawings and specifications that reflect the precise manner and number of things desired by the owner in the finished building. As discussed in chapter 1, bid documents are sent out to construction managers or general contractors. Often, we daresay most often, jobs are put out to bid and actual construction begun before the bid documents are complete. Even if allowed to complete the construction drawings before they are bid, design professionals rarely get all the design information onto their drawings for the contractors.

The number and severity of those omissions largely determine whether a project will be rife with costly change orders and delays. To the extent that those omissions can be reduced in scale and scope before the contractor bids on them, everyone will be better off. But given their inevitability, it is essential that construction contracts anticipate errors and omissions and ensure that the resulting change orders are reasonably priced and not used to gouge owners, who as we have seen, are rendered virtually powerless due to contractors' superior information and market power once construction begins. In short, the contract has to level a playing field currently slanted steeply in favor of contractors.

When a general contractor assumes the risk of accepting a contract with a fixed price or lump sum—or in other words, when he commits to build and provide every item shown on the bid documents within a specified time for an immutable price—he becomes a guarantor of performance of the work. Accepting such a contract is risky business. To construct a building—say a hospital—the contractor must bring together tens of thousands of different pieces of material shown on the drawings. He has to coordinate the daily schedules of each of the suppliers, subcontractors, fabricators, and general work staff, a team that can easily number in the hundreds for a moderately sized project. If a subcontractor fails to perform as prescribed, the contractor must step into the breach, secure another subcontractor willing to complete the defaulting subcontractor's work, and assume any cost increases charged by the completing subcontractor.

And the risks do not stop there. Everything about the construction of the modern structure bears a risk disproportionate to the return on investment for each participant in the process. Years after a building is completed, each of the team members remain liable for problems that may, and often do, arise. Some problems are common to all in business—a passerby can trip over a crack in a sidewalk and sue the owner, the architect, and the contractor for injuries resulting from a slip and fall. Others can be more far-reaching in nature, like cracks that appear in walls along the exterior of a brick building two years after completion.

The owner of a building also assumes a series of risks, few of them insurable, that the architects, engineers, and construction team that erect the structure rarely understand or appreciate. These include acquiring the land and numerous governmental approvals; retaining the right architect to provide design services that match the owner's business goals (a process that is much more risky than most owners ever come to recognize); securing construction and long-term financing; hiring a construction manager or general contractor; assuming certain unanticipated site risks such as the existence of unobservable hazardous materials or subsurface rock; insuring the project appropriately during and after construction; verifying that all installed machinery and equipment is in working order; approving and paying for all work, overseeing labor and services on the project; ensuring that any deficiencies in the work are corrected before occupancy; training employees of the building to maintain and operate the facility after completion; and last but hardly least, assuming all costs for delays and additional scope added to the project if not addressed in the original design documents.

It is sometimes said that "the owner has traditionally borne the risk of loss since he is the one who initiates the entire construction process."[43] This bizarre custom is thoroughly entrenched; the courts have long upheld it. The notion that the owner must bear the risk of construction has perpetuated the use of mutable-cost contracts that are the root of the construction industry's economic inefficiency. Why should owners bear the economic risks of constructing the buildings that they buy any more than the purchasers of automobiles, chewing gum, or major surgery bear the risks of their production?[44]

This is not to argue, however, that owners should allow themselves to remain pushovers. Owners cannot know everything about construction, but they can know, and should know, that they are innocent babes in need of help, serious help, from experienced intermediaries and/or some other trusted, informed party with an economic incentive to keep the fixed contract from turning into a mutable one. In other words, owners need to retake control of the overall process and stop allowing themselves to be victimized.[45]

Architects and engineers also bear risk on a project. Unlike the early architect who served as the "master builder," today's architect typically plays only a limited role as the designer and the licensed professional who is responsible to governmental authorities for ensuring compliance with applicable building codes. Since most architects no longer visit the project construction site on a daily basis, their role as the ombudsman for the owner during the so-called construction administration phase has diminished considerably in recent decades. The fee structure for architects varies greatly: from 4 percent for large-scale government and institutional projects to 20 percent for custom residential or complex commercial retail projects. Often, they must share portions of this fee with the project engineers and assume liability for their work. (This under the legal theory that the one who retains a party is responsible for it.) Architects often must perform their design services quickly, within the confines of the fast-track system, all while complying with an ever-increasing complex of local, state, and federal rules, regulations, and codes that are in constant flux. Architects are liable for all design errors and omissions in the many drawings, specifications, sketches, and submittals individually prepared for each project, so they usually purchase up to several million dollars of professional liability insurance.[46] That is not much if the case is actively litigated, especially given that contractors eager to generate change orders invariably accuse architects of design errors or omissions in the construction documents.

The contractor or construction manager is expected to bring the project to fruition precisely within the confines of the approved project schedule, despite a host of uncertainties and unanticipated problems lurking around each corner. Experienced contractors ameliorate those numerous risks contractually, accepting some but imposing most on owners. By law, contractors must build everything shown or "reasonably inferable" on the drawings and specifications prepared by the design team. What is "reasonably inferable" is never as clear-cut as the contractor would wish. As a result, the risks and responsibilities of the contractor involve a host of pitfalls. Good contractors will carefully analyze the project drawings and specifications to ensure that all details of the required work, labor, materials, and services are identified and properly priced for the job by each of its subcontractors and suppliers bidding to work on the project. They also try to understand the project site and assume some of the risk for any observable surface and subsurface conditions. They also secure the necessary bonds for the performance of the work and payment to each of the subcontractors during the course of the project. Under OSHA and the laws of many states, responsibility for the safety and comfort of the workers employed at the site falls on the contractor. Good contractors also provide warranties of the work installed, agree to correct all defective work at its own cost, and promise to complete the project on schedule or face damages and/or penalties for late completion.

During the course of a given project, the design and construction team members will also be engaged in several other projects, each fraught with risks of its own. To be sure, none of the projects will proceed along the scheduled path without surprises, problems, or changes. Because of those multiple risks, many construction managers and contractors try to include in each construction budget a contingency of 10 percent to cover the problems and mistakes that arise during the course of almost every project. In other words, owners are requested to fund the mistakes or misjudgments of the construction team.

Contractors often make mistakes in the preparation of their bids. Estimating a project from the architect's drawings and specifications is part art and part science. On many fast-track projects, the CM requires the subcontractors to bid on construction documents that may be perhaps less than 50 percent complete. These bid documents could lack "minor" details such as wall openings, pipes, and reinforcements in concrete floor slabs. Subcontractors who bid on these documents in a fast-track project are expected to draw on their expertise and account for the cost of the missing details on their bid proposal. Under the definition of a guaranteed maximum price, or GMP, if they omit an item that is reasonably inferable from the bid documents, they must provide it during construction even if they did not include it in their bid. To cover themselves, bidders in such situations may assume that all material quantities will increase by perhaps 20 percent and that material cost and even labor may increase 1 or 2 percent before the materials are actually purchased. The subcontractor plays a delicate game here with the CM. By adding too much padding, it may underbid and lose the job. If the cushion is too thin, it may take it on the chin. Often, while the CM may foster heated competition amongst subcontractors for the base bid award, it will then permit the successful subcontractor some latitude in submitting change orders for work not specifically shown on the bid documents, although it could be reasonably inferable. CM's frequently have long-established relationships, as do GCs, with their subcontractors through the many projects they may have worked together. The CM's loyalty to the owner is therefore often conflicted by its loyalty to a subcontractor.

The construction process starts and ends with risk for all sides. Here, the more sophisticated or knowledgeable party—usually the contractor—can insulate itself from its own mistakes and protect its profits at the expense of the other parties, usually the designers and owners. This is not to say, however, that windfall profits are the norm. Chances are slim that the architect, the engineers, or the construction team will earn profits of more than 10 percent, even on a well-managed project. The average profit for architectural firms in 2003 as reported by the American Institute of Architects was 10.5 percent. Construction firms in 2003 averaged 5.1 percent return on assets and 17 percent return on equity.[47]

Clearly, the incentives of the major players on the supply side are not closely aligned, and the interests of the owner (buyer) and general contractor (seller) are antithetical. It is therefore imperative to negotiate fair and logical contracts with each of the team members lest one party or another bear too much of the risk and cost of the project. A good contract does not empower one party at the expense of another but rather aligns the incentives of all parties to produce the result to which the contract is instrumental. A well-designed contract is especially important in construction to leverage the greater market and informational power that contractors wield after beginning work on a job. Aggrieved parties usually litigate, though courtrooms are almost invariably the worst place to settle disputes—unless you're an attorney billing $500 per hour. "Litigation," attorney Bryant Byrnes reminds anyone who has forgotten, "is the quickest way to turn a large sum of money into a small sum of money." In a recent suit between general contractor LMB and the Venetian Resort Hotel and Casino in Las Vegas, lawyers made off with $9.6 million. And they earned every penny, creating a whopping 11,000 exhibits that totaled 3 million pages. That massive pile was made possible by the fact that in this very litigious industry, everyone has long learned to document everything. Ironically, just a few more pages in the original contract could have saved those 3 million pieces of paper, and countless additional reams in the thousands of other construction cases that go to court each year.[48]

Even more fascinating is the industry's avowed preference to arbitrate rather than litigate disputes. Seemingly faster, fairer, and less costly than litigation, arbitration is relatively rare because most experienced construction counsel rightly steer their clients away from it. Arbitration of construction disputes, it turns out, is not necessarily quicker or less costly than the courts.[49]

Despite the crucial importance of a good contract, some construction companies, even fairly sizable ones, try to avoid entering into any formal written contracts with owners at all. Others try to induce owners to sign what amount to one-way deals: the owners pay a large sum of money for the privilege of having the contractor decide when work will begin, and how and when it will be completed. Contractors are quite honest about this with each other. One guru advises: "No retainage [typically 5–10 percent of the contract price held by the owner until final completion] will be owing when Mr. X enjoys the use of his new facility. Callbacks will be handled on a warranty basis, not by holding my money as a club. Also, the question of a bond may come up, if needed. Then I tell the owner the cost of the bond will be added to the contract as an extra." Other contractors proffer contracts that are so short and general they are better called agreements rather than contracts. If anything goes wrong, they are largely ineffective. Contractors like them because they know that "the simpler the contract, the quicker it's signed."[50]

A good contract reflects a fair allocation of risks to each party. A careful and skillful recognition of each side's risk is the first step to achieving an equtable risk allocation agreement. Effective contracts should outline the rights and responsibilities of the owner as well as the contractor. No contract is ever complete, but it should be as comprehensive as possible. At the very least, a good contract seeks to avoid potential surprises, puts everyone "on the same page" and lowers the cost of resolving any disputes that may occur down the line. Unless those representing the owner have at least as much experience in the business and legal realities of the construction world as the contractor does, chances are small that the equities will be fairly allocated.[51]

It is strongly recommended that construction agreements should identify and address common problems fairly and logically and not be skewed in favor of owners, or any other interest for that matter. The goal is to avoid problems, not to "get the other guy." For example, owners have been known to work over contractors on occasion by withholding final payments. That can be quite a burden on contractors, especially as some contracts stipulate that up to 10 percent of the contract be withheld until the project is completely finished, "punch list" and all.

It behooves both contractors and owners to settle their differences out of court if at all possible. Alternate dispute resolution (ADR) ranges from a candid chat over a cup of coffee to nonbinding mediation to small claims court to binding arbitration. A good contract will spell out which of those is best for different types of disputes.[52] For disputes up to a specified amount (precluding costly legal and expert fees), ADR has substantial merits.

As noted above, contractors are extremely reluctant to assume all the risks of building. But even those who eschew change order gaming still insist on the contractual right to change orders for unforeseen events. In his contracts, David Gerstel tells owners that "Change orders can be required for reasons including but not limited to: Subsurface Conditions: Conditions below existing grade requiring extra efforts to accomplish excavation or drilling. Example: Boulders."[53] That seems reasonable enough, but consider this: how many contractors will issue a change order *reducing* their bill if subsurface or other hidden conditions turn out to be *better* than expected?

And aren't conditions more or less predictable over a large number of projects? If construction firms were bigger they could lose 5 basis points because of a hidden condition on one or two projects but make up for it on their 100 other projects that experienced fewer hidden difficulties than expected. In other words, why should owners shoulder the burden of a risk that can be diversified away? Imagine your reaction if your bank told you that you no longer had any money in your checking account because one of the bank's borrowers defaulted. You'd find it preposterous. But add a room onto your house that requires any excavation and you will find yourself agreeing to the "unanticipated rock clause." Yes, each project is different, but it isn't completely new. The basics, and even many of the specifics, are the same from project to project. Construction firms need to learn to better generalize from past experiences.[54]

Granted, on some types of projects a large degree of uncertainty that cannot be insured or diversified away may indeed exist. In that case, a hybrid contract that is neither fixed price nor carte blanche may be the best choice. One such hybrid is called GMPBUA or guaranteed maximum price based unit assumptions. Such contracts allow contractors to raise prices, but not above contract levels for each type of input involved in the job. These contracts are more complex than standard ones, but they allow the contractor and the owner to share the onus of uncertainty. (Of course GMPBUA contracts also reduce one of the major benefits of fixed price contracting, the reduction in the number of *owner* defaults and bankruptcies. Under mutable contracting, owners sometimes must abandon projects before completion because they cannot finance the unexpected extra charges.)[55]

Another type of hybrid contract provides bonuses for completing work early and penalties for completing it late. Such contracts will work to make the industry more competitive as long as the terms are fixed and not subject to contractors' claims for extra reimbursement. Such contracts, and many others, do have their place. Owners and contractors need to realize that, above a certain threshold of size and complexity, each project needs a specially tailored contract to ensure that everyone's interests are aligned as much as possible, that everyone's duties and responsibilities are spelled out as fully and clearly as possible, and that everyone knows how to try to settle any disputes that may arise.[56]

In terms of the industry's efficiency, the key is to eliminate excuses for altering contracts after work has begun. Sixty percent of construction contracts are nominally fixed price, with the price set either through bidding or negotiation. GMP contracts constitute another 20 percent or so. The remaining 20 percent are various open-ended arrangements, for example, time and materials, cost plus fee, or fees based on unit costs. If owners can keep those contracts truly fixed to the base contract or to the GMP, and perhaps decrease the use of the various open-ended arrangements, which by their very nature are mutable price, the construction industry will quickly improve.

An Industry Open to Innovation

Construction firms still build most houses using a technique developed in Chicago in 1833. Pressed for time building churches and other wood frame structures for a burgeoning town, Augustine D. Taylor developed what was then called the "balloon frame." The balloon frame used lightweight two-by-four studs, which could be easily nailed, instead of the heavier, traditional ten inch square timbers with their complex mortise and tenon connections. Taylor constructed buildings fast and cheap using the new technique, and it quickly spread. Balloon framing was improved by a further modification: simply running the studs from floor to floor rather than all the way from the first floor sill to the rafter (roof) plate. This technique became known as platform framing and is used predominantly to this day in wood frame structures in the United States.[57]

It is a good technique, no doubt about it. (Czechs who learned of it in the mid-twentieth century were so agog that one of them purchased a two by four and carried it home with him on the airplane, so the story goes.) Chicago and San Francisco sprang up seemingly overnight because of the productivity improvement that balloon framing wrought. And over the next 170 or so years there have been other improvements: prefabricated trusses and stairs, pre-hung doors, pre-engineered lumber and the like. But most of the improvements are related to better materials, not better techniques for turning them into buildings.[58]

161

Most construction firms today are too small to develop break-through construction improvements like balloon framing. But under a fixed-price system, that could change quickly. Once owners stop subsidizing small, inefficient players, size should quickly win out. Large integrated firms are much better equipped to hire and retain better business managers, people capable of hedging risks, obtaining the best external financing available, and investing in research and development. Large firms could also manage labor more effectively, sustain labor relations, and effect changes in building codes and other governmental regulations that cause inefficiencies. In addition, they would have the ability to use and disseminate innovative processes and materials.

In the future, bigger contractors will make better use of computer technology than most construction firms traditionally have. As the Office of Technology Assessment noted *twenty years ago,* "computer-based technologies can significantly reduce the cost of making modifications to existing plans while preventing errors from creeping into areas unaffected by the change."[59] Today, they can do that and a whole lot more. Firms like Autodesk have created incredible products that, if used by a significant portion of contractors, could greatly increase construction industry productivity. Design programs can automatically retrieve accurate prices and availability times from online databases, double check that every material needed for a particular design in the proper quantity has been included in the bid, and even submit purchase orders. Such software will reduce a major coordination problem that plagues construction today: the disconnect between the ideas, experience, and knowledge of the design team and the contractors.[60]

Fortune magazine knew in 1947 that size mattered. "The search for reform in the house building business," it noted, "becomes primarily a search for large-scale operations. . . . Efficient house production requires firms big enough to mobilize capital and organize production in systematic, repetitive operations. They must be big enough to assume full managerial responsibility instead of dividing it with subcontractors; to oppose strength to strength in dealing with labor; to buy supplies in quantity; to counter the rapacity of the suppliers of building materials; and to take the responsibility of making a fair price to the customer."[61]

How do we *know* all this? The same way that *Fortune* did: it has already happened in other markets. *Fortune* rightly extolled the virtues of Levitt and Sons.[62] In just four years, 1947 to 1951, Levitt and Sons transformed potato farms in central Nassau County, Long Island, into a thriving community of 70,000 persons comfortably housed in 17,437 single family dwellings nestled amidst nine community swimming pools, fourteen playgrounds, twelve baseball and two football fields, ten basketball and ten handball courts, an archery range, and numerous parks. The company was a victim of its own success. Its original plans called for the creation of only 2,000 homes and far fewer amenities; it paid $250 per acre at first but by the end it had to pony up $3,750 per acre for land of the same quality. (Levitt and Sons learned from that mistake, purchasing all of the land for Levittown, Pennsylvania, at the outset.) Nevertheless, the profits came down like a torrent because, as an early historian of the company put it, when it came to construction, advertising, and sales, "every operation was meticulously planned in advance, and represented years of thought and experimentation."[63]

The company at first rented their houses only to veterans. Levitt and Sons preferred specializing in construction, so it soon began to encourage renters to buy. In 1950 and again in 1953 it sold large chunks of its remaining portfolio of homes to a Philadelphia company for some $15 million. It also retailed newly constructed homes itself. Owners of corner homes had to pay a little more for the bigger lots they enjoyed, and different model years had slightly different prices, but otherwise everyone paid the same amount. Later, it offered its homes to nonveterans who, of course, were not entitled to Veterans Administration subsidies but were otherwise treated the same as veterans. The company was able to maintain such a narrow range of prices because it had tremendous control over its costs. If it added an amenity it made up for it by eliminating or downgrading something else. As land prices edged upward, it found ways to cut costs without cutting too many corners. Simply moving the kitchen to the front of the house saved money because water pipes did not have to be run as far and under the concrete slab that formed the floor of the Levitt homes.

163

Levitt and Sons knew that it could not pass costs along to owners via change orders, so it buckled down and figured out how to continue to provide buyers with a lot of bang for their buck. By 1955, its model 1950 ranches regularly sold in the secondary market for $1,000 more than the 1949 model. The 1950 model was still a steal, though, a good $1,000 to $2,000 cheaper than comparable houses built by traditional contractors.

Organization, mass production, and vertical integration were key, and they would be again in a modern-day transformation of the industry. From its timber stands and lumber mill at Blue Falls, California, rough cut lumber traveled by rail to Levitt and Sons' wood shop in Roslyn, Long Island, where it was cut precisely to size, loaded onto pallets, and trucked to the construction site. It bought piping, but cut it to size and preassembled it in its own shop. The company also owned and operated its own nail factory, the excess production of which it sold into the open market. It even owned its own construction supply company, North Shore Supply.

Levitt and Sons used subcontractors in name but not in spirit. In short, the "subcontractors" were really employees, but it was convenient for tax purposes to treat them as separate firms. As an early historian of Levittown explained, "Contrary to popular practice, the subcontractors worked only for Levitt. They worked on a fee or piece rate basis.... All subcontractors were subject to the supervision of Levitt's own project engineers and superintendents who maintained close control over all operations. Production schedules were set up and rigidly maintained." Because they all essentially worked for the same company, teams composed of two to three nonunion laborers worked together almost seamlessly, ensuring a minimum of downtime between each of the seventeen major production steps between site preparation and landscaping. Interestingly, Levitt and Sons paid its laborers *more* than union scale because worker productivity warranted it. When humming nicely, the teams reportedly could finish a house in twenty-four minutes. That's right, minutes.[64] Due to its large capital and its tremendous business expertise, Levitt and Sons enjoyed a $7 million line of credit with a large New York bank.

Freed from the opiate of change orders, Levitt and Sons grew so efficient that it could guarantee prices on custom work. It won contracts for constructing schools in Pennsylvania, for example, by promising to complete them for 40 percent less than previous contractors had actually charged on identical plans (after change orders, that is, not bids). It not only fulfilled the contract, it did so in spades, completing the schools for less than half what other contractors charged! Honest-to-goodness competition is a wonderful thing.[65]

Levittown, Long Island was more than a mere business success. By 1955 it was already showing signs of maturity—few tenants, a mix of vets and nonvets, swarms of kids, more and more leaves to rake each fall, and architectural diversity as some homeowners put on garages, others dormers, and still others swimming pools, decks, Florida rooms, and the like. It would be easy to mock Levittown for its suburban blandness—many people have done so—but as the detractors note, people bought them. They also *liked* them.

Levitt and Sons is not the only construction success story. Fox & Jacobs, which built 35 percent of the homes, including 65 percent of the lower and middle income ones, in Dallas, Texas, had a factory that churned out parts of houses eighteen hours a day, five days a week. Trucks then hauled the pieces to home sites where up to 300 men put the pieces together, assembly-line style, except, as in Levitt and Son operations, it was the men who moved rather than the product. (The experts who argued that one cannot build homes, even mobile homes, as one does automobiles were only half right.)[66]

Co-founder Dave Fox called himself a housing "manufacturer" and used terms like "continuous production." The scheduling was as precise as any factory. It could be precise because the firm was highly vertically integrated, owning everything from the aforementioned factory, to the bulldozers that prepared the lot, to the concrete mixers that poured the pad on which each of its homes rested, Levitt-style. Fox bought only one finished component, roof trusses, for the simple reason that he found a firm that could make them to his specifications cheaper than he could.

Fox's designs, aided by computers, kept plumbing and electrical lines at a minimum. The utility room, kitchen, and both bathrooms, for instance, shared a single wall that sheltered all the home's plumbing. Ventilation was kept similarly compact, reducing both materials and labor costs. Even in the late 1970s, the carpenters all used nail guns, the painters used sprayers and one-coat paints. Interestingly, top Fox & Jacobs executives were not contractors at all but veterans of Frito-Lay, Texas Instruments, and Procter & Gamble.

Fox & Jacobs houses were inexpensive but not cheap. They cost considerably less than average homes though they were more energy efficient and had overall better quality. To put it another way, they built real houses at mobile home prices. Much of that cost savings had to do with the company's scale, its limited use of subcontractors, and its superior management. Some of it, though, was attributable to the limited government interference that the firm faced and the relatively easy Texas climate and landscape. At about 5,000 homes a year, Fox & Jacobs is small, but it is a subsidiary of a much larger construction firm, Centex.[67]

While the Levitts were at the forefront of industry change half a century ago, today's homebuilders are leading a modern-day transformation of the industry. Large-scale development home building continues to be the closest thing the industry has to a commoditized industrial product. Since the days of Levitt, the large-scale residential market has become a highly sophisticated, heavily capitalized sector of the construction industry. Toll Brothers, one of the nations most successful homebuilders, designs and builds large-scale developments comprised of what they refer to as "the Estate Home," but what others sometimes deride as "McMansions." Formed by two brothers in 1967, the company went public in 1986. Today it has a capitalization of $4.9 billion. It has built over 13.5 million single family homes since the mid 1990s.

Companies such as Toll Brothers are also major purchasers of land throughout the United States. As recently as 1986, Toll Brothers controlled land that could support nearly 80,000 homes. Other major home builders have acquired even more land for future construction. K. Hovnanian controls land for more than 100,000 homes; Pulte Homes holds 350,000 sites; and a coterie of other homebuilders similarly control hundreds of thousands more.[68] By finding their way through a growing morass of governmental approvals and regulations required for building a new community, these home builders have fine-tuned their operations through extensive research and experience to maximize profits. Building as much as it does enables Toll Brothers to retain a loyal group of subcontractors that regularly proceed through the steps needed to complete hundreds of homes at a time under tight time and budget constraints to maximize profits. The company has learned through its research, that the high end residential purchaser desires top quality finishes and fixtures as standard rather than optional add-ons. According to company executives, "the more options we sold, the less we made." The company discovered along the way that an option like a whirlpool tub decreased profits since this "change order" led to construction errors, delays, and additional costs that could not be passed on to the purchaser.

Toll Brothers has decreased the cost of its residences by implementing production methods that minimize field labor and help drive down costs. For example, the company has developed a prebuilt wall panel and roof truss system that ships directly from its own factories to the home site.[69] Other large homebuilders have found their own methods for achieving greater efficiencies.

It is no coincidence that Levitt and Sons, Fox & Jacobs, Toll Brothers, and others are all speculative homebuilders. Rather than building to order on the basis of only nominally fixed contracts, they build houses on standard plans and offer them to the public for fixed prices.[70] No change orders here. They do it right or they suffer the cost themselves. Part of doing it right for firms like Levitt and Sons entailed mass-producing designs that satisfied the lowest common denominator; in the case of today's homebuilders like Toll Brothers, it means providing luxury options. Not all buildings can be mass-produced on such simple yet functional plans, but we need not lament. The real lesson those companies taught is not about mass production and standardization per se, but rather about fixed prices and competition. Construction industry productivity will improve rapidly once owners stop allowing contractors to go over budget and past deadline. Owners will do that after they receive help from construction intermediaries and better contracts. Strange as it may seem, the key to a better construction process starts with pieces of paper with the right words on them, where relationships are properly aligned, and information flows freely.

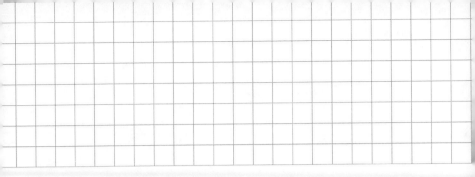

Practical Advice to Owners for Getting Started Now

Where is the construction industry likely headed? As we have seen, the industry has many impediments holding it back from becoming a true twenty-first century industry. As long as there are no truly national, well-capitalized construction companies, there will be only incremental advances in research and new technology to encourage consolidation in the industry. As an industry widely recognized to be low profit, there is little likelihood that any one or group of contractors could aggregate enough capital or borrowing power to secure control over even a regional market.

Ideas that reshape an industry rarely transform that industry overnight. While Thomas Edison may have invented the electric light in 1879, it took over forty years before electric lights lit the newly constructed skyscrapers of our nation. The steel industry, which had years of large profitability, took nearly three decades to consolidate.[1] So it is unlikely that the low profitability, mom-and-pop nature of the construction industry, which has been in place since the founding of our nation, will magically transform itself without great vision and substantial private investment. But could it happen?

Until there is a radical transformation of the construction industry, there is much that can be done to ameliorate many of the flaws and weakness described in this book. Whether you are a corporate vice president charged with overseeing your company's new headquarters or a school superintendent trying to maximize the newly authorized bond issue for new schools, knowing the right questions to ask can be a daunting experience. You are in charge. It is tempting to act as if you know what is what, even when you don't. How do you solve the Gladwellian construction industry mystery?[2]

By following the rules set out here, you will do better and be able to save 5, 10, perhaps 15 percent or more over what less knowledgeable owners would pay in comparable situations. Do not be intimidated by any architect, contractor, or construction manager who challenges these suggestions. Do not accept the standard retort, "This is how it's always been done." Remember, these companies want your business and have room to be flexible. If you explain that the project you proffer mandates the following requirements set out below, you will be rewarded with a team that accepts your business goals, ensuring a fair profit to the contractor and enabling you, the owner, to harvest considerable cost savings.

Secure the Right Contract

As highlighted in chapter 6, your primary goal is to enter into agreements with all team members that will ensure a construction agreement that is not mutable. Securing a true fixed-price contract using the Equitable Risk Allocation Agreement model for your project will require your architect and engineers to deliver to you a set of construction documents for bidding that are fully detailed, complete in all respects, and coordinated with each other. (Owners often assume, incorrectly, that finished architectural drawings are 100 percent complete. Unfortunately, they typically are not.) To accomplish this, your agreement with the architect—who will likely enter into separate agreements with each of the engineers—must contain language such as the following:

> The Architect agrees that an essential part of its services is to provide a fully detailed set of construction documents to enable the

Owner to secure a fixed-price contract from the selected contractor. To assist the Owner in accomplishing this objective, the Architect agrees to provide for bid issue 100 percent complete construction documents that have been fully coordinated with each of the engineers and other designers on the project.

This provision requires the architect to do nothing more than what is the standard for any architect in the nation. If the architect objects to this provision, the owner should question the architect's ability and intention to submit complete drawings and specifications—a red flag signaling that any errors or omissions could open the owner to costly contractor change orders and delay claims.

Once this provision is in place, the next objective is to ensure that a corollary provision is included in the construction manager or contractor agreement, which should provide the following:

The Construction Manager (or Contractor) has been provided full opportunity to review the Construction Documents and field conditions so as to ensure that it fully understands the design intent shown and that all elements for construction shown thereon have been included in the contract price. It is agreed that the contract price includes all necessary work, labor, and material expressly or impliedly required for the project. The Construction Manager (or Contractor), agrees to waive any claim for extra cost or delay related to any error or omission in the Construction Documents that reasonably should have been observed prior to commencing work on the project.

By including this provision, the owner protects against a "creeping" price. Only legitimate additions to the project, for example the owner's decision to add a new floor or additional lighting that were not part of the original scope of work on the approved drawings, will add cost to the project.

A second important feature of securing a fixed-price contract is to resist efforts to have your project managed on the "fast-track." Time is money and other arguments for commencing construction as quickly as possible are well known, but beware that the owner's risk rises rapidly using fast-track. Under fast-track, no construction manager can or will provide realistic assurances that the initial proposed project budget or preliminary GMP will be finalized into a final GMP of the same amount, let alone that the final construction cost will be less than the GMP. Construction managers explain that they have no control over the material marketplace or over the cost of labor. Moreover, since fast-track construction commences before the project design is finalized, the owner effectively loses the opportunity to re-bid the project if the final GMP prepared by the construction manager far exceeds the owner's budget. Reducing scope at that point will have an enormous ripple effect and likely impact the schedule, negating any advantage the fast-track process might have yielded.

By agreeing to a fast-track process, the owner gives up control over the pricing and schedule to the construction manager who bears little risk if the budget is exceeded or the project encounters serious delays. By avoiding the fast-track and permitting the architect extra time to complete the critical construction documents, the owner has the opportunity to secure a fixed price for the work shown on the drawings. If there are errors or omissions detected, the construction manager or contractor will be given the time to assist in identifying them *before* they impact the schedule and lead to large claims.

The Owner's Best Friend: The On–Site Owner's Representative

Depending on the size of the project, the owner will be required to make thousands of decisions, many highly technical. In all but aesthetic decisions, the owner will probably not be sufficiently versed to participate intelligently in the decision making and will be forced to rely on the experience of the architect or the construction team. On projects of any complexity, a hospital for instance, or for projects costing several million dollars or more, retaining an owner's representative to oversee construction becomes imperative.

In many parts of the United States the use of a qualified independent representative of the owner during the construction phase is uncommon; owners rely on the local contractor and the part-time visits of the architect. For costly or complex projects, the value of the owner's representative is incalculable. A good one has many years of construction experience that will likely more than offset its fee. The qualified owner's representative also acts as the owner's ombudsman, the arbiter of any conflicts that may arise. The daily presence of someone versed in the technical issues of the project at the site will garner increased respect from the construction team, thereby reducing the likelihood that disputes will arise in the first place. On large-scale projects with hundreds of workers and constantly revised work directives, problems are magnified. Large projects such as these call not just for one owner's representative, but an entire a team of experienced individuals who can track change orders, review requisitions and make decisions on the thousands of items that cross their desks weekly.

Similarly, the role of the architect should be enhanced for these types of projects. If the architect has extensive experience overseeing construction—and not every architectural firm has someone with good field experience—then retaining their services for daily oversight to ensure compliance with the approved design documents is worth every penny. Contractors often have numerous questions in the field regarding the designer's intent. This is most often seen during layout and mechanical trades coordination and to a lesser extent in the fine finish trades toward the end of the project. The hands-on involvement of the architect can keep your project moving effectively forward.

Selecting the Best Agreements

Use of standard form agreements from professional groups such as the American Institute of Architects, the Associated General Contractors, or those provided by a construction manager or general contractor will give the architect or the contractor a material advantage during contract negotiations. Standard form agreements do not protect owners from the consequence of asymmetric information and lack of an intermediary. Nor does the use of these form agreements with a few additional pages of riders undercut the inherent advantages to the design and construction team members who very much

desire to provide services with agreements that have served them well in the past.

To more fairly allocate the risk and protect the owner, contractual provisions are needed in the following areas:

- A complete narrative of the owner's business goals for the project that sets standards, tasks, and responsibilities for each team member as to meeting project dates, budgets, and usability requirements.
- The requirement that the construction manager or general contractor have an experienced project executive, specifically named in the agreement, who is capable of directing all phases of the work and running the critical weekly project meetings.
- Limiting the construction manager fee to its true profit (often 2 to 3 percent of the total cost of the work), without allowance for any additional markups on the construction manager's general conditions costs (those reimbursable at cost to the construction manager for cleanup, insurance, hoists, etc.), insurance costs, or subcontractors. Additional markups are often undetected by less experienced owner teams.
- Narrowly defining the construction manager's allowable general conditions costs to identifiable line items that must be supported by auditable invoices if they are to be reimbursed. Such costs are generally allowable for the construction manager's project management, field office equipment and supplies, site protection, hoists, site and cleanup labor, project security, and other direct expenses such as permits, nonlocal travel, and photocopies. The construction manager's charge for its home-office personnel should be a prorated portion of their annual salaries plus benefits as they undoubtedly will be assigned to one or more of the construction manager's other ongoing projects.

- Based on an itemized list of general conditions, the establishment of a not-to-exceed "cap" on general conditions costs, tied to the total cost of all subcontractor work on the project. The only exception to this limitation should occur when the project, through no fault of the construction manager, must be extended, in which case the direct costs of the construction manager (and not a prorated portion of established general conditions) for the period of such extension should be paid to the construction manager.

Design–Build

Perhaps the most direct method for controlling costs with a fixed-price contract is for an owner to use a design-build agreement. As discussed briefly in chapter 1, the owner contracts with a sole source provider—usually a company that includes architects, engineers, and contractors—who will provide both the design for the project as well as construction of a completed facility for a fixed sum.

By combining the design effort with the construction team, the owner eliminates the possibility of contractor claims alleging errors and omissions in the design documents. Similarly, unless the owner chooses to change the design after it has been approved, there are only a few instances where delay claims can be validly asserted to increase the fixed price shown in the contract.

Design-build is still most effective on buildings that do not require numerous unique design elements. Factories, warehouses, medical and laboratory research facilities, and many schools and highways lend themselves to this type of construction. Special design-build agreements should be carefully drafted to ensure that all design elements needed by the owner are included in the fixed construction cost of the project.

Insurance Costs for the Construction Team

Insurance costs are typically shown as a separate line item of reimbursable cost in contractor and construction manager contracts, and are calculated as a percentage of the cost of the work, usually from 1.75 to 2.5 percent, depending on the insurability of the contractor or construction manager. In most instances, the contractor advises the owner of the purported allocable cost for insurance to be borne by the owner as determined by the contractor's insurer. The contractor's insurance costs, however, are rarely audited to confirm the actual premium paid, or to confirm whether it was purchased at all. Moreover, the contractor will frequently maintain high deductibles and self-insured retentions to reduce premiums, but not pass the savings along to the owner. Accordingly, owners should request information on the construction manager's deductibles and self-insured retentions that could add costs to the budget. In addition, the owner must insist on documentation supporting the applicable insurance in writing directly from the issuing insurer, clearly setting forth all contract insurance requirements and applicable endorsements. Contractors have been known to furnish owners with fake certificates of insurance and then pocket the premiums. Finally, the contract must specifically provide for an audit of all annual insurance premiums that appear on the contractor's payment applications for insurance line items.

Winning the Change Order and Scheduling Games

Owners too often allow contractors to play the change order game unimpeded. According to one study, "less than half of the internal auditors whose companies regularly enter into construction contracts actually examine compliance issues and the propriety of construction costs." These are not kitchen renovations we're talking about here either, but make or break "multimillion and sometimes billion dollar-plus construction projects."[3] According to this view, some owners deserve to pay too much. But they do not. The seriousness and widespread nature of such unchecked cost overruns can best be appreciated by setting up a Google Alert for "construction cost overruns." To get a fuller sense of the nation's exposure in this area, one can visit www.brokenbuildings.com, which tracks the problem.

The complexity of the construction process and the numbers of firms and individuals involved at every level of a project will, inevitably, result in human error or unanticipated additional construction costs. Whether an error on the drawings, the discovery of pre-existing site conditions not determined by usual analysis, or delays from abnormal weather conditions, contractor change orders are not necessarily unwarranted. Nevertheless, change orders have a bad reputation with many owners and architects and should be carefully reviewed in every instance.

Too often, the "winner's curse" compels contractors to seek out excuses for change orders to make up the profit given away during the bid process. Owners without protective provisions in their agreements are without effective defenses when faced with the prospect of paying for an unwarranted or costly change order. The owner must accede to the cost, challenge it in some fashion, or refuse to have the work done. The latter two choices are costly and time consuming. Even if the contractor makes some concession on the first few change orders, as others ensue the owner usually gives up just to end the painful process.

At the very least, the contract should provide that no change order shall be chargeable to the owner unless it clearly states a fixed amount for a defined scope of work, the additional time that will be added to the project schedule, and the owner's signed approval in advance of any work performed. To avoid unwarranted change orders and to minimize their cost, owners would be wise to do the following:

- Use agreements that require the contractor to identify all errors and omissions during the bid process and specify that obvious or inferable information that could be provided by the architect prior to the start of construction will not be the basis for a later change order.
- Insist that all change orders be fully supported with documentation that demonstrates the full cost proposed by each subcontractor as well as any impact on the completion schedule. This will enable the owner to discuss with the architect any

possible alternatives to be pursued to minimize cost and delay. The contractor should not be allowed to reserve its rights to present additional delay claims at a later date.

- Establish in the contract a fixed cost for contractor profit (fee) but exclude additional overhead if the change order work does not require additional supervision that is otherwise covered by the contract's general conditions. An owner should reject any request for payment of home office overhead as this is included in the base general conditions costs.

- Provide for a one-day or shorter process to review disputed change orders by an arbiter selected in advance. The arbiter could be a mutual friend or the dean of the local school of architecture or engineering. The agreement should include a "no hostage" provision that states that in the event of a dispute over the amount of a proposed change order, the owner can order the work to proceed and not delay the project while the dispute is addressed by the parties either during or after the work is completed.

- Under no circumstances should a contractor be allowed to hold the project hostage, that is, stop work on the entire project or delay it because of a dispute over the cost of a change order. AIA standard agreements are often vague on this point, leaving owners without recourse. Provisions should be inserted that require the contractor to proceed with disputed change order work and provide recourse or resolution to an arbitration, if the amounts are small, or litigation, if the dispute is large.

Change orders almost always adversely impact the schedule, whether the contractor acknowledges so initially or "reserves its rights to calculate such impacts at a future date," a phrase contractors commonly use to conclude a change order request. The owner needs to promptly respond to such contractor language with firm command of what the real impacts to the project schedule are likely to be. To effectively do this, the owner or, ideally, its construction-savvy owner's representative, should be intimately familiar with industry-standard project management and scheduling software. For owners who build infrequently, it should consider purchasing scheduling software that is compatible with what its CM or GC uses. If the owner builds frequently, it should consider purchasing a full software suite (e.g., Primavera or Prolog), and make the CM or GC contractually required to use it as well.

In both instances, the electronic version, not simply a print out that can hide manual overrides made to the file, of the contractor's schedule should be evaluated using the software. Armed with the electronic version of the CM's schedule, the contractually required monthly update schedules issued by the CM can be "electronically" shadowed by the owner to verify that the project is actually progressing per the contract schedule. If a scheduling discrepancy is detected, action can be taken quickly to force the CM to address the problem immediately and mitigate further cost or delay to the project.

For complex projects, the owner may also require a separate weekly scheduling meeting with the CM—at least until buyouts are complete, the building is weathertight, and the mechanical trades are "roughed in."

The owner should ensure that there are milestone dates for substantial completion and final completion. These are the key dates that must be achieved by the construction team to enable the owner to plan accordingly, whether it is a corporation moving in its employees, a landlord commencing leaseholds, or a school beginning a new semester. Any revision to these dates must be accompanied by written notice from the contractor along with a detailed reason for the extension request. If the contractor, through its own actions, falls behind in the schedule, the contract should provide that the owner can demand that the delay period be overcome by overtime or weekend work at the expense of the contractor. Delays that are caused by the owner or its architect or engineers are compensable to the contractor. Similarly, delays to the opening caused by a contractor should be chargeable to the responsible subcontractor and/or construction manager. The contract should require the CM to submit with every delay claim a so-called critical path schedule analysis in electronic form that the owner can review prior to agreeing to any impact it may cause to the completion date.

Learn with Whom You Are Doing Business

It is essential that the owner have a complete business profile of all project members. Doing the requisite due diligence on the business and financial backgrounds of your architects, engineers, and construction team is a critical first step to a successful project. The following questions, at a minimum, should be raised and answered:

- Are each of the team members licensed in the state where the project is being performed? Homeowner contractors in many states now are required to have licenses that ensure that they will honor warranties and guarantees of performance if problems occur following construction.
- Use resources such as the internet and public documents to determine if team members have been subject to lawsuits or judgments that would warn you away from using them or, at the very least, make further inquiry into the background of any complaints filed against them. As owner, you are entrusting hundreds of thousands, and all too often millions, of dollars to companies that are small businesses. Caveat emptor!
- Check to see that contractors or construction managers have a satisfactory payment history to their subcontractors. Calls to prior owners will disclose any history or mechanics liens that evidenced problems in payment. Check bankruptcy files for predecessor companies who have failed financially with the principals who are now offering services on your new facility. Run a business search and secure a wealth of business information on each firm and its principals.
- Inquire about whether the contractor and its subs can secure payment and performance bonds. Such bonds are only available to financially secure contractors with a successful history of completed projects.

Treating the planning stage of each project with the same due diligence that one takes in checking out any substantial financial matter will reap dividends and avoid countless headaches.

Contingencies, Allowances, and Savings Clauses

Contractors are adept at defining budgetary issues that are difficult, if not impossible, for owners to interpret or contest. Many are self-serving; some have evolved over time to avoid risks that the contractor wishes to sidestep. In some cases, these provisions exist solely to cover up mistakes made by the construction manager or the subcontractors with costs passed on to the owner.

When construction managers or contractors use the term "contingency," they almost always use it to define matters that cannot be anticipated. Fair, but necessary costs that are bound to arise during every project should not be considered a contingency. Last-minute owner-initiated changes are valid contingencies; prudent owners may wish to keep a small percentage in their own budgets for such last-minute changes.

Contingencies are prudent during design phase project budgeting with a CM, but owners should resist conceding that the contractor's proposal includes a line item for contingencies during the construction process. Construction managers often insist that at least five percent be added to their budget or GMP, then fail to inform the unsophisticated owner that the funds will be allocated as they see fit, for example to correct the errant placement of a wall or supplement a subcontractor who bid too low and cannot finish the job for the amount budgeted.

If an owner wishes to concede to a construction manager's request for a contingency, the total control over such funds ought to rest exclusively with the owner. In that case, if the construction manager reports that contingency funds are needed to bail out a subcontractor or replace an incorrectly built wall, the owner can make the decision whether to allocate a portion of the contingency monies on a case-by-case basis. Sometimes, permitting such discretionary funds can show good faith to those working on a complex, costly project. What must be made clear, however, is that the contingency fund belongs to the owner. It is not there to clean up messes made by subcontractors who cannot get it right.

The term "allowance" is used when one or more discrete elements of the project have not been finalized, whether by the architect or the owner, prior to the design documents being issued for final pricing by the construction manager or contractor. For example, the owner may be uncertain as to the final selection of kitchen equipment to be installed. This may be so for a number of reasons. To enable the contractor to finalize a budget number, an allowance, that is, a number that reasonably reflects the maximum permissible cost for these items, is inserted into the budget. Only if the owner ultimately approves equipment of a higher standard than that reflected in the allowance will the budget be increased. By establishing realistic allowances an owner is in no danger of seeing the project budget increased.

Construction managers on fast-track projects sometimes insist on a savings clause that entitles them to a share of any savings that they achieve by bringing in the final construction cost for less than the GMP. While sounding fair, such clauses are generally proposed when the construction manager envisions the opportunity to play with the GMP to concoct false savings. Since the GMP will likely be based on incomplete drawings, it is only understandable that the construction manager will establish a highly conservative GMP, if only for a better chance to show the owner it can buy the subcontractors for less than the corresponding GMP line items as the buyout process proceeds. With a savings clause, where the so-called savings are to be shared on a percentage basis, say 60 percent to the owner and 40 percent to the construction manager, the construction manager has a large incentive to price the preliminary budget high.

It is important to remember that the construction manager is being paid a fee to establish a realistic budget and negotiate contracts with the trades that stay within the budget. There is no need for an additional incentive for the construction manager. Moreover, absent an independent source to determine if the budget amounts are realistic, the asymmetry of information in this business deal rests heavily in favor of the construction manager. Once contingency and allowance line-items are in the budget, they are almost invariably spent. Holding the line on these items is almost impossible, as the information related to these costs rests solely with the construction manager. Where an owner has control over the project, these items will reflect actual items designed and approved on the basis of the project budget in detail.

Architects, Engineers, and Other Design Consultants

Architects, engineers, and those who contribute design ideas for a project are only as valuable as their ability to contribute designs that add value and avoid excessive cost to the project. With today's emphasis on "starchitects," many owners fail to understand that some types of design elements may be difficult to build in the field and will add incremental or premium cost to the project for which there will be little or no return.

When dealing with the design team, consider the following:

- Owners should ascertain not only whether an architect has previously designed "pretty" buildings. They should be equally, if not more, concerned with whether the architect knows how to prepare construction documents from which the contractor can build with available materials and in the time frame called for in the contract. Ensure that prior clients of the architect did not face costly overruns because of the inadequacy of the construction drawings. Similarly, ask about the experience of the individuals who will be assigned by the architect to work with the contractors in the field. If they lack actual field experience, the potential for costly conflicts increases.
- For large or complex projects, it is not uncommon for the design team to need as long as a year or more to finalize the design documents before bidding can take place. The typical phases are concept, schematic, design development, and con-

struction documents. Thousands of decisions must be made and detailed drawings of great complexity must be prepared for each phase. However, for relatively straightforward, repetitive projects such as residential or office towers, architects may find it appropriate to proceed from the schematic phase, where critical decisions on design and the overall parameters of the project have been set, directly to the construction document phase, in effect bypassing design development. In this way, a project that might otherwise take as much as a year to design can be cut to nine or ten months. The owner can then get the construction documents out to bid and start construction several months sooner. The benefit to the architect? He or she gets the full fee and frees up the design team for other projects that much faster. A true win-win situation.

- By virtue of the U.S. Copyright Act, which automatically conveys intellectual property rights to a designer upon conception of the design, all designers own the proprietary rights to their design documents unless they convey them away by a written contract.[4] Owners do not wish to be held hostage in the event of a dispute with a member of the design team. As these disputes can and do arise, it is imperative that the equities here be balanced fairly. Accordingly, the contract with the architect and all other designers for the project should allow the architect to retain the copyright but grant a license to the owner for the right to use all of the design documents developed for the particular project through to completion, even in the event of a dispute. No right should be conveyed to the owner for any further use of the design documents, for example, a second, similar building, without the consent of the architect and fair compensation for such use.

- Should the owner choose not to retain an owner's representative for assistance during the construction phase, the architect should be retained to provide full-time representation or daily visits to the site. This is not typical, as standard form agreements only call for the architect to visit the site "at intervals appropriate to the phase of the work." But in fact, the architect is often needed at the job site on a daily basis. Questions abound from the construction manager or the contractors during the work—from requests for clarification of the design intent to necessary design changes needed to address field conditions. An experienced field operative who has worked closely with construction teams can vastly improve the quality of the work and the speed at which necessary issues can be resolved.

To prevent your organization—your business, your government agency, your family—from paying more than it has to for its physical infrastructure, it is absolutely essential that you understand the construction industry's history, its economic structure, and the incentives facing its major players. *Broken Buildings* has avoided a banal list of business dos and don'ts. Such a list would have had a short shelf life, because contractors could quickly adapt to it. Instead, *Broken Buildings* has been written to help you, the potential purchaser of an office building, a home, a highway, a dam, to understand how the construction industry functions, why it is so inefficient, and so likely to try to bust your budget. Armed with the most powerful weapon in any business arsenal—information—you will have a fighting chance to get the building you want, when you want it, for the price you agreed upon.

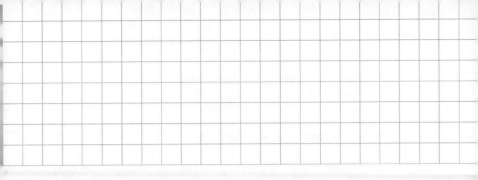

Notes

The epigraph appearing on page v by architect Moshe Safdie appears as quoted in Martin Mayer, *The Builders: Houses, People, Neighborhoods, Governments, Money* (New York: W. W. Norton and Company, 1978), 253.

1. Barry B. LePatner and Sidney M. Johnson, *Structural and Foundation Failures: A Casebook for Architects, Engineers and Lawyers* (New York: McGraw-Hill Book Company, 1982).

2. U.S. Congress, House Committee on Science and Technology, *Structural Failures in Public Facilities*, March 15, 1984, House Rep. 98-621, 8, 9, 12, 13.

3. Thomas L. Friedman, *The World Is Flat: A Brief History of the Twenty-first Century* (New York: Farrar Strauss & Giroux, 2005).

Chapter One

1. Ernesto Henriod et al., *The Construction Industry: Issues and Strategies in Developing Countries* (Washington, D.C.: The World Bank, 1984), 30–31; Andre Manseau and George Seaden, eds., *Innovation in Construction: An International Review of Public Policies* (London: Spon Press, 2001), 2–3; National Research Council Committee on the International Construction Industry, *Building for Tomorrow: Global Enterprise and the U.S. Construction Industry* (Washington, D.C.: National Academy Press, 1988), 11.

2. U.S. Census Bureau Projections by Age, Sex, Race and Hispanic Origins, 2004; Arthur C. Nelson, "Toward a New Metropolis: The Opportunity to Rebuild America" (Brookings Institution, December 2004). Throughout this book, we cite statistics compiled by various government agencies, including the Census Bureau and the Bureau of Economic Analysis, all from various unpublished online sources. As these agencies frequently change their Web sites but are unlikely to remove data already in digital form, we point readers only

to the agency where the data originated trusting that they will be able to navigate the agencies' sites, whatever they may look like in the future, and find the data alluded to herein.

3. John Gertner, "Chasing Ground," *New York Times,* October 16, 2005.

4. Booth Mooney, *Builders for Progress: The Story of the Associated General Contractors of America* (New York: McGraw-Hill 1965), 8.

5. From its initial publication in 1939, this book has been read by generations of young people. It tells the story of Mike and his steam shovel, Mary Ann, as they dig canals, cut wide mountain passes, and excavate building foundations together. Mike and Mary Ann travel to Popperville to accept one final challenge—build the town cellar in just one day or be replaced by more modern machinery. The end of the story is a testament to hard work and ingenuity that continues to delight readers of all ages.

6. LowerManhattan.info Web site: Envisioning the Future / Looking Ahead / Transportation: http://www.lowermanhattan.info/future/looking_ahead/transportation/airport.aspx (accessed March 26, 2007).

7. Malcom Gladwell, "Open Secrets," *New Yorker,* January 8, 2007.

8. Jonathan R. Macey, "A Pox on Both Your Houses: Enron, Sarbones-Oxley and the Debate Concerning the Relative Efficacy of Mandatory Versus Enabling Rules," *Washington University Law Quarterly* 81 (2003): 329.

9. For one of many egregious cases, see the February 2005 news release from the office of Charlie Crist, the attorney general of Florida, "Crist Sues Ex-contractor over Hurricane Service Plans," http://myfloridalegal.com/newsrel.nsf/newsreleases/F1C7A871CA0662B785256F9D00570C0D (accessed April 16, 2005).

10. Raphael Lewis and Sean P. Murphy, "Artery Errors Cost More than $1b," *Boston Globe,* February 9, 2003, http://www.boston.com/globe/metro/packages/bechtel/020903.shtml (accessed April 16, 2005).

11. See, for example: Peter Keating, "How to Fix the MTA," *New York,* February 28, 2005, http://nymag.com/nymetro/news/features/11161/ (March 26, 2007); Stuart W. Elliott, "Cabbie's Climb to Buy 11 Madison," *The Real Deal,* March 2004, http://www.therealdeal.net/issues/March_2004/1078688203.php (March 26, 2007); Memo in Support: MTA Reform (A. 7998), Sponsored by Assembly Members Brodsky, Nolan et. al., http://www.straphangers.org/mtareform/supportmemo.htm (March 26, 2007); and Skyscraper Press Web site, installment 39, November 14, 2005, http://www.greatgridlock.net/NYC/nycpress.html (March 26, 2007).

12. Annual report to SEC 2005, Las Vegas Sands Corp., p. 48. Legal Proceedings.

13. Hubble Smith, *Las Vegas Review Journal,* December 21, 2005.

14. U.S. Census Bureau, County Business Patterns, 1998–2002.

15. The classic treatment of this problem, which is known as adverse selection, is described by George Akerloff, "The Market for 'Lemons': Quality Uncertainty and the Market Mechanism," *Quarterly Journal of Economics* (August 1970): 488–500.

16. "H. Wayne Huizenga Chairman Huizenga Holdings, Inc.," The Horatio Alger

Association of Distinguished Americans, http://www.horatioalger.com/members/member_info.cfm?memberid=hui92.

17. For details see Robert E. Wright, *The Wealth of Nations Rediscovered: Integration and Expansion in American Financial Markets, 1780–1850* (New York: Cambridge University Press, 2002).

18. James Surowiecki, *The Wisdom of Crowds: Why the Many Are Smarter Than the Few and How Collective Wisdom Shapes Business, Economies, Societies and Nations* (New York: Doubleday, 2004).

19. Other observers have hinted at this. See, for example, Leo Grebler, *Large Scale Housing and Real Estate Firms: Analysis of a New Business Enterprise* (New York: Praeger, 1973), 157.

20. Douglass C. North, *Understanding the Process of Economic Change* (Princeton: Princeton University Press, 2005), 122.

21. Jay MacDonald ("Don't Let Shoddy Contractors Demolish Your Budget," Bankrate.com [May 10, 2006] at http://biz.yahoo.com/brn/060510/18447.html) argues that the Better Business Bureau *can* be helpful. We agree but note that it often is not.

Chapter Two

1. Alex Frangos, "Construction Sticker Shock: Optimism, Pricey Materials Help to Fuel a 10% Leap in the Cost of a New Building," *Wall Street Journal,* March 23, 2005, B1.

2. Department of Commerce, Bureau of Economic Analysis. Chart: "Percentage Contribution to Private GDP by Sector, 1959–1999."

3. Department of Commerce, Bureau of Economic Analysis. Chart: "GDP by Industry Group as a Percentage of GDP, 2000."

4. Donald Adams, "Residential Construction Industry in the Early Nineteenth Century," *Journal of Economic History* 35 (1975): 794; Steven Allen, "Why Construction Industry Productivity is Declining," *Review of Economics and Statistics* 67 (1985): 661; David Arditi and Krishna Mochtar, "Trends in Productivity Improvement in the U.S. Construction Industry," *Construction Management and Economics* (2000): 15–27; W. C. Clark, "The Construction Industry: Outlook for 1930," *Review of Economic Statistics* 12 (1930): 23; George H. Hull, Jr., "The Construction Industry and Business Depressions," *Annals of the American Academy of Political and Social Science* 154 (1931): 148–52; National Research Council Committee on the International Construction Industry, *Building for Tomorrow: Global Enterprise and the U.S. Construction Industry* (Washington, D.C.: National Academy Press, 1988), ix, 1–2; Robert E. Yuskavage and Erich Strassner, "Gross Domestic Product by Industry for 2002," *Survey of Current Business* (May 2003): 9.

5. U.S. Census Bureau, Chart: "Total Construction Put in Place, 1993–2004."

6. U.S. Census Bureau, County Business Patterns. Chart: "Total Employment in Construction, 1998–2004."

7. U.S. Bureau of Labor Statistics, Chart: "Employment and Monthly Earnings. Total Non-Agricultural, Goods Producing Employment in the U.S., 1950–2000."

189

8. U.S. Bureau of Labor Statistics, Chart: "Employment and Monthly Earnings. U.S. Employment by Sector, 1980–2001."

9. Following a long tradition that dates back to at least Frank Lloyd Wright, we often use the term "home" instead of "house" or "housing" because the latter especially seems too inhuman, too akin to the term "stabling," as of horses. For a discussion, see Burnham Kelly, "Problems and Potential: The Housing Industry Today," in Burnham Kelly, ed., *Design and the Production of Houses* (New York: McGraw Hill, 1959), 2.

10. U.S. Census Bureau. Chart: "Relative Importance of Maintenance and Improvements, 1963–2003."

11. Kelly, "Problems and Potential," 8; Peter Philips, "The United States: Dual Worlds: The Two Growth Paths in U.S. Construction," in Gerhard Bosch and Peter Philips, eds., *Building Chaos: An International Comparison of Deregulation in the Construction Industry* (New York: Routledge, 2003), 162.

12. U.S. Census Bureau, Chart: "Value of Construction Put in Place, 2006." Despite frequent claims to the contrary, the Social Security system as currently constituted is not doomed to failure, provided U.S. GDP grows quickly enough. See Dean Baker and Mark Weisbrot, *Social Security: The Phony Crisis* (Chicago: University of Chicago Press, 1999).

13. The standard metric, derived from U.S. Bureau of Labor Statistics and U.S. Census Bureau times series by Paul Teicholz, professor emeritus of civil engineering at Stanford University, measures constant contract dollars per field-work hour to conclude that construction industry productivity declined nearly 0.5 percent per year from 1964 to 1999, while labor productivity in other nonfarm industries rose 1.7 percent annually. True: some firms do better than this, and where mechanization has been applied, specific task productivity has been observed to increase. Such capital-intensive methods however are spread thin and unevenly across an industry still filled with small family-owned firms. Also true: construction today turns out a higher quality product (i.e., buildings that perform more functions), which conventional output measures do not capture. Yet quality improvements have been common in all industries, and comparable data is unavailable. Possibly true: construction statistics are too flawed to accurately determine productivity in the sector. See Paul Teicholz, "Reverse Productivity Declines," *Engineering News Record*, December 13, 1999; Paul Teicholz, "U.S. Construction Labor Productivity Trends, 1970–1998," *Journal of Construction Engineering and Management*, September/October 2001. For evidence of selective improvements, see "Study Concludes Productivity Is Up, Just Not Enough," *Engineering News Record*, July 5, 2004; Eric Allmon, Carl T. Haas, John D. Borcherding, and Paul M. Goodrum, "U.S. Construction Labor Productivity Trends," *Journal of Construction Engineering and Management* 126 (March/April 2000): 97–105; Eddy Rojas and Peerapong Aramvareekul, "Is Construction Labor Productivity Really Declining?" *Journal of Construction Engineering and Management* 129 (January–February 2003): 41–46.

14. Robert Jensen, "Operation Breakthrough: The Systems, the Sites and the Designers Are Chosen. The Question Now: On What Standards Should the Program Be Judged?" *Architectural Record* (April 1970): 138.

15. Chuck Kluenker, "Risk vs. Conflict of Interest: What Every Owner Should Consider When Using Construction Management," *CM eJournal* (January 2001): 1–18.

16. Michael Horman and Russell Kenley, "Quantifying Levels of Wasted Time in Construction with Meta-Analysis," *Journal of Construction Engineering & Management* 131 (January 2005): 52–61.

17. The authors are aware that construction data is notoriously difficult to obtain and compare. Precise data are not central to the discussion here because we use only general descriptive statistics and simple "eye-ball" tests. Some series may be somewhat off. Others are misleading because they do not differentiate between contract construction and "force account" or do-it-yourself work. Some series include maintenance, others do not, and so forth. For a discussion of some of the difficulties with construction statistics, which has been a longstanding problem, see Business Roundtable, *More Construction for the Money: Summary Report of the Construction Industry Cost Effectiveness Project* (January 1983), 11, 17–19, 73–74; Peter Cassimatis, *Economics of the Construction Industry* (New York: National Industrial Conference Board, 1969), 3–4; Gerald Finkel, *The Economics of the Construction Industry* (Armonk, N.Y.: M. E. Sharpe, 1997), 56–63; Burnham Kelly, "Problems and Potential: The Housing Industry Today," in Burnham Kelly, ed., *Design and the Production of Houses* (New York: McGraw Hill, 1959), 24–25; Marc Linder, *Projecting Capitalism: A History of the Internationalization of the Construction Industry* (Westport, Conn.: Greenwood Press, 1994), 165–69, 182; Andre Manseau and George Seaden, eds., *Innovation in Construction: An International Review of Public Policies* (London: Spon Press, 2001), 3. Ernest Fisher of Columbia University once noted that "more facts are known, literally, about a single agricultural product, peanuts, than about urban real estate."

18. David Arditi and Krishna Mochtar, "Trends in Productivity Improvement in the U.S. Construction Industry," *Construction Management and Economics* (2000): 15–27; Gerald Finkel, "The American Construction Industry: An Overview," in Hamid Azari-Rad, Peter Philips, and Mark Prus, eds., *The Economics of Prevailing Wage Laws* (Burlington, Vt.: Ashgate, 2005), 44–49; C. A. Foster, "Construction Management and Design-Build / Fast Track Construction: A Solution Which Uncovers a Problem for the Surety," *Law and Contemporary Problems* 46 (1983): 116–17n119; Preston Haskell, "Construction Industry Productivity," Working Paper (December 2004); Michael Horman and Russell Kenley, "Quantifying Levels of Wasted Time in Construction with Meta-Analysis," *Journal of Construction Engineering and Management* 131 (January 2005): 52–61; Manseau and Seaden, *Innovation in Construction,* 2–3; Teicholz, "Labor Productivity Declines in the Construction Industry: Causes and Remedies," *AECBytes Viewpoint* (April 14, 2004); Richard L. Tucker, "Construction Technologies," in *Technology and the Future of the U.S. Construction Industry* (Washington, D.C.: AIA Press, 1986), 87. Paul M. Teicholz, "Reverse Productivity Declines," *Engineering News Record* (December 13, 1999), 59; "U.S. Construction Labor Productivity Trends, 1970–1998," *Journal of Construction Engineering and Management* (September/October 2001), 427.

19. Natalie Keith, "The Reality of Risk: Design and Construction Industries Creating New Standards for Building Security," *New York Construction,* September 1, 2004.

20. Business Roundtable, *More Construction for the Money: Summary Report of the Construction Industry Cost Effectiveness Project* (January 1983), 11.

21. Bureau of Labor Statistics data indicate that the absolute value of percentage changes in year-to-year construction employment were very high in the 1940s and 1950s but dropped to about the same level as changes in manufacturing employment (around 5 percent), by the early 1960s. In the mid-1970s, the two series again diverge, with manufacturing changes dropping to around 2 percent and construction to around 5 or 6 percent. Construction productivity was flat, or at best very low, over all three periods.

22. Rojas and Aramvareekul, "Is Construction Labor Productivity Really Declining?" Lawrence White to Robert E. Wright, private communication, February 27, 2006.

23. John D. Allison, "An Analysis of Levittown, New York, with Particular Reference to Demand Satisfaction from Mass Produced Low Cost Housing" (Ph.D. diss., New York University, 1956), 71; Peter Philips, "The United States: Dual Worlds: The Two Growth Paths in U.S. Construction," in Gerhard Bosch and Peter Philips, eds., *Building Chaos: An International Comparison of Deregulation in the Construction Industry* (New York: Routledge, 2003), 162.

24. Luke Grant, "Seasonal Occupation in the Building Trades: Causes and Effects," *Annals of the American Academy of Political and Social Science* 33 (1909): 129–37; M. R. Lefkoe, *The Crisis in Construction: There Is An Answer* (Washington, D.C.: Bureau of National Affairs, Inc., 1970), 45.

25. According to the National Archives Web site records of the Temporary National Economic Committee (Record Group 144.1, 1938–41), the TNEC was "a joint Congressional-Executive branch committee, composed of members of both houses of Congress and representatives of several Executive departments and commissions, by joint resolution of Congress, June 16, 1938 (52 Stat. 705). Functions: Studied monopoly and concentration of economic power, and made recommendations for legislation" (http://www.archives .gov/research/guide-fed-records/groups/144.html). See also "The Industry Capitalism Forgot," *Fortune* (August 1947), 61; Business Roundtable, *More Construction,* 91; John Keats, *The Crack in the Picture Window* (Boston: Houghton Mifflin, 1956); Kelly, "Problems and Potential," 4.

26. Except where otherwise noted, this section is based on Gerhard Bosch and Peter Philips, *Building Chaos: An International Comparison of Deregulation in the Construction Industry* (New York: Routledge, 2003); Gerald Finkel, *The Economics of the Construction Industry* (Armonk, N.Y.: M.E. Sharpe, 1997), 3–5; Ernesto Henriod et al., *The Construction Industry: Issues and Strategies in Developing Countries* (Washington, D.C.: World Bank, 1984); William W. Lewis, *The Power of Productivity: Wealth, Poverty, and the Threat to Global Stability* (Chicago: University of Chicago Press, 2004). See especially the main empirical studies underlying Lewis's *The Power of Productivity,* all of which registered users can download gratis from the McKinsey Global Institute at http://www.mckinsey.com: "U.S.

Productivity Growth, 1995–2000: Understanding the Importance of Information Technology Relative to Other Factors" (Washington, 2001). See also other McKinsey reports: "India: The Growth Imperative" (Mumbai, 2001); "Why the Japanese Economy Is Not Growing: Micro Barriers to Productivity Growth" (Washington, 2000); "Poland's Economic Performance" (Washington, 2000); "Driving Productivity and Growth in the UK Economy" (London, 1998); "Productivity Led Growth for Korea" (Seoul, Washington, 1998); "Productivity: The Key to an Accelerated Development Path for Brazil" (Sao Paulo, Washington, 1998); "Boosting Dutch Economic Performance" (Amsterdam, 1997); "Removing Barriers to Growth and Employment in France and Germany" (Frankfurt, Paris, Washington, 1997); "Australia's Economic Performance" (Sydney, 1995); "Sweden's Economic Performance" (Stockholm, 1995). Another useful source for international comparison is Manseau and Seaden, *Innovation in Construction*.

27. Allan Collard-Wexler, "Plant Turnover and Demand Fluctuations in the Ready-Mix Concrete Industry," Working Paper (November 10, 2005); Alberto Salvo, "Inferring Conduct under the Threat of Entry: The Case of the Brazilian Cement Industry" (paper delivered at the London School of Economics, October 2004).

28. For a further explication of the difficulties that arise from a lack of clear property rights, see Hernando de Soto, *The Mystery of Capital: Why Capitalism Triumphs in the West and Fails Everywhere Else* (New York: Basic Books, 2000). The mortgage market has long been a crucial aspect of the U.S. construction industry. Clark, "The Construction Industry," 23–29.

29. Adam Smith, *An Inquiry into the Nature and Causes of the Wealth of Nations* (New York: Modern Library, 1937), book 1, chapters 1–3.

30. Martin Mayer, *The Builders: Houses, People, Neighborhoods, Governments, Money* (New York: W. W. Norton and Company, 1978), 105.

31. "Japan's Construction Industry" *Asia Pulse* (October 2003). The "Big Six" are Kajima, Takenaka, Obayashi, Kumagai, Taisei, and Shimizu. For an overview, see Sidney Levy, *Japan's Big Six: Case Studies of Japan's Largest Contractors* (New York: McGraw-Hill, 1993), 13.

32. Levy, *Japan's Big Six*, 21–22.

33. Richard A. Belle, Harvey M. Bernstein, and Andre Manseau, "The U.S. Federal Policy in Support of Innovation in the Design and Construction Industry," in Manseau and Seaden, *Innovation in Construction*, 373; Mayer, *Builders*, 3–4.

34. U.S. Census Bureau, County Business Patterns, 1998–2002. Charts: "Construction Industry Fragmentation: Percentage of Firms of Different Sizes" and "Construction Industry Fragmentation: Number of Firms of Different Sizes."

35. Business Roundtable, *More Construction*, 12; Cassimatis, *Economics of the Construction Industry*, 26–41; Ryan Conley, "Large Companies Change Complexion of Ocala, Fl., Construction Industry," *Ocala Star-Banner* (August 15, 2004); Finkel, *The Economics of the Construction Industry*, 32–33; Leo Grebler, *Large Scale Housing and Real Estate Firms: Analysis of a New Business Enterprise* (New York: Praeger, 1973), 158; Kelly, "Problems and Potential," 9–11; M. R. Lefkoe, *The Crisis in Construction* , 26; McConnell, *State of the U.S. Construction Industry*, 3.

193

36. United States Department of Labor: Bureau of Labor Statistics.

37. U.S. Census Bureau, County Business Patterns, 1998–2002. Charts: "Heavy Construction Firms by Number of Employees" and "Commercial Construction Firms by Number of Employees."

38. "Mechanics' Liens and Surety Bonds in the Building Trades," *Yale Law Journal* 68 (1958): 167; David Gerstel, *Running a Successful Construction Company* (Newtown, Conn.: Taunton Press, 2002), 18–20, 84; William Keating, "Emerging Patterns of Corporate Entry Into Housing" (Center for Real Estate and Urban Economics Institute, University of California, Berkeley, 1973), 28–34; National Research Council, *Building for Tomorrow*, 27–31; Lefkoe, *The Crisis in Construction*, 26; Vernon Swaback, "Production Dwellings: An Opportunity for Excellence," *Land Economics* 47 (1971): 332.

39. Marc Linder, *Projecting Capitalism: A History of the Internationalization of the Construction Industry* (Westport, Conn.: Greenwood Press, 1994), 170, 178.

40. Linder, *Projecting Capitalism*, 17.

41. Bosch and Philips, introduction to *Building Chaos*, 3; Cassimatis, *Economics of the Construction Industry*, 29–36; Gerstel, *Running a Successful Construction Company*, 14.

42. Gerstel, *Running a Successful Construction Company*, 15.

43. John D. Allison, "An Analysis of Levittown, New York, with Particular Reference to Demand Satisfaction from Mass Produced Low Cost Housing," 2.

44. The classic exposition of this point is Ronald Coase, "The Nature of the Firm," 4 *Economica* (1937): 386–405. For its extension to cover postcontractual opportunistic behavior, see Benjamin Klein, Robert Crawford, and Armen Alchian, "Vertical Integration, Appropriable Rents, and the Competitive Contracting Process," *Journal of Law and Economics* 21 (1978): 297–326. For its explicit application to construction firms, see Howard Seymour, *The Multinational Construction Industry* (New York: Croom Helm, 1987), 31–33 and Lawrence Wai Chung Lai, "The Coasian Market-Firm Dichotomy and Subcontracting in the Construction Industry," *Construction Management and Economics* (2000): 355–62.

45. For further explication of these points, see Oliver Williamson and Sidney Winter, eds., *The Nature of the Firm: Origins, Evolution, and Development* (New York: Oxford University Press, 1993).

46. A superb introduction is still Alfred D. Chandler, Jr., *The Visible Hand: The Managerial Revolution in American Business* (Cambridge, Mass.: Harvard University Press, 1977).

47. John Buttrick, "The Inside Contract System," *Journal of Economic History* 12 (1952): 205–21.

48. David Nasaw, *Andrew Carnegie* (New York: Penguin Press, 2006).

49. George Baker and George D. Smith, *The New Financial Capitalists: Kohlberg Kravis Roberts and the Creation of Corporate Value* (New York: Cambridge University Press, 1998).

50. Armen Alchian, "Uncertainty, Evolution, and Economic Theory," *Journal of Political Economy* 58 (1950): 211–21; Cassimatis, *Economics of the Construction Industry*, 57–60; Grebler, *Large Scale Housing and Real Estate Firms*, 40–71.

51. Cassimatis, *Economics of the Construction Industry*, 123.

52. Gerstel, *Running a Successful Construction Company*, 228.
53. Maged Georgy, Luh-Maan Chang, and Lei Zhang, "Engineering Performance in the U.S. Industrial Construction Sector," *Cost Engineering* 47 (2005): 27–36.
54. John Crispo, "Labour-Management Relations in the Construction Industry: The Findings of the Goldenberg Commission," *Canadian Journal of Economics and Political Science* 29 (1963): 349.
55. "Mechanics' Liens and Surety Bonds in the Building Trades," *Yale Law Journal* 68 (1958): 139; "Allocation of Risk in the Construction Industry: The Non-professional Owner and His Construction Manager," *Law and Contemporary Problems* 46 (1983): 145; Finkel, *The Economics of the Construction Industry*, 64–71; Burnham Kelly, *Design and the Production of Houses* (New York: McGraw Hill, 1959), xii.
56. Leo Grebler and Leland Burns, *Construction Cycles in the United States, 1950–1978* (April 1981); Philips, "The United States: Dual Worlds," in *Building Chaos*, 162.
57. Patricia Hillebrandt, *Economic Theory and the Construction Industry* (London: Macmillan, 1974), 11; Michael Horman and Russell Kenley, "Quantifying Levels of Wasted Time in Construction with Meta-Analysis," *Journal of Construction Engineering and Management* 131 (January 2005): 52–61.
58. Bosch and Peter, introduction to *Building Chaos*, 10; Robert Eccles, "Bureaucratic Versus Craft Administration: The Relationship of Market Structure to the Construction Firm," *Administrative Science Quarterly* 26 (1981): 449–69; Gerstel, *Running a Successful Construction Company*, 229.
59. Allison, "An Analysis of Levittown, New York, with Particular Reference to Demand Satisfaction from Mass Produced Low Cost Housing," 73–74.
60. Gerstel, *Running a Successful Construction Company*, 233; Behlul Usdiken, Zeynep Sozen, and Hayat Enbiyaoglu, "Strategies and Boundaries: Subcontracting in Construction," *Strategic Management Journal* 9 (1988): 633–37.
61. Albert Dietz, Castle Day, and Burnham Kelly, "Design and the Industrialized House," in Burnham Kelly, ed., *Design and the Production of Houses* (New York: McGraw Hill, 1959), 138–39; Eccles, "Bureaucratic Versus Craft Administration," 452.
62. "Mechanics' Liens and Surety Bonds in the Building Trades," *Yale Law Journal* 68 (1958): 138–71; Robert Axelrod, *The Evolution of Cooperation* (New York: Basic, 1984); Paul DiMaggio, ed., *The Twenty-First-Century-Firm: Changing Economic Organization in International Perspective* (Princeton: Princeton University Press, 2001); Robert Eccles, "The Quasi-Firm in the Construction Industry," *Journal of Economic Behavior and Organization* 2 (1981): 335–57; Gerstel, *Running a Successful Construction Company*, 22, 197; Charles Goetz and Robert Scott, "Principles of Relational Contracts," *Virginia Law Review* 67 (1981): 1,089–1,150; Lefkoe, *The Crisis in Construction*, 32; Philips, "The United States: Dual Worlds," in *Building Chaos*, 163; Oliver Williamson, "The Logic of Economic Organization," in Oliver Williamson and Sidney Winter, eds., *The Nature of the Firm: Origins, Evolution, and Development* (New York: Oxford University Press, 1993), 90–116.
63. As quoted in Mayer, *Builders*, 249.
64. "Mechanics' Liens and Surety Bonds in the Building Trades," *Yale Law Journal*

195

68 (1958): 138–71; Douglas Dyer and John Kagel, "Bidding in Common Value Auctions: How the Commercial Construction Industry Corrects for the Winner's Curse," *Management Science* 42 (1996): 1,471; Eccles, "The Quasi-Firm in the Construction Industry," 335–57; Charles Foster, "Competition and Organization in Building," *Journal of Industrial Economics* 12 (1964): 163–74; Arthur Stinchcombe, "Bureaucratic and Craft Administration of Production: A Comparative Study," *Administrative Science Quarterly* 4 (1959): 168–87.

65. Ralph Stephenson, *Project Partnering for the Design and Construction Industry* (New York: John Wiley & Sons, 1996), 386–425.

66. Except where otherwise noted, these cases are adapted from Stephenson, *Project Partnering for the Design and Construction Industry,* 62–86, 109–111.

67. Norma Cohen, "Lipton Plans Building Shake-Up: In a Setback for the Construction Industry, a Leading Property Developer Aims to Break with Tradition and Cut Prices," *Financial Times,* August 26, 2003.

68. "The Rise of the Green Building," *Economist,* December 4, 2004, 18.

Chapter Three

1. "The Industry Capitalism Forgot," *Fortune* 36 (August 1947), 61–67, 167–70.

2. Martin Mayer, *The Builders: Houses, People, Neighborhoods, Governments, Money* (New York: W. W. Norton and Company, 1978), 21; Richard Plunz, *A History of Housing in New York City: Dwelling Type and Social Change in the American Metropolis* (New York: Columbia University Press, 1990): 151, 153–56, 161, 165–67; H. H. Vivian, "A Novel Attempt at Co-operative Production in the Building Trades," *Economic Journal* 6 (1922): 270–72.

3. Plunz, *A History of Housing in New York City,* 101.

4. George H. Hull, Jr., "The Construction Industry and Business Depressions," *Annals of the American Academy of Political and Social Science* 154 (1931): 148–52; Royal E. Montgomery, "Graft in the Building Trades," *University Journal of Business* 4 (1926): 312.

5. Richard Bender, *A Crack in the Rear-View Mirror: A View of Industrialized Building* (New York: Van Nostrand Reinhold Company, 1973),56; Gerald Finkel, *The Economics of the Construction Industry* (Armonk, N.Y.: M. E. Sharpe, 1997), 85; Gilbert Herbert, *Pioneers of Prefabrication: The British Contribution in the Nineteenth Century* (Baltimore: Johns Hopkins University Press, 1978); Mayer, *Builders,* 257.

6. Jim Barlow, "Edison Built It, but Few Came," *Houston Chronicle,* January 28, 1997, 1; Jeanette Almada, "New Life for Abandoned and Derelict Edison Homes," *New York Times,* January 14, 1996, 9. History Channel television video, "Modern Marvels: Failed Inventions: Edison," available at http://www.thehistorychannel.com/broadband/clipview/index.jsp?id=mm_edison_broadband.

7. William Keating, "Emerging Patterns of Corporate Entry Into Housing" (Center for Real Estate and Urban Economics Institute, University of California, Berkeley, 1973), 6–7; Mayer, *Builders,* 264; Bernard Spring, "Advances in House Design," in Burnham Kelly, ed., *Design and the Production of Houses* (New York:

McGraw Hill, 1959), 60; Robert E. Wright and George D. Smith, *Mutually Beneficial: The Guardian and Life Insurance in America* (New York: New York University Press, 2004), 338, 458 n10.

8. Albert Dietz, Castle Day, and Burnham Kelly, "Design and the Industrialized House," in Burnham Kelly, ed., *Design and the Production of Houses* (New York: McGraw Hill, 1959), 160.

9. Bender, *A Crack in the Rear-View Mirror*, 58; Mayer, *Builders*, 264; Spring, "Advances in House Design," 60.

10. Bender, *A Crack in the Rear-View Mirror*, 58–61; Kelly, "Problems and Potential," 32; Carl Koch, "Design and the Industrialized House," in Kelly, ed., *Design and the Production of Houses*, 107–8.

11. Bender, *A Crack in the Rear-View Mirror*, 28, 60; Dietz et al., "Design and the Industrialized House," 162; Keating, "Emerging Patterns of Corporate Entry Into Housing," 7–11; Koch, "Design and the Industrialized House," 95.

12. "The Industry Capitalism Forgot," *Fortune* 36 (August 1947), 61–67, 167–70.

13. Kelly, "Problems and Potential," 12, specifically the chart, "U.S. Nonfarm Housing Starts, 1935–1957."

14. Miles Colean, "Housing Prospects in 1956," *Banking* (October 1955), 44–45.

15. Some sixty years later, Metropolitan Life and New York Life would later reap large dividends. Peter Cooper Village and Stuyvesant Town in lower Manhattan sold at auction for $5.4 billion. In 2006, New York Life sold Manhattan House for over $620 million.

16. Mayer, *Builders*, 27–28.

17. Bender, *A Crack in the Rear-View Mirror*, 84–89; Koch, "Design and the Industrialized House," 95.

18. Dietz et al., "Design and the Industrialized House," 174–87; Mayer, *Builders*, 268–70.

19. Bender, *A Crack in the Rear-View Mirror*, 89.

20. As quoted in Mayer, *Builders*, 257.

21. Dietz et al., "Design and the Industrialized House," 148; Koch, "Design and the Industrialized House," 99.

22. "The Industry Capitalism Forgot," *Fortune* 36 (August 1947), 61–67, 167–70.

23. Mayer, *Builders*, 86–91.

24. Leo Grebler, *Large Scale Housing and Real Estate Firms: Analysis of a New Business Enterprise* (New York: Praeger, 1973), 35–38; Mayer, *Builders*, 91–93.

25. Burnham Kelly, "Building and Land Use Controls," in Burnham Kelly, ed., *Design and the Production of Houses*, 358.

26. Charles Foster, "Competition and Organization in Building," *Journal of Industrial Economics* 12 (1964): 163–74; Keating, "Emerging Patterns of Corporate Entry into Housing," 14–15, 75.

27. As quoted in Keating, "Emerging Patterns of Corporate Entry into Housing," 2; emphasis added.

28. Robert Jensen, "Operation Breakthrough: The Systems, the Sites and the Designers Are Chosen. The Question Now: On What Standards Should the Program Be Judged?" *Architectural Record* (April 1970), 139; Keating, "Emerging Patterns of Corporate Entry into Housing," 2–4; M. R. Lefkoe, *The Crisis in Con-*

197

struction: There Is An Answer (Bureau of National Affairs, Inc.: Washington, D.C., 1970), 137–39.

29. Companies identified through the online database, Hoover's Company Information, 2005; Bender, *A Crack in the Rear-View Mirror*, 116; John Kenneth Galbraith, *The New Industrial State* 2d rev. ed. (Boston: Houghton Mifflin Company, 1971), esp. 115–127; Grebler, *Large Scale Housing and Real Estate Firms*, 14–18, 126–45; Keating, "Emerging Patterns of Corporate Entry Into Housing," 24, 34–44, 59–83, 87–95; Mayer, *Builders*, 248; Vernon Swaback, "Production Dwellings: An Opportunity for Excellence," *Land Economics* 47 (1971): 321.

30. For further company information, see the following Web sites: Boise Cascade, LLC: http://www.bc.com/; Centex: http://www.centex.com/; Champion Homes: http://www.championhomes.net/; Fleetwood: http://www.fleetwood.com/; KB Homes: http://www.kbhomes.com/; Lennar: http://www.lennar.com; Ryan Homes: http://www.ryanhomes.com/; Skyline Homes: http://www.skylinehomes.com/. See also M. Edgar Barrett and Jonathan N. Brown, "Stirling Homex," Harvard Business School Case (March 1, 1973); Bender, *A Crack in the Rear-View Mirror*, 91–102; Dietz et al., "Design and the Industrialized House," 149, 173–74; Kelly, "Problems and Potential," 30–31; Mayer, *Builders*, 27, 265–66; Keating, "Emerging Patterns of Corporate Entry Into Housing," 44–56; Timothy Luehrman and William Teichner, "Fleetwood Enterprises, Inc.: 1990," Harvard Business School Case, June 19, 1992. Grebler, *Large Scale Housing and Real Estate Firms*, 21–33.

31. Swaback, "Production Dwellings," 322–24.

32. Bender, *A Crack in the Rear-View Mirror*, 57.

33. Peter Cassimatis, *Economics of the Construction Industry* (New York: National Industrial Conference Board, 1969), 22, 110–15; Finkel, *The Economics of the Construction Industry*, 86.

34. Bender, *A Crack in the Rear-View Mirror*, 1, 5–10, 63–76, 132–35.

35. Mayer, *Builders*, 272–82.

36. Richard Conner, "Contracting for Construction Management Services," *Law and Contemporary Problems* 46 (1983): 5; Edward Davis and Lindsay White, "How to Avoid Construction Headaches," *Harvard Business Review* (March–April 1973): 87–93.

37. As quoted in Conner, "Contracting for Construction Management Services," 7.

38. Business Roundtable, *More Construction for the Money: Summary Report of the Construction Industry Cost Effectiveness Project* (January 1983), 26.

39. Alex F. Ferrini, "Construction Manager Owner Agreements: Beware," *LePatner Report* (Winter 2005): 1, 3–4.

40. "Allocation of Risk in the Construction Industry: The Nonprofessional Owner and His Construction Manager," *Law and Contemporary Problems* 46 (1983): 165; William D. Booth, *Marketing Strategies for Design-Build Contracting* (New York: Chapman and Hall, 1995), 169; Business Roundtable, *More Construction for the Money*, 56; C. A. Foster, "Construction Management and Design-Build/Fast Track Construction: A Solution Which Uncovers a Problem for the Surety," *Law and Contemporary Problems* 46 (1983): 95–125; Ralph Stephenson, *Project*

Partnering for the Design and Construction Industry (New York: John Wiley & Sons, 1996), 23.

41. See the Emcor Group, Inc., Web site: http://www.emcorgroup.com/. See also Business Roundtable, *More Construction for the Money*; Finkel, *The Economics of the Construction Industry*, 88.

42. Ryan Conley, "Large Companies Change Complexion of Ocala, Fl., Construction Industry," *Ocala Star-Banner*, August 15, 2004; Daniela Deane, "Home from the Factory; Pulte Says Its New Way of Manufactured Building Is Faster, Better," *Washington Post*, December 11, 2004, F01.

43. John Gertner, "Chasing Ground," *New York Times*, October 16, 2005.

44. Finkel, *The Economics of the Construction Industry*, 55. Data taken from charts published annually in *Fortune* magazine between 1995 and 2005: "Average List Position of Engineering and Construction Companies in the Fortune 1000," "Revenue of Engineering and Construction Companies in the Fortune 1000," and "Employees, Construction and Engineering Firms in the Fortune 1000."

45. Gary Berman, "Are Foxes Watching the Owner's Hen House? An Examination of the Architect's and Construction Manager's Roles in Managing and Administering the Design and Construction Process," *CM eJournal* (2003).

46. Paul Greenbeck, "The Pricing Decision in the Micro-business: A Study of Accountants, Builders and Printers," *International Small Business Journal* 17 (April–June 1999).

Chapter Four

1. Douglass C. North, *Understanding the Process of Economic Change* (Princeton: Princeton University Press, 2005), 60.

2. James Surowiecki, "The Financial Page: The Customer is King," *New Yorker*, February 15, 21, 2005, 104.

3. "Mechanics' Liens and Surety Bonds in the Building Trades," *Yale Law Journal* 68 (1958): 143–44; "Allocation of Risk in the Construction Industry: The Nonprofessional Owner and His Construction Manager," *Law and Contemporary Problems* 46 (1983): 150; William D. Booth, *Marketing Strategies for Design-Build Contracting* (New York: Chapman and Hall, 1995), 168–69; Patricia Hillebrandt, *Economic Theory and the Construction Industry* (London: Macmillan, 1974), 154–59; M. R. Lefkoe, *The Crisis in Construction: There Is An Answer* (Washington, D.C.: Bureau of National Affairs, Inc., 1970), 27–29; Peter Philips, "The United States: Dual Worlds: The Two Growth Paths in U.S. Construction," in Gerhard Bosch and Peter Philips, eds., *Building Chaos: An International Comparison of Deregulation in the Construction Industry* (New York: Routledge, 2003), 163.

4. Peter Cassimatis, *Economics of the Construction Industry* (New York: National Industrial Conference Board, 1969), 117; Albert Dietz, Castle Day, and Burnham Kelly, "Design and the Industrialized House," in Burnham Kelly, ed., *Design and the Production of Houses* (New York: McGraw Hill, 1959), 140; Douglas Dyer and John Kagel, "Bidding in Common Value Auctions: How the Com-

mercial Construction Industry Corrects for the Winner's Curse," *Management Science* 42 (1996): 1,470.

5. Hillebrandt, *Economic Theory and the Construction Industry*, 153.

6. Gerstel, *Running a Successful Construction Company*, 131.

7. Booth, *Marketing Strategies for Design-Build Contracting*, 115; emphasis added.

8. Mark Federle and Steven Pigneri, "Predictive Model of Cost Overruns," *Transactions of the AACE International* (1993): L.7.2.

9. Business Roundtable, *More Construction for the Money: Summary Report of the Construction Industry Cost Effectiveness Project* (January 1983), 56; Philips, "The United States: Dual Worlds,"163.

10. Dennis Applegate and Curtis Matthews, "Building Controls into Capital Construction," *Internal Auditor* (June 2002): 54.

11. Booth, *Marketing Strategies for Design-Build Contracting*, 118, 169; emphasis added.

12. Booth, *Marketing Strategies for Design-Build Contracting*, 117.

13. Mary Powers, "Deal Cut to Expedite Miami Arts Center Job: Owner, Contractors and Architect Settle Claims and Set New Schedule for Much-Troubled Project," *Engineering News-Record* 253 (August 30 and September 6, 2004): 12.

14. John E. Osborn, "Navigating Troubled Waters with School Construction," *Construction Law* 15 (June 1, 2004): 137.

15. Tom Witkowski, "Columbus Center: Cassin Reflects on Lessons Learned," *Boston Business Journal*, January 21, 2005.

16. "Work Wrapping Up On New Ballpark," Associated Press. Broadcast on TodaysTHV.com March 21, 2007: http://www.todaysthv.com/sports/story.aspx?storyid=43200.

17. "Price Increases Concern Contractors; Material Shortages Drive Price Increases in Project Bidding According to PinnacleOne Survey of Construction Industry," *Rocky Mountain Construction*, January 10, 2005; Peter Reina, "Multiyear Jobs, Even Small Ones, Are Biggest Risks for Overruns," *Engineering News-Record* 250 (May 26, 2003).

18. Stephen Daniels, "Cost Engineering: Battling Cost Overruns," *Engineering News-Record* 241 (September 28, 1998): 35.

19. See, for example, "Building a Plant on Schedule, on Budget," *Management Review* (August 1972): 44–45; Edward Davis and Lindsay White, "How to Avoid Construction Headaches," *Harvard Business Review* (March–April 1973): 87–93; John Hoffman, "Know 5 Problems and You'll Plan a Better Building," *Banking* 68 (September 1976): 64, 66; Kwaku Tenah, "Project Delivery Systems for Construction: An Overview," *Cost Engineering* 43 (January 2001): 30–36.

20. Larry Rocha e-mail to Barry LePatner, May 5, 2005.

21. Gary S. Berman, "The Morphing of the Architect's Role and How It Is Impacting the CM," *CM eJournal* (2002) presented at the Construction Management Association of America National Conference, http://cmaanet.org/user_images/final_architect_paper_for_cmejournal.pdf; Charles Foster, "Competition and Organization in Building," *Journal of Industrial Economics* 12 (1964): 163–74; Dean Kashiwagi and John Savicky, "The Cost of 'Best Value' Construction," *Journal of Facilities Management* 2 (2003): 285–95.

22. Martin Mayer, *The Builders: Houses, People, Neighborhoods, Governments, Money* (New York: W. W. Norton and Company, 1978), 31.

23. John Flood and Andrew Caiger, "Lawyers and Arbitration: The Juridification of Construction Disputes," *Modern Law Review* 56 (1993): 412; Ralph Stephenson, *Project Partnering for the Design and Construction Industry* (New York: John Wiley & Sons, 1996).

24. Khaled Nasser, "Cost Contingency Analysis for Construction Projects Using Spreadsheets," *Cost Engineering* 44 (September 9, 2002): 26–31.

25. Stephenson, *Project Partnering for the Design and Construction Industry*, 63–86.

26. Gerstel, *Running a Successful Construction Company*, 131–33; C. A. Foster, "Construction Management and Design-Build / Fast Track Construction: A Solution Which Uncovers a Problem for the Surety," *Law and Contemporary Problems* 46 (1983): 119.

27. Ernesto Henriod et al., *The Construction Industry: Issues and Strategies in Developing Countries* (Washington, D.C.: The World Bank, 1984), 59.

28. As quoted in Richard Conner, "Contracting for Construction Management Services," *Law and Contemporary Problems* 46 (1983): 14.

29. FMI Corporation report, "Why Contractors Fail?" *Engineering News Record*, June 5, 2006.

30. Kelly, "Problems and Potential," 32.

31. Business Roundtable, *More Construction for the Money*, 13.

32. Leslie M. Kusek, "Know Your Markets: Construction Industry Firms Must Understand Their Business and Markets," *Michigan Contractor Builder*, January 22, 2005.

33. Kimberly Griffiths, "An Inevitable Evolution: The Construction Industry Is Not Immune to the Changing Face of Distribution; It's Just a Bit Slower to Change," *Industrial Distribution*, October 1, 2004.

34. As quoted in Mayer, *Builders*, 34; emphasis added.

35. Herbert Applebaum, *Royal Blue: The Culture of Construction Workers* (New York: Holt, Rinehart and Winston, 1981), 56–57.

36. Steve Brown, "Construction Industry Hit with Rising Materials Prices," *Dallas Morning News* (May 21, 2004); Federle and Pigneri, "Predictive Model of Cost Overruns"; Campbell Fraser, "The Influence of Personal Characteristics on Effectiveness of Construction Site Managers," *Construction Management and Economics* (2000), 29–36; Pat King, "Alaska Construction Industry Expects to See Boom This Summer," *Alaska Journal of Commerce*, June 10, 2003; Todd Milbourn, "Construction Industry Watches as Plywood Prices Skyrocket," *Modesto Bee*, October 21, 2003; Judy Rapp, "Managing Risk: Keeping Your Company Safe," *Northwest Construction*, May 1, 2004; Jeremy Vermilyea, "Construction Law: Managing Risk with Construction Contract Documents," *Northwest Construction*, May 1, 2004.

37. William Bender, "Simplified Risk Assessment for Construction Clients," *AACE International Transactions* (2004): R.05.1–R.05.9; Hillebrandt, *Economic Theory and the Construction Industry*, 162–70; see North, *Understanding the Process of Economic Change*, 13–14.

38. Gerstel, *Running a Successful Construction Company*, 16–17.

201

39. Mayer, *Builders,* 49.
40. Business Roundtable, *More Construction for the Money,* 24–25, 53–57; Gerstel, *Running a Successful Construction Company,* 205, 221–22; Kelly, "Problems and Potential," 32–37.

41. Gerstel, *Running a Successful Construction Company,* 51–99, 118.
42. Gerstel, *Running a Successful Construction Company,* 288; Samuel Kitchell, *Kitchell Corporation: Building People, Building Success* (New York: Newcomen Society of the United States, 1991), 16.
43. As quoted in Mayer, *Builders,* 27.
44. Mayer, *Builders,* 36.
45. Gerstel, *Running a Successful Construction Company,* 45–50; Leo Grebler, *Large Scale Housing and Real Estate Firms: Analysis of a New Business Enterprise* (New York: Praeger, 1973), 16; Hillebrandt, *Economic Theory and the Construction Industry,* 120; Susanne Sclafane, "Alternative Markets Ease Construction Woes: One Broker Cites Option Starting with a Home Warranty and Ending with a Captive," *National Underwriter: Property & Casualty,* October 4, 2004, 14, 29.
46. Tammy Galvin, "Neumann Homes," *Training,* November 2002, 32. "2006 Giants Results," HousingZone.Com, Reed Business Information. http://www.housingzone.com/giants.html (March 26, 2007).
47. Grebler, *Large Scale Housing and Real Estate Firms,* 44–47, 159; Hillebrandt, *Economic Theory and the Construction Industry,* 167.
48. Burnham Kelly, "Building and Land Use Controls," in Burnham Kelly, ed., *Design and the Production of Houses* (New York: McGraw Hill, 1959), 359–60; Kelly, "Problems and Potential," 47; Carl Koch, "Design and the Industrialized House," in Burnham Kelly, ed., *Design and the Production of Houses* (New York: McGraw Hill, 1959), 102–5; Lefkoe, *The Crisis in Construction,* 135–36; National Research Council Committee on the International Construction Industry, *Building for Tomorrow: Global Enterprise and the U.S. Construction Industry* (Washington, D.C.: National Academy Press, 1988), 66–80.
49. See the American Council for Construction Education web site: http://www.acce-hq.org.
50. Business Roundtable, *More Construction for the Money,* 60–61.
51. Henry Kelly, "Technology and the Construction Industry: An Introduction," in *Technology and the Future of the U.S. Construction Industry* (Washington, D.C.: AIA Press, 1986), 9; Alton S. Bradford, "Computers and Construction," in *Technology and the Future of the U.S. Construction Industry* (Washington, D.C.: AIA Press, 1986), 23.
52. James Marston Fitch and William Bobenhausen, *American Building: The Environmental Forces That Shape It,* 2nd ed. (New York: Oxford University Press, 1999), 357.
53. Fitch and Bobenhausen, *American Building,* 357–58; National Research Council, *Building for Tomorrow,* 73–76.
54. National Research Council, *Building for Tomorrow,* 358; Vernon Swaback, "Production Dwellings: An Opportunity for Excellence," *Land Economics* 47 (1971): 332.
55. National Research Council, *Building for Tomorrow,* 73–76.

56. Gerstel, *Running a Successful Construction Company*, 134.

57. As quoted in Mayer, *Builders*, 33, 249.

58. For an overview, see Maged Georgy, Luh-Maan Chang, and Lei Zhang, "Engineering Performance in the U.S. Industrial Construction Sector," *Cost Engineering* 47 (2005): 27–36.

59. Business Roundtable, *More Construction for the Money*, 30.

60. Alice Agogino and Sherry Hsi, "Interface Considerations for Multimedia Case Studies in Design," paper presented at the HCI International 5th International Conference on Human-Computer Interaction, August 8–13, 1993, Orlando, Florida.

61. Lawrence P. Grayson, *The Making of an Engineer: The Illustrated History of Engineering Education in the United States and Canada* (New York: John Wiley & Sons, 1993), 264.

62. "A Little Learning," *Economist*, July 26, 2003; "But Can You Teach It?" *Economist*, May 22, 2004. See also these articles, all published in Philip Altbach, Patricia Gumport, and D. Bruce Johnstone, eds., *In Defense of American Higher Education* (Baltimore: Johns Hopkins University Press, 2001): Nannerl Keohane, "The Liberal Arts and the Role of Elite Higher Education," 181; Jules LaPidus, "Graduate Education and Research," 271–72; and Arthur Levine, "Higher Education as a Mature Industry," 51.

63. Sidney Levy, *Japan's Big Six: Case Studies of Japan's Largest Contractors* (New York: McGraw-Hill, 1993), 22–23; Linder, *Projecting Capitalism*, 119–66; National Research Council, *Building for Tomorrow*, 25–27.

64. Richard A. Belle, Harvey M. Bernstein, and Andre Manseau, "The U.S. Federal Policy in Support of Innovation in the Design and Construction Industry," in Andre Manseau and George Seaden, eds., *Innovation in Construction: An International Review of Public Policies* (London: Spon Press, 2001), 375; Richard Bender, *A Crack in the Rear-View Mirror: A View of Industrialized Building* (New York: Van Nostrand Reinhold Company, 1973), 110; Cassimatis, *Economics of the Construction Industry*, 124–26; Albert Dietz, "Housing Industry Research," in Burnham Kelly, ed., *Design and the Production of Houses* (New York: McGraw Hill, 1959), 241; Elhanan Helpman, *The Mystery of Economic Growth* (Cambridge, Mass.: Belknap Press, 2004), 46–48; Henry Kelly, "Technology and the Construction Industry," 9; Levy, *Japan's Big Six*, 26, 227–64; Marc Linder, *Projecting Capitalism: A History of the Internationalization of the Construction Industry* (Westport, Conn.: Greenwood Press, 1994), 182–88; Dorothy Nelkin, *The Politics of Housing Innovation: The Fate of the Civilian Industrial Technology Program* (Ithaca: Cornell University Press, 1971), 8; U.S. Department of Commerce, *A Competitive Assessment of the U.S. International Construction Industry* (February 1989), 73.

65. See the web site of the Construction Industry Institute at the University of Texas at Austin: http://www.construction-institute.org/; Business Roundtable, *More Construction for the Money*, 27; Dietz, "Housing Industry Research," 243–48; Dietz et al., "Design and the Industrialized House," 152.

66. FIATECH, "FIATECH: What's in It for You?" http://www.fiatech.org/.

67. See ATLSS web site at http://www.atlss.lehigh.edu/. See also Dietz, "Housing

Industry Research," 241–44; Henry Kelly, "Technology and the Construction Industry," 10.

68. Belle et al., "The U.S. Federal Policy in Support of Innovation in the Design and Construction Industry," 376–81.
69. Kelly, "Problems and Potential," 6–7.
70. Except where otherwise noted, this section is based on Nelkin, *Politics of Housing.*
71. Arthur D. Little, Inc., *Patterns and Problems of Technical Innovation in American Industry: Report to National Science Foundation, U.S. Department of Commerce* (September 1963), 133.
72. Kelly, "Problems and Potential," 24; Henry Kelly, "Technology and the Construction Industry," 9–10.
73. *Technology and the Future of the U.S. Construction Industry* (Washington, D.C.: AIA Press, 1986); Nelkin, *Politics of Housing,* 9.
74. "Egan Slams Public Sector's Progress," *Contract Journal,* January 31, 2007, http://www.contractjournal.com/Articles/2007/01/31/53468/egan-slams-public-sectors-progress.html.
75. Michael P. Gallaher, Alan C. O'Connor, John L. Dettbarn, and Linda T. Gilday, "Cost Analysis in Inadequate Interoperability in the U.S. Capital Facilities Industry," NIST GCR 04-867 (Research Triangle Park, N.C.: RTI International and McLean, Va. Logistics Management Institute, August 2004); Gerstel, *Running a Successful Construction Company,* 20–21, 24–25, 30–36; Daisy Keung, Sai-On Cheung, Kevin Cheung, and Henry Suen, "Web-based Project Cost Monitoring System for Construction Management," *AACE International Transactions* (2003): IT.09.1–IT.09.11; Tom Sawyer, "Online Management Tools Excel at Empowering Project Teams," *Engineering News-Record* (October 11, 2004).
76. Gallaher et al., "Cost Analysis in Inadequate Interoperability in the U.S. Capital Facilities Industry," v.
77. Jim Stafford, "Stillwater, Okla.-Created 'intelliRock' System Stirs Up Construction Industry," *Daily Oklahoman,* February 6, 2004.
78. Business Roundtable, *More Construction for the Money,* 26–27.
79. Dietz, "Housing Industry Research," 240–41; Lefkoe, *The Crisis in Construction,* 139; Martin Meyerson, foreword to Burnham Kelly, ed., *Design and the Production of Houses* (New York: McGraw Hill, 1959), xii; National Research Council, *Building for Tomorrow,* 15, 55–62, 85–92; Nelkin, *Politics of Housing,* 12.
80. "Gehry's New Venture," *Principal's Report* (November 2003): 2; Peter Goddard, "Inside Gehry's Mind," *Toronto Star,* March 17, 2001; Jim Glymph e-mail to Barry LePatner, May 4, 2005; Bien Perez, "Building a New Dimension Software Reduces Errors, Cuts Costs," *South China Morning Post,* November 23, 2004.
81. Paul Siodmok, "Computer Aided Design," *Design Council Bulletin,* January 5, 2005.
82. Christopher Palmeri, "Frank Gehry's High-Tech Secret," *Business Week Online,* October 6, 2003, http://www.businessweek.com/magazine/content/03_40/b3852132.htm.
83. Gregory Beck, Phillip Bernstein, Jeffrey Inaba, Mikyoung Kim, and Eliza-

beth Padjen, "Roundtable: Designers without Borders," *Architecture Boston* 7 (November–December 2004): 20–29.

84. Elaine S. Silver, "GSA to Require Building Information Models by FY 2006," *Engineering News Record*, January 21, 2005.

Chapter Five

1. J. C. Conklin, "More Women Entering Construction Industry," *Dallas Morning News*, March 17, 2002; Kevin Harlin, "New York State Construction Industry Recruiting Underused Labor Sources," *Times Union*, May 15, 2001; Herbert Applebaum, *Royal Blue: The Culture of Construction Workers* (New York: Holt, Rinehart and Winston, 1981), 130–33.

2. Allan Mandelstamm, "The Effects of Unions on Efficiency in the Residential Construction Industry: A Case Study," *Industrial and Labor Relations Review* 18 (1965): 503–21; Martin Mayer, *The Builders: Houses, People, Neighborhoods, Governments, Money* (New York: W. W. Norton and Company, 1978), 36.

3. "The Industry Capitalism Forgot," *Fortune* 36 (August 1947), 61–67, 167–70; Steven Allan, "Union Work Rules and Efficiency in the Building Trades," *Journal of Labor Economics* 4 (1986): 212–42; Business Roundtable, *More Construction for the Money: Summary Report of the Construction Industry Cost Effectiveness Project* (January 1983), 31–41; Peter Cassimatis, *Economics of the Construction Industry* (New York: National Industrial Conference Board, 1969), 125; Gerald Finkel, *The Economics of the Construction Industry* (Armonk, N.Y.: M. E. Sharpe, 1997), 118–22; Alan Gustman and Martin Segal, "Wages, Wage Supplements, and the Interaction of Union Bargains in the Construction Industry," *Industrial and Labor Relations Review* 25 (1972): 179–85; Robert Jensen, "Operation Breakthrough: The Systems, the Sites and the Designers Are Chosen. The Question Now: On What Standards Should the Program Be Judged?" *Architectural Record* (April 1970), 138; William Keating, "Emerging Patterns of Corporate Entry Into Housing" (Center for Real Estate and Urban Economics Institute, University of California, Berkeley, 1973), 113–17; M. R. Lefkoe, *The Crisis in Construction: There Is An Answer* (Bureau of National Affairs, Inc.: Washington, D.C., 1970), 34–37; Kenneth McCaffree, "Regional Labor Agreements in the Construction Industry," *Industrial and Labor Relations Review* 9 (1956): 595–609; Jeffrey Perloff and Robin Sickles, "Union Wage, Hours, and Earning Differentials in the Construction Industry," *Journal of Labor Economics* 5 (1987): 174–210; Stephen Sobotka, "Union Influences on Wages: The Construction Industry," *Journal of Political Economy* 61 (1953): 127–43.

4. Cassimatis, *Economics of the Construction Industry*, 109–110; J. E. Covington, "Union Security Elections in the Building and Construction Industry under the Taft-Hartley Act," *Industrial and Labor Relations Review* 4 (1951): 547–48; John Crispo, "Labour-Management Relations in the Construction Industry: The Findings of the Goldenberg Commission," *Canadian Journal of Economics and Political Science* 29 (1963): 349; John Dunlop, "Labor-Management Relations," in Burnham Kelly, ed., *Design and the Production of Houses* (New York: McGraw Hill, 1959), 259–63; Luke Grant, "Seasonal Occupation in the Build-

ing Trades: Causes and Effects," *Annals of the American Academy of Political and Social Science* 33 (1909): 129–37.

5. Ronald Filipelli, *Labor in the USA: A History* (New York: Alfred Knopf, 1984); Finkel, *The Economics of the Construction Industry*, 125–26; Donna Rilling, *Making Houses, Crafting Capitalism: Builders in Philadelphia, 1790–1850* (Philadelphia: University of Pennsylvania Press, 2001); Robert E. Wright, *The First Wall Street: Chestnut Street, Philadelphia, and the Birth of American Finance* (Chicago: University of Chicago Press, 2005), 104–17.

6. Daniel Jacoby, "The Transformation of Industrial Apprenticeship in the United States," *Journal of Economic History* 51 (1991): 887–910; George Sikes, "The Apprentice System in the Building Trades," *Journal of Political Economy* 2 (1894): 397–423.

7. John R. Commons, "The New York Building Trades," *Quarterly Journal of Economics* 18 (1904): 409–36; Finkel, *The Economics of the Construction Industry*, 81; Royal E. Montgomery, "Graft in the Building Trades," *University Journal of Business* 4 (1926): 309–27; New York State Organized Crime Task Force, *Corruption and Racketeering in the New York City Construction Industry* (Ithaca: Cornell University Press, 1988); Jean Sexton, "Controlling Corruption in the Construction Industry: The Quebec Approach," *Industrial and Labor Relations Review* 42 (1989): 524–35; George Strauss, "Business Agents in the Building Trades: A Case Study in a Community," *Industrial and Labor Relations Review* 10 (1957): 237–51.

8. Commons, "New York Building Trades," 409–36; Samuel Donnelly, "The Trade Agreement in the Building Trades," *Annals of the American Academy of Political and Social Science* 27 (1906): 48–54; Sikes, "The Apprentice System in the Building Trades," 404.

9. Cassimatis, *Economics of the Construction Industry*, 18, 105–108; Covington, "Union Security Elections," 545; Dunlop, "Labor-Management Relations," 264; Finkel, *The Economics of the Construction Industry*, 127, 131.

10. Lipsky and Farber, "Composition of Strike Activity," 388–404; Albert Rees and Arthur Okun, "The Construction Industry Stabilization Committee: Implications for Phase II," *Brookings Papers on Economic Activity* 3 (1971): 767.

11. Business Roundtable, *More Construction for the Money*, 37–39; Finkel, *The Economics of the Construction Industry*, 79; Rees and Okun, "Construction Industry Stabilization," 760–68.

12. Bureau of Labor Statistics, "Union Members in 2004," *News*, January, 27, 2005; Business Roundtable, *More Construction for the Money*, 33; Filipelli, *Labor in the USA*, 284–87; Finkel, *The Economics of the Construction Industry*, 128; Robert Flanagan, "Has Management Strangled U.S. Unions?" *Journal of Labor Research* 26 (2005): 33–63; Richard Newman, "Construction Industry Tries to Woo Tomorrow's Hard Hats in Lincroft, N.J.," *The Record* (New Jersey), March 26, 2002; David van den Berg, "Unions to Train Students at Construction Industry Expo in Collinsville, Ill." *Belleville News-Democrat*, October 21, 2003.

13. Burnham Kelly, "Problems and Potential: The Housing Industry Today," in Burnham Kelly, ed., *Design and the Production of Houses* (New York: McGraw Hill, 1959), 33–35; Mayer, *Builders*, 250–52.

14. As quoted in Mayer, *Builders,* 242.

15. Business Roundtable, *More Construction for the Money,* 25; Peter Philips, "The United States: Dual Worlds: The Two Growth Paths in U.S. Construction," in Gerhard Bosch and Peter Philips, eds., *Building Chaos: An International Comparison of Deregulation in the Construction Industry* (New York: Routledge, 2003), 164–76; Frank H. T. Rhodes, *The Creation of the Future: The Role of the American University* (Ithaca: Cornell University Press, 2001); Peter Smith, *The Quiet Crisis: How Higher Education is Failing America* (New York: Anker Publishing Co., 2004).

16. "But Can You Teach It?" *Economist,* May 22, 2004; "A Little Learning," *Economist,* July 26, 2003; Business Roundtable, *More Construction for the Money,* 34–35; Finkel, *The Economics of the Construction Industry,* 137–46. See also the following articles all published in Philip Altbach, Patricia Gumport and D. Bruce Johnstone, eds., *In Defense of American Higher Education* (Baltimore: Johns Hopkins University Press, 2001): Arthur Levine, "Higher Education as a Mature Industry," 51; Nannerl Keohane, "The Liberal Arts and the Role of Elite Higher Education," 181; and Jules LaPidus, "Graduate Education and Research," 271–72.

17. Gerstel, *Running a Successful Construction Company,* 211; emphasis in original.

18. As quoted in Mayer, *Builders,* 241.

19. John D. Allison, "An Analysis of Levittown, New York, with Particular Reference to Demand Satisfaction from Mass Produced Low Cost Housing," (Ph.D. diss., New York University, 1956), 71.

20. Dunlop, "Labor-Management Relations," 273–77; Finkel, *The Economics of the Construction Industry,* 115.

21. Applebaum, *Royal Blue,* 54.

22. The literature here is vast and complex. For some representative studies, see Andrea Gabor, *The Capitalist Philosophers: The Geniuses of Modern Business, Their Lives, Times, and Ideas* (New York: Times Business, 1999); Paul E. Johnson, *A Shopkeeper's Millennium: Society and Revivals in Rochester, New York, 1815–1837* (New York: Hill and Wang, 1978); Daniel Nelson, *Frederick W. Taylor and the Rise of Scientific Management* (Madison: University of Wisconsin Press, 1980); Marvin Weisbord, *Productive Workplaces: Organizing and Managing for Dignity, Meaning, and Community* (San Francisco: Jossey-Bass, 1987).

23. Robert Sharoff, "Drawing a Line on Drugs," *Builder* 20 (March 1997): 154–57.

24. "No Offense, Buddy," *Occupational Hazards* 65 (November 2003): 7; Jonathan Gerber and George Yacoubian, "An Assessment of Drug Testing within the Construction Industry," *Journal of Drug Education* 32 (2002): 53–68; Richard Korman, "Drug Problems Persist," *Engineering News Record* 236 (May 13, 1996): 10; Jack Naudi, "Drug, Alcohol Testing Reduces St. Louis Construction Industry Deaths," *St. Louis Post-Dispatch,* July 9, 2003; Andy Pearson, "The Secret Epidemic," *Building* (November 19, 2004); Debra Rubin, "Construction Shuns Drug Programs," *Engineering News Record* 219 (August 27, 1987): 60; Robert Sharoff, "Drawing a Line on Drugs," *Builder* 20 (March 1997): 154–57; Sherie Winston, "Unions Tackle the Costs of Drug Use," *Engineering News Record* 253 (September 27, 2004): 32–35. Except where otherwise noted, this section is based on Applebaum, *Royal Blue: The Culture of Construction Workers* (New York:

Holt, Rinehart and Winston, 1981); E. E. LeMasters, *Blue-Collar Aristocrats: Life-Styles at a Working-Class Tavern* (Madison: University of Wisconsin Press, 1975).
25. Mayer, *Builders*, 249.
26. Business Roundtable, *More Construction for the Money*, 54–55.
27. Ibid., 24.
28. Gerstel, *Running a Successful Construction Company*, 22.
29. Business Roundtable, *More Construction for the Money*, 23; emphasis in original.
30. Ibid., 24.
31. Ibid., 33; John A. Kuprenas and Abdallah S. Fakhouri, "A Crew Balance Case Study: Improving Construction Productivity," *CM eJournal* (January 2001).
32. John Pencavel, "Unionism Viewed Internationally," *Journal of Labor Research* 26 (2005): 65–97.
33. As quoted in Alex Frangos, "Construction Sticker Shock: Optimism, Pricey Materials Help to Fuel a 10% Leap in the Cost of a New Building," *Wall Street Journal*, March 23, 2005, B1. See also Jenalia Moreno, "Career Building without College: Skilled Workers Can Have Their Pick of Jobs in the Understaffed Construction Trades," *Washington Post*, May 15, 2005.
34. Gerhard Bosch and Peter Philips, introduction to Gerhard Bosch and Peter Philips, eds., *Building Chaos: An International Comparison of Deregulation in the Construction Industry* (New York: Routledge, 2003), 10–23.
35. Business Roundtable, *More Construction for the Money*, 43.
36. Richard A. Belle, Harvey M. Bernstein, and Andre Manseau, "The U.S. Federal Policy in Support of Innovation in the Design and Construction Industry," in Andre Manseau and George Seaden, eds., *Innovation in Construction: An International Review of Public Policies* (London: Spon Press, 2001), 381.
37. "Small Companies 'Losing' 21 Working Weeks a Year," *Global News Wire*, September 3, 2004.
38. New York State, *Corruption and Racketeering*, 59.
39. Business Roundtable, *More Construction for the Money*, 11.
40. As quoted in Mayer, *Builders*, 349.
41. Business Roundtable, *More Construction*, 45; Mayer, *Builders*, 36–37; Dorothy Nelkin, *The Politics of Housing Innovation: The Fate of the Civilian Industrial Technology Program* (Ithaca: Cornell University Press, 1971), 13; Philips, "The United States: Dual Worlds," 184.
42. Mayer, *Builders*, 47, 243, 296–300.
43. Cassimatis, *Economics of the Construction Industry*, 120; Kelly, "Problems," 24; Mayer, *Builders*, 37; Nelkin, *Politics of Housing*, 14.
44. Albert Dietz, James Murray, Burnham Kelly, and Carl Koch, "Construction Advances," in Burnham Kelly, ed., *Design and the Production of Houses* (New York: McGraw Hill, 1959), 204–20; Burnham Kelly, "Building and Land Use Controls," in Burnham Kelly, ed., *Design and the Production of Houses* (New York: McGraw Hill, 1959), 302–47; Lefkoe, *The Crisis in Construction*, 51.
45. As quoted in Mayer, *Builders*, 73, 71–74.
46. Mayer, *Builders*, 51–52.
47. Mayer, *Builders*, 77.
48. Mayer, *Builders*, 78.

208

49. For details, see Anon., "Mechanics' Liens and Surety Bonds in the Building Trades," *Yale Law Journal* 68 (1958): 138–71; New York State Lien Law Sections 2, 3, and 4; Arthur Corbin, "Third Parties as Beneficiaries of Contractors' Surety Bonds," *Yale Law Journal* 38 (1928): 1–24.

50. Anon., "Allocation of Risk in the Construction Industry: The Nonprofessional Owner and His Construction Manager," *Law and Contemporary Problems* 46 (1983): 150–52, 165; Richard Conner, "Contracting for Construction Management Services," *Law and Contemporary Problems* 46 (1983): 11–12; New York State, *Corruption and Racketeering*, 108–12; John E. Osborn, "Navigating Troubled Waters with School Construction," *Construction Law* 15 (June 1, 2004): 137.

51. Gerstel, *Running a Successful Construction Company*, 45.

52. As quoted in Mayer, *Builders*, 328–29.

53. Kelly, "Problems and Potential," 42; Carl Koch, "Design and the Industrialized House," in Burnham Kelly, ed., *Design and the Production of Houses* (New York: McGraw Hill, 1959), 99.

54. According to Wikipedia, the Davis-Bacon Act of 1931 is a United States federal law that established the requirement for paying prevailing wages on public works projects. The Copeland Anti-Kickback Act precludes a contractor or subcontractor from inducing an employee to give back to its employer any part of the compensation to which he or she is entitled under his or her contract of employment. The Eight-hour Law, an act adopted in 1868 by the United States Congress, provides that eight hours shall constitute a day's work in all government employment.

55. For a spirited defense of prevailing wage laws, including the federal Davis-Bacon Act and similar state statutes, as policy instruments, see Hamid Azari-Rad, Peter Philips, and Mark Prus, "Introduction: Prevailing Wage Regulations and Public Policy in the Construction Industry," in Hamid Azari-Rad, Peter Philips, and Mark Prus, eds., *The Economics of Prevailing Wage Laws* (Burlington, Vt.: Ashgate, 2005), 3–27.

56. Steven G. Allen, "Much Ado About Davis-Bacon: A Critical Review and Evidence," *Journal of Law and Economics* 26 (1983): 707–36; Business Roundtable, *More Construction*, 44; Finkel, *The Economics of the Construction Industry*, 77–78; Gerald Finkel, "The American Construction Industry: An Overview," in Hamid Azari-Rad, Peter Philips, and Mark Prus, eds., *The Economics of Prevailing Wage Laws* (Burlington, Vt.: Ashgate, 2005), 53–57; Daniel Kessler and Lawrence Katz, "Prevailing Wage Laws and Construction Labor Markets," *Industrial and Labor Relations Review* 54 (2001): 259–74; Lefkoe, *The Crisis in Construction*, 19–23; Arthur S. Miller, "Government Contracts and Social Control: A Preliminary Inquiry," *Virginia Law Review* 41 (1955): 46–48; Armand Thieblot, "The Twenty-Percent Majority: Pro-Union Bias in Prevailing Rate Determinations," *Journal of Labor Research* 36 (Winter 2005): 99–134.

57. Mayer, *Builders*, 338–40.

58. As quoted in Mayer, *Builders*, 377.

59. Between 1965 and 1975, over 600,000 units of affordable housing were built under HUD's Section 221(d)(3) and Section 236 programs. This was the first time the private sector was invited to participate in producing low- and

209

moderate-income housing, previously the sole domain of public housing authorities. Under Section 236, the Federal Housing Authority insured forty-year loans were provided with a below-market interest rate.

60. Mayer, *Builders*, 128, 210–11.

61. William Keating, "Emerging Patterns of Corporate Entry into Housing," (Center for Real Estate and Urban Economics Institute, University of California, Berkeley, 1973), 18–19.

62. Cassimatis, *Economics of the Construction Industry*, 121; Finkel, *The Economics of the Construction Industry*, 18; Lefkoe, *The Crisis in Construction*, 49–50, 55–79, 88, 127; Mayer, *Builders*, 37.

63. Allison, "An Analysis of Levittown, New York, with Particular Reference to Demand Satisfaction from Mass Produced Low Cost Housing," 78; Belle et al., "The U.S. Federal Policy in Support of Innovation in the Design and Construction Industry," 376.

Chapter Six

1. Ralph Stephenson, *Project Partnering for the Design and Construction Industry* (New York: John Wiley & Sons, 1996), 24.

2. Richard Bender, *A Crack in the Rear-View Mirror: A View of Industrialized Building* (New York: Van Nostrand Reinhold Company, 1973), 166–67; David Gerstel, *Running a Successful Construction Company* (Newtown, Conn.: Taunton Press, 2002), 121–41.

3. Martin Mayer, *The Builders: Houses, People, Neighborhoods, Governments, Money* (New York: W. W. Norton and Company, 1978), 38.

4. Mayer, *Builders*, 38.

5. William D. Booth, *Marketing Strategies for Design-Build Contracting* (New York: Chapman and Hall, 1995), 114; David Gerstel, *Running a Successful Construction Company*.

6. The best recent discussion of the economics of construction bonds and guarantees is Will Hughes, Patricia Hillebrandt, and John Murdoch, *Financial Protection in the UK Building Industry: Bonds, Retentions and Guarantees* (London: E&FN Spon, 1998).

7. Dennis Applegate and Curtis Matthews, "Building Controls into Capital Construction," *Internal Auditor* (June 2002): 53.

8. Patrick Bajari and Steven Tadelis, "Incentives versus Transaction Costs: A Theory of Procurement Contracts," *Rand Journal of Economics* 32 (Autumn 2001): 387–407.

9. Timothy Jacobson, *Waste Management: An American Corporate Success Story* (Washington, D.C.: Gateway Business Books, 1993).

10. Benjamin Friedman, *The Moral Consequences of Economic Growth* (New York: Alfred A. Knopf, 2005), 428–32; Leo Grebler, *Large Scale Housing and Real Estate Firms: Analysis of a New Business Enterprise* (New York: Praeger, 1973), 47–52, 55–61.

11. Business Roundtable, *More Construction for the Money*, 58.

12. James Marston Fitch and William Bobenhausen, *American Building: The Envi-*

ronmental Forces That Shape It, 2nd ed. (New York: Oxford University Press, 1999), 359.

13. U.S. Census Bureau. Chart: "Share of Public and Private Construction, 1993–2004."

14. "Allocation of Risk in the Construction Industry: The Nonprofessional Owner and His Construction Manager," *Law and Contemporary Problems* 46 (1983): 146–47; Michael Ceschini, "Does Uncle Sam Want You?" *Mid-Atlantic Construction,* October 1, 2004; Gerald Finkel, *The Economics of the Construction Industry* (Armonk, N.Y.: M. E. Sharpe, 1997), 76–82; Arthur S. Miller, "Government Contracts and Social Control: A Preliminary Inquiry," *Virginia Law Review* 41 (1955): 27–58; Stephenson, *Project Partnering,* 369.

15. Bender, *A Crack in the Rear-View Mirror,* 110; Charles Foster, "Competition and Organization in Building," *Journal of Industrial Economics* 12 (1964): 163–74.

16. Richard A. Belle, Harvey M. Bernstein, and Andre Manseau, "The U.S. Federal Policy in Support of Innovation in the Design and Construction Industry," in Andre Manseau and George Seaden, eds., *Innovation in Construction: An International Review of Public Policies* (London: Spon Press, 2001), 383; Mark Federle and Steven Pigneri, "Predictive Model of Cost Overruns," *Transactions of the AACE International* (1993): L.7.6; Dean Kashiwagi and John Savicky, "The Cost of 'Best Value' Construction," *Journal of Facilities Management* 2 (2003): 285–95; Sidney Levy, *Japan's Big Six: Case Studies of Japan's Largest Contractors* (New York: McGraw-Hill, 1993), 16.

17. William Keating, "Emerging Patterns of Corporate Entry into Housing," (Center for Real Estate and Urban Economics Institute, University of California, Berkeley, 1973), 12–14.

18. Grebler, *Large Scale Housing and Real Estate Firms,* 33–35; Robert Jensen, "Operation Breakthrough: The Systems, the Sites and the Designers Are Chosen. The Question Now: On What Standards Should the Program Be Judged?" *Architectural Record* (April 1970), 137–50; Keating, "Emerging Patterns," 19, 22–27; Mayer, *Builders,* 264–67; Harry St. John, "The Energy Market for High-Technology Companies," *Journal of Marketing* 42 (1978): 46–53.

19. See Qualitel's Web site: http://www.qualitel.org. See also "Opt for Pre-Fab System, Domestic Construction Industry Told," *Bernama, The Malaysian National News Agency* (January, 18 2005); Andre Manseau and George Seaden, eds., *Innovation in Construction: An International Review of Public Policies* (London: Spon Press, 2001); Mayer, *Builders,* 284–87; Yuthana Priwan, "Thailand Officials Attempt to Boost Construction Industry," *Bangkok Post,* September 13, 2003.

20. As quoted in St. John, "The Energy Market for High-Technology Companies," 51.

21. Guarantors are not insurers; guarantees are not insurance. "A guarantor promises to perform, or pay for the nonperformance of, an act which a third party is contractually bound to perform for the promisee." A suretyship is much the same as guaranty, except the surety is jointly liable. Robert Harmon, "Insurance – Rate Regulation – Construction and Effect of Guaranty Bond Agreement," *Michigan Law Review* 60 (1962): 806.

22. C. A. Foster, "Construction Management and Design-Build / Fast Track Con-

211

struction: A Solution Which Uncovers a Problem for the Surety," *Law and Contemporary Problems* 46 (1983): 123; Business Roundtable, *More Construction for the Money: Summary Report of the Construction Industry Cost Effectiveness Project* (January 1983), 45.

23. Other types of construction manager contracts also exist but most essentially turn the construction manager either into a general contractor or into the owner's partner. The discussion here is limited to those working for a set fee as that makes them owners' agents or employees. "Allocation of Risk in the Construction Industry: The Nonprofessional Owner and His Construction Manager," *Law and Contemporary Problems* 46 (1983): 147–49, 159; Richard Conner, "Contracting for Construction Management Services," *Law and Contemporary Problems* 46 (1983): 9–12; Finkel, *The Economics of the Construction Industry*, 111; Foster, "Construction Management," 101, 104; Kwaku Tenah, "Project Delivery Systems for Construction: An Overview," *Cost Engineering* 43 (January 2001): 30–36.

24. That is why analysts urge owners to perform their own construction management if they have the requisite expertise. Conner, "Contracting for Construction Management Services," 8.

25. Conner, "Contracting for Construction Management Services," 8; M. R. Lefkoe, *The Crisis in Construction: There Is An Answer* (Washington, D.C.: Bureau of National Affairs, Inc., 1970), 132–33; Thomas Ulen, "The Efficiency of Specific Performance: Toward a Unified Theory of Contract Remedies," *Michigan Law Review* 83 (1984): 347–49.

26. Surety bonds are an example of a larger set of contractual arrangements known as "self-help enforcement." For further details, see Charles Goetz and Robert Scott, "Principles of Relational Contracts," *Virginia Law Review* 67 (1981): 1,089–1,150; Ulen, "Efficiency of Specific Performance," 341–403.

27. "Mechanics' Liens and Surety Bonds in the Building Trades," *Yale Law Journal* 68 (1958): 138–71; "Allocation of Risk in the Construction Industry: The Nonprofessional Owner and His Construction Manager," *Law and Contemporary Problems* 46 (1983): 159, 163–64; Arthur Corbin, "Third Parties as Beneficiaries of Contractors' Surety Bonds," *Yale Law Journal* 38 (1928): 15–16; Foster, "Construction Management," 95–125; Barry LePatner and David Pfeffer, "Professional Liability Insurance For Construction Projects: Now You See It, Now You Don't," http://www.lepatner.com/prof-insur.htm; William J. McConnell, Jr., *State of the U.S. Construction Industry 2005/2006* (Vertex Engineering Services, Inc., 2006), 17.

28. Lefkoe, *The Crisis in Construction*, 28, 133–34; Donna Rilling, *Making Houses, Crafting Capitalism: Builders in Philadelphia, 1790–1850* (Philadelphia: University of Pennsylvania Press, 2001).

29. Mayer, *Builders*, 287–96.

30. Ibid., 298–300.

31. Gerstel, *Running a Successful Construction Company*, 133–41; Kitchell, *Kitchell Corporation*, 13, 15.

32. Bender, *A Crack in the Rear-View Mirror*, 165.

33. Lefkoe, *The Crisis in Construction*, 136–42.

34. In the short run, bids may simply increase as contractors compensate for the additional risk by raising their bids. The change in the nature of competition, from strategic bidding and change order gaming to construction cost, quality, and time, would soon lead to the qualitative changes described here, we believe.

213

35. Peter Cassimatis, *Economics of the Construction Industry* (New York: National Industrial Conference Board, 1969), 31, 55–68; Lefkoe, *The Crisis in Construction*, 36–49; Barbara Stevens, "Single-Site Economies in the Construction of Multi-Family Housing," *Land Economics* 51 (1975): 50–57.

36. Dennis Applegate and Curtis Matthews, "Building Controls into Capital Construction," *Internal Auditor* (June 2002): 49–55; Stephenson, *Project Partnering*, 1.

37. Anon., "Mechanics' Liens and Surety Bonds in the Building Trades," *Yale Law Journal* 68 (1958): 164–71; Anon., "Allocation of Risk in the Construction Industry: The Nonprofessional Owner and His Construction Manager," *Law and Contemporary Problems* 46 (1983): 159; Corbin, "Third Parties as Beneficiaries," 19–24; Finkel, *The Economics of the Construction Industry*, 72–76; Robert Wallick and John Stafford, "The Miller Act: Enforcement of the Payment Bond," *Law and Contemporary Problems* 29 (1964): 514–30;

38. "Miami-Dade Commission Votes on MIA Construction," CBS 4, March 20, 2007, http://cbs4.com/topstories/local_story_079101944.html (accessed March 23, 2007).

39. Steven G. Allen, "Unionization and Productivity in Office Building and School Construction," *Industrial and Labor Relations Review* 39 (1986): 187–201.

40. Barry LePatner, *Structural and Foundation Failures: A Case Book for Architects, Engineers, and Lawyers* (New York: McGraw Hill, 1997).

41. AIA Document B141, 1997; emphasis added.

42. Barry LePatner, "Riders in a Storm," *Architecture* (February 1999), 106–9; Barry LePatner, "Seeing the Light," *Architecture* (March 1999); Barry LePatner and Victoria Drogin, "Drafting Construction Contracts for Today's Complex Projects," *New York Law Journal*, March 31, 1999.

43. Anon., "Allocation of Risk in the Construction Industry: The Nonprofessional Owner and His Construction Manager," *Law and Contemporary Problems* 46 (1983): 145.

44. Anon., "Allocation of Risk," 148; Bender, "Simplified Risk Assessment."

45. LePatner and Drogin, "Drafting Construction Contracts," Barry LePatner, "Owner's Counsel, Be Very Careful: Drafting Agreements for Your Clients' New Construction Projects Ain't What It Used To Be," *New York Law Journal*, March 27, 2006.

46. While professional liability insurance for architects and engineers may provide $1 million, $2 million, or even $5 million, these amounts are eroded by the payment of attorney and expert fees, thus leaving potentially far less actually available to pay valid claims.

47. CFMA Construction Industry Financial Survey Results (2003), http://enr.construction.com/resources/special/archives/cfma_2003.asp.

48. Belle et al., "The U.S. Federal Policy in Support of Innovation in the Design

and Construction Industry," 381; Gerstel, *Running a Successful Construction Company,* 177–78; John L. Smith, "Construction Firm Scales the Heights of Litigation to Win Venetian Judgment," *Las Vegas Review-Journal,* April 6, 2005; Dwight Zink, "Impacts and Construction Inefficiency," *Cost Engineering* 32 (November 1990): 21–23.

49. American Institute of Architects, AIA Document A207, 1997, Section 4.6, obligates the parties to arbitrate all disputes in the event a mandatory nonbinding mediation is unsuccessful. Barry B. LePatner, "Construction Arbitration: Uprooting the Myths," *Legal Times,* June 30, 1986, 33.

50. Booth, *Marketing Strategies,* 158, 153.

51. Jeff Alden, "Drafting Residential Construction Agreements," *Bench & Bar of Minnesota* 61 (2004): 28–29; Gerstel, *Running a Successful Construction Company,* 177–78, 189–93; LePatner, "Owner's Counsel, Be Very Careful."

52. Gerstel, *Running a Successful Construction Company,* 195–97.

53. Gerstel, *Running a Successful Construction Company,* 186.

54. Business Roundtable, *More Construction for the Money,* 27.

55. "Allocation of Risk in the Construction Industry: The Nonprofessional Owner and His Construction Manager," *Law and Contemporary Problems* 46 (1983): 145; Foster, "Construction Management," 121.

56. Stephenson, *Project Partnering,* 102–3.

57. Don O. Carlson, "Modular Structures and Related Techniques," in *Technology and the Future of the U.S. Construction Industry* (Washington, D.C.: AIA Press, 1986), 46.

58. Mayer, *Builders,* 253–56; Henry Kelly, "Technology and the Construction Industry: An Introduction," in *Technology and the Future of the U.S. Construction Industry* (Washington, D.C.: AIA Press, 1986), 4–5.

59. Kelly, "Technology and the Construction Industry," 6.

60. Daisy Keung, Sai-On Cheung, Kevin Cheung, and Henry Suen, "Web-based Project Cost Monitoring System for Construction Management," *AACE International Transactions* (2003): IT.09.1–IT.09.11; Scott Unger, "The Strategic Impact of Web-Based Communication on Costs, Schedule, Scope and Quality Across the Design and Construction Life Cycle," Constructw@re White Paper (January 2005).

61. "The Industry Capitalism Forgot," *Fortune* 36 (August 1947): 61–67, 167–70.

62. This section is based on John D. Allison, "An Analysis of Levittown, New York, with Particular Reference to Demand Satisfaction from Mass Produced Low Cost Housing," (Ph.D. diss., New York University, 1956).

63. Ibid., 31.

64. Ibid., 74, 79.

65. Ibid., 207.

66. Bender, *A Crack in the Rear-View Mirror,* 165; Burnham Kelly, *The Prefabrication of Houses* (New York: John Wiley and Sons, 1951), 51–55; Burnham Kelly, "Problems and Potential: The Housing Industry Today," in Burnham Kelly, ed., *Design and the Production of Houses* (New York: McGraw Hill, 1959), 4.

67. Mayer, *Builders,* 229–43, 268.

68. Gertner, "Chasing Ground."

69. Ibid.

70. Allison, "An Analysis of Levittown, New York, with Particular Reference to Demand Satisfaction from Mass Produced Low Cost Housing,"6.

Chapter Seven

1. David Nasaw, *Andrew Carnegie* (New York: Penguin Press, 2006).

2. Malcom Gladwell, "Open Secrets," *New Yorker,* January 8, 2007.

3. Dennis Applegate and Curtis Matthews, "Building Controls into Capital Construction," *Internal Auditor* (June 2002): 49–55.

4. Copyright Act of 1976, Pub. L. No. 94-553 (codified as 17 U.S.C., as amended by a 1990 amendment identified as "The Architectural Works Copyright Protection Act of 1990," Pub. L. 101-650).

Index

221

223